The Official
Arsenal
Yearbook 2005

hamlyn

Acknowledgements
The publisher would like to thank Julian Flanders, Joe Cohen,
Chas Newkey-Burden, Ivan Ponting, Stuart MacFarlane and
Vic Akers for their help throughout this project.

Produced for Hamlyn by Butler and Tanner

First published in 2005 by Hamlyn,
a division of Octopus Publishing Group Ltd,
2–4 Heron Quays, London E14 4JP

ISBN 0 600 613380
EAN 9780600613381

A CIP catalogue record for this book is available from the British Library

Printed and bound in the UK by Butler and Tanner

10 9 8 7 6 5 4 3 2 1

Executive Editor Trevor Davies
Match Reports Chas Newkey-Burden
Project Editor Julian Flanders at Butler and Tanner
Additional Material Ivan Ponting
Design Kathie Wilson at Butler and Tanner
Production Ian Paton
All images copyright © Arsenal Football Club Plc /Stuart MacFarlane

All statistics are correct to 31 May, 2005

CONTENTS

DIRECTORS

Peter Hill-Wood (Chairman)
David Dein (Vice-Chairman)
Sir Roger Gibbs
Richard Carr
Daniel Fiszman
Ken Friar OBE
Lady Nina Bracewell-Smith

Managing Director
Keith Edelman

Manager
Arsène Wenger

Secretary
David Miles

MAJOR HONOURS

League Champions 1930/1931, 1932/1933, 1933/1934, 1934/1935,
1937/1938, 1947/1948, 1952/1953, 1970/1971, 1988/1989,
1990/1991, 1997/1998, 2001/2002, 2003/2004

FA Cup Winners 1929/1930, 1935/1936, 1949/1950, 1970/1971,
1978/1979, 1992/1993, 1997/1998, 2001/2002, 2002/2003, 2004/2005

League Cup Winners 1986/1987, 1992/1993

European Fairs Cup Winners 1969/1970

European Cup Winners Cup Winners 1993/1994

FA Youth Cup Winners 1965/1966, 1970/1971, 1987/1988, 1993/1994,
1999/2000, 2000/2001

CLUB INFORMATION

Address Arsenal Stadium, Avenell Road, Highbury, London N5 1BU

Club 020-7704-4000
Box Office 020-7704-4040
Recorded Ticket Information 020-7704-4242
Commercial Department 020-7704-4100
Website www.arsenal.com
Information info@arsenal.co.uk
Arsenal Membership www.arsenal.com/membership
0870-343-070

Junior Gunners 020-7704-4160/4150
Arsenal Travel Club 020-7704-4150/4160

ARSENAL IN THE COMMUNITY
t 020-7704-4140
f 020-7704-4141
e bnicholas@arsenal.co.uk

ARSENAL MERCHANDISE
The Gunners Shop 020-7704-4120
Arsenal World of Sport 020-7272-1000
Mail Order Credit Line 020-7704-2020

Arsenal Museum contact Iain Cook on 020-7704-4100

MANAGER'S MESSAGE

The 2004/2005 season was a successful year for Arsenal Football Club. Patrick Vieira, as captain, lifted the Club's tenth FA Cup after a hard-fought victory on penalties over Manchester United at Cardiff's Millennium Stadium. The team also finished second in the Premiership. The eighth time in eight years they have done so – an excellent example of their consistency.

While we failed to make any real progress in the UEFA Champions League, losing out to Bayern Munich, I am positive that the Club's time will come. We must be patient.

Thierry Henry, despite being out injured for the last six games, was crowned the league's 'Golden Boot' after having scored 25 goals. In fact, the team scored the most goals it has ever managed over one season in the Premiership with 87, which also stood as the highest goal count for any Club last season. An excellent achievement. In addition, the team, playing some wonderful football, set a new record for consecutive unbeaten league games – 49 matches.

I am very proud of the squad for what they achieved as I genuinely believe that the unbeaten record will stand for a long time. This Club has a great tradition and a record like that one is almost like having another trophy. I am also happy for the fans because they play a large part in the team's successes. Both at Highbury and away from home they are amazing.

Here at Arsenal we have a young team with some promising players fighting for a number of different places. Next season is our last at Highbury and I am certain that with the right mixture of talent, desire and spirit we can, in 2005/2006, challenge in the league and leave this great stadium with the Premiership title it deserves.

ARSÈNE WENGER

AUGUST

FA Community Shield
Sunday 8 August 2004 at the Millennium Stadium, Cardiff, 3.00 p.m.
Attendance: 63,317 Referee: Mike Dean

W D D D W W [11 goals scored, 5 conceded]   W L L D W W [8 goals scored, 3 conceded]

ARSENAL 3
Gilberto 49, Reyes 59,
Silvestre o.g. 79

1 MANCHESTER UNITED
Smith 55

Substitutes						Substitutes	
Manuel **ALMUNIA**	24	Jens **LEHMANN**	1	1	Tim **HOWARD**	Roy **CARROLL**	13
Philippe **SENDEROS**	20	Ashley **COLE**	3	2	Gary **NEVILLE**	Phil **NEVILLE** ▶	3
▶ Gael **CLICHY**	22	Pascal **CYGAN**	18	27	Mikael **SILVESTRE**	(Fortune, 50 mins) ◀	
◀ (Aliadiere, 69 mins)		Kolo **TOURE**	28	25	Quinton **FORTUNE**	Darren **FLETCHER** ▶	24
▶ Sebastian **SVARD**	28	**LAUREN**	12	12	David **BELLION**	(Keane, 50 mins) ◀	
◀ (Fabregas, 87 mins)		Jermaine **PENNANT**	21	16	Roy **KEANE**	Diego **FORLAN** ▶	21
▶ Justin **HOYTE**	31	Francesc **FABREGAS**	15	11	Ryan **GIGGS**	(Giggs, 51 mins) ◀	
◀ (Reyes, 80 mins)		**GILBERTO**	19	18	Paul **SCHOLES**	Kieran **RICHARDSON** ▶	23
▶ Jeremie **ALIADIERE**	30	José Antonio **REYES**	9	14	Alan **SMITH**	(Scholes, 18 mins) ◀	
◀ (Bergkamp, 61 mins)		Dennis **BERGKAMP**	10	22	John **O'SHEA**	Chris **EAGLES** ▶	33
▶ Robin **VAN PERSIE**	11	Thierry **HENRY**	14	19	Eric	(Smith, 73 mins) ◀	
◀ (Henry, 45 mins)					**DJEMBA-DJEMBA**	Jonathan **SPECTOR** ▶	29
						(O'Shea, 82 mins) ◀	

MATCH REPORT

So the Community Shield is a meaningless game? Try telling that to the thousands of Arsenal fans who flocked to the Millennium Stadium in Cardiff to watch the Champions take on FA Cup holders Manchester United. Try, indeed, telling that to the players from both teams who produced a hugely competitive and entertaining match.

After a testing summer of media speculation over the future of captain Patrick Vieira, the Arsenal fans welcomed the chance to get together and watch their heroes in action. And their heroes didn't disappoint with a glorious performance ending in a 3–1 victory.

Arsenal were missing Sol Campbell, Patrick Vieira and Robert Pires so in came Pascal Cygan, Jermaine Pennant and, most notably, Francesc Fabregas. The 17-year-old Spanish midfielder played with the composure and assurance of a seasoned professional. At the other end of the age scale, stand-in captain Dennis Bergkamp played with the energy and determination of a player much younger than his 35 years.

The Arsenal fans give their heroes a rousing reception as the team take the field for the new season's traditional curtain raiser.

But more than anyone, it was José Antonio Reyes who inspired Arsenal to this victory and he was a constant threat to Manchester United with his pacy, probing runs. Shortly after the break, he ghosted through the United defence and rounded goalkeeper Tim Howard only to shoot wide of the goal. But within minutes he atoned for this miss, running again at United in a move that ended with him setting up Gilberto to comfortably tap home the opening goal in the 49th minute.

On 55 minutes, Alan Smith charged down a Kolo Toure clearance and fired an unstoppable shot past Jens Lehmann to bring Manchester United fans hope. Four minutes later, Reyes dashed that hope when he punished uncertainty in the United defence and blasted home from close range.

On 79 minutes, Gary Neville and David Bellion got into a muddle in front of their goal and Ashley Cole ghosted into the box and played a cross that deflected off Mikael Silvestre and into the net, completing victory for Arsenal.

Substitute Jeremie Aliadiere came on for Bergkamp in the second half but after just eight minutes on the field was stretchered off after falling awkwardly in a challenge and damaging his anterior cruciate ligament. This was the only dark spot in an enjoyable afternoon in Cardiff for the Arsenal faithful.

As Dennis Bergkamp lifted the trophy, there was much cause for optimism among the Arsenal fans for the campaign ahead. Reyes had shone brightly, suggesting an even greater campaign for him in 2004/2005, Bergkamp had shown that he'd lost none of his skill or hunger despite his advancing years and Fabregas had graced the midfield, suggesting he has a long, bright future ahead of him at Arsenal.

The passion on show in the stands and on the pitch throughout the afternoon showed how much this match meant to both teams, but it was Arsenal who tasted victory. Season 2004/2005 was less than a week away and the Arsenal fans spoke with one voice: bring it on.

Gilberto slides in the opener from a Reyes pass.

Ten minutes later José Antonio Reyes makes it 2–1.

Ashley Cole's attempted cross deflects off Mikael Silvestre's knee and into the net for Arsenal's third.

D D L L L L [4 goals scored, 11 conceded]

D D D W W W [9 goals scored, 5 conceded]

EVERTON 1
Carsley 64

4 ARSENAL
Bergkamp 23, Reyes 39,
Ljungberg 54, Pires 83

Substitutes						Substitutes	
Richard **WRIGHT**	1	Nigel **MARTYN**	25	1	Jens **LEHMANN**	Manuel **ALMUNIA**	24
Steve **WATSON**	2	Alessandro **PISTONE**	3	3	Ashley **COLE**	Robert **PIRES** ▶	7
▶ Tony **HIBBERT**	22	Alan **STUBBS**	4	18	Pascal **CYGAN**	(Reyes, 65 mins) ◀	
◀ (Stubbs, 45 mins)		Joseph **YOBO**	20	28	Kolo **TOURE**	Jermaine **PENNANT** ▶	21
▶ Marcus **BENT**	7	Gary **NAYSMITH**	15	12	**LAUREN**	(Ljungberg, 64 mins) ◀	
◀ (McFadden, 45 mins)		Leon **OSMAN**	21	8	Fredrik **LJUNGBERG**	Mathieu **FLAMINI** ▶	16
▶ Duncan **FERGUSON**	10	Thomas **GRAVESEN**	16	15	Francesc **FABREGAS**	(Gilberto, 69 mins) ◀	
◀ (Osman, 71 mins)		Lee **CARSLEY**	26	19	**GILBERTO**	Justin **HOYTE**	31
		Kevin **KILBANE**	14	9	José Antonio **REYES**		
		Kevin **CAMPBELL**	9	10	Dennis **BERGKAMP**		
		James **McFADDEN**	11	14	Thierry **HENRY**		

MATCH REPORT

Watching their team play Everton at Goodison Park, the Arsenal fans could have been forgiven for wondering if Euro 2004 and the rest of the summer was just a strange dream. Arsenal looked just as invincible and threatening as they did throughout the unbeaten 2003/2004 Premiership campaign. It was all there again: the pacy, flowing moves, the passes that cut seemingly effortlessly through the bewildered opposition, the palpable team spirit during goal celebrations. Has there ever been a better time to be an Arsenal supporter?

Dennis Bergkamp's first goal of the season, on 23 minutes, put Arsenal firmly on the road to victory.

José Antonio Reyes gets between two Everton defenders to head home Arsenal's second.

The Gunners were once again without Sol Campbell and Patrick Vieira, with Robert Pires only making the bench. Proving once again the depth and quality of the squad, the eleven on the field swept Everton aside. It was a team effort and even before the goalscoring started Kolo Toure had bravely blocked a shot from James McFadden, and Freddie Ljungberg had made three threatening runs into the Everton half.

An afternoon of goalscoring delight began with Dennis Bergkamp's goal on 23 minutes. The Dutchman was fed by Thierry Henry on the right of the penalty area and hammered home an unstoppable shot. A great way to mark the 500th league appearance of his career.

Arsenal's lead was doubled 16 minutes later when José Antonio Reyes met a Freddie Ljungberg cross with his head. On 54 minutes Ljungberg got himself on the scoresheet. Francesc Fabregas fed Henry who gifted the Swedish midfielder with an easy chance to make it 3–0.

Far from taking their feet off the gas, Arsenal continued to attack, Bergkamp and Henry came close to scoring before Everton grabbed a consolation goal through Lee Carsley. Not that the home side were ever threatening to wrestle control of the game from the rampant Gunners. With eight minutes left, substitute Pires smashed a fourth goal home to complete the goal fest.

Much of the talk during the summer about Arsenal and Everton had centred around two players out injured for this match – Patrick Vieira and Wayne Rooney. Arsenal showed that they are anything but a one-man team in this match. The rest of the Premiership must have looked on in sympathy for Everton and in fear of their own forthcoming plight when Arsenal roll into town.

At 17 years and 103 days, Fabregas became Arsenal's youngest ever Premiership player and this result moved another record into the Gunners' sights. Victory over Everton left Arsenal standing two games – against Middlesbrough and Blackburn – away from beating Nottingham Forest's record of 42 league games unbeaten: a record that has stood for 26 years.

The opening league match of the season saw goals galore leading to a victory that took Arsenal within touching distance of breaking another record: it's like the summer break never happened.

Freddie Ljungberg accepts José Antonio Reyes' congratulations after putting the Gunners 3–0 ahead.

Seven minutes from time substitute Robert Pires wraps things up with Arsenal's fourth goal.

D D W W W W [16 scored, 5 conceded]   L L L L L D [5 scored, 15 conceded]

ARSENAL 5   3 MIDDLESBROUGH

Henry 25, 90, Bergkamp 54,   Job 43, Hasselbaink 50,
Pires 65, Reyes 65   Queudrue 53

Substitutes			Jens **LEHMANN**	**1**		**1**	Mark **SCHWARZER**	Substitutes	
Manuel **ALMUNIA**	**24**		Ashley **COLE**	**3**		**3**	Franck **QUEUDRUE**	**8**	Szilard **NEMETH** ▸
▸ Robert **PIRES**	**7**		Pascal **CYGAN**	**18**		**23**	Colin **COOPER**		(Zenden, 78 mins) ◂
◂ (Ljungberg, 61 mins)			Kolo **TOURE**	**28**		**5**	Chris **RIGGOTT**	**12**	Carlo **NASH**
▸ Mathieu **FLAMINI**	**16**		**LAUREN**	**12**		**2**	Michael **REIZEIGER**	**9**	Massimo **MACCARONE**
◂ (Reyes, 78 mins)			Fredrik **LJUNGBERG**	**8**		**7**	George **BOATENG**	**20**	Guidoni **DORIVA**
Robin **VAN PERSIE**	**11**		Francesc **FABREGAS**	**15**		**15**	Ray **PARLOUR**	**21**	Stuart **PARNABY** ▸
Justin **HOYTE**	**31**		**GILBERTO**	**19**		**14**	Gaizka **MENDIETA**		(Reiziger, 74 mins) ◂
			José Antonio **REYES**	**9**		**32**	Boudewijn **ZENDEN** ▧		
		▧	Dennis **BERGKAMP**	**10**		**18**	Jimmy-Floyd		
			Thierry **HENRY**	**14**			**HASSELBAINK**		
						16	Joseph-Desire **JOB**		

MATCH REPORT

Hands up who thought the unbeaten run was over when Middlesbrough went 3–1 ahead? On a hot afternoon at Highbury this extraordinary match saw Arsenal equal Nottingham Forest's all-time league record sequence of 42 unbeaten games. But equally as significant for the Highbury faithful was the evidence that this Gunners side can not only dominate matches from start to finish but also come back from a two-goal deficit to win.

Before Thierry Henry gave Arsenal a thoroughly deserved lead, Dennis Bergkamp, Freddie Ljungberg and Reyes had all come close to breaking the deadlock. Henry did just that when he ran onto a long diagonal pass from Reyes and calmly lobbed Mark Schwarzer. Another game, another goal from the gifted Frenchman.

Shortly before the interval, Henry nearly doubled the lead when his dipping free-kick hit the

As cool as you like… Thierry Henry lobs the Boro keeper to give Arsenal the lead.

The comeback begins as Dennis Bergkamp beats Mark Schwarzer with a shot from the edge of the box.

It's two goals in a minute as first Robert Pires taps in the third…

… and then José Antonio Reyes scores with a cracking right-foot volley.

Having topped the game with his first goal Thierry Henry tails it with his second, stroking home Pires's pass.

woodwork but it was Middlesbrough who, against the run of play, were to score just before half-time. After good work from Jimmy-Floyd Hasselbaink, Joseph-Desire Job fired a powerful shot past Jens Lehmann.

It is sometimes said that conceding a goal just before the half-time interval is a cruel blow to a team's morale for the second half. Five minutes after the break Highbury was stunned as Hasselbaink punished some poor defending and made it 2–1 to the visitors. Just three minutes later it was 3–1 to Middlesbrough as Queudrue fired a cheeky, swerving shot past Lehmann.

Far from rolling over at such a blow, the goal sparked a memorable and breathtaking comeback that showed the true depths of this Arsenal side's grit. First, Bergkamp picked up the ball and powered forward and on reaching the edge of the box shot hard and true into the corner of Schwarzer's goal. Although this goal still left Arsenal 3–2 behind, there was already a sense of something special in the air.

With the home fans roaring their heroes on, a Robert Pires goal hauled Arsenal level after some fantastic work by Henry. As the crowd celebrated Pires' strike, Reyes quickly restored Arsenal's lead with a fantastic right-footed volley. Cue bedlam for Arsenal fans and despair for the visitors who, in fairness, deserved more for their efforts.

Even after seven goals and scarcely believable excitement, there was still time for one more goal as Henry comfortably made it five with a gentle touch. Little over half an hour previously, Gunners' fans had been in shock as they faced a 3–1 home defeat. How wonderfully typical it is of this Arsenal side to turn that scenario into a 5–3 victory.

There were shades of the 4–2 home victory against Liverpool during the climax of the previous Premiership campaign here. Perhaps there is a way of beating this Arsenal side but as the players left the field at the end of an extraordinary afternoon, no one seemed any closer to discovering how.

D W W W W W [16 scored, 7 conceded]　　W W L D D L [6 scored, 6 conceded]

ARSENAL 3　0 BLACKBURN ROVERS

Henry 50, Gilberto 58, Reyes 79

Substitutes					Substitutes
		Jens **LEHMANN**	1	1	Brad **FRIEDEL**		
Manuel **ALMUNIA**	24	Ashley **COLE**	3	2	Lucas **NEILL**	13	Peter **ENCKELMAN**
▸ Fredrik **LJUNGBERG**	8	Pascal **CYGAN**	18	6	Craig **SHORT**	5	Garry **FLITCROFT**
◂ (Pennant, 77 minutes)		Kolo **TOURE**	28	33	Michael **GRAY**	4	Lorenzo **AMORUSO**
▸ José Antonio **REYES**	9	**LAUREN**	12	23	Vratislav **GRESKO**	11	Javi **DE PEDRO** ▸
◂ (Bergkamp, 77 mins)		Jermaine **PENNANT**	21	7	Brett **EMERTON**		(Tugay, 77 mins) ◂
▸ Mathieu **FLAMINI**	16	Francesc **FABREGAS**	15	8	Kerimoglu **TUGAY**	22	Dwight **YORKE** ▸
◂ (Fabregas, 86 mins)		**GILBERTO**	19	14	Nils- Eric **JOHANSSON**		(Stead, 63 mins) ◂
Justin **HOYTE**	31	Robert **PIRES**	7	22	Dominic **MATTEO**		
		Dennis **BERGKAMP**	10	10	Paul **DICKOV**		
		Thierry **HENRY**	14	9	Jon **STEAD**		

MATCH REPORT

Arsenal returned to the top of the Premiership and set a new record of 43 unbeaten league matches with an impressive victory over a determined and hard-working Blackburn Rovers side. The Champions needed patience and solid effort more than skills and tricks.

The Gunners had to work hard for their victory and the goalless first half saw plenty of chances for both sides. Thierry Henry forced a couple of good saves from Brad Friedel. For the visitors, Craig Short, Jonathan Stead and former Arsenal man Paul Dickov all came close to scoring.

Cesc Fabregas proved that the praise he had been receiving of late was thoroughly deserved with another mature and commanding performance in midfield. The young Spaniard almost scored twice as the first half came to a close. He first shot narrowly wide and then saw an effort on goal accidentally diverted over the bar by team-mate Robert Pires.

Five minutes into the second half Blackburn's brave and admirable resistance was broken when Henry found space between two Blackburn defenders to fire home a Dennis Bergkamp cross. Blackburn's sense of despair was

Thierry Henry nips *between two Blackburn defenders to score.*

palpable. For so long it seemed they were going to at least thwart Arsenal's efforts to score and here they were behind.

But even worse was to come for the visitors. Eight minutes later Arsenal doubled the lead when Gilberto met a Henry corner with a powerful header which found its way into Friedel's goal via Fabregas' knee. On 77 minutes, substitutes Freddie Ljungberg and José Antonio Reyes came on for Jermaine Pennant and Dennis Bergkamp respectively, and within minutes Reyes was on the scoresheet.

With characteristic ease, Thierry Henry rushed clear of the Blackburn defence only to see his shot saved by Friedel. However, Henry was able to reclaim possession and pass to Reyes who finished comfortably to continue his fine run of goals and secure the three points for Arsenal.

Blackburn had put in a more than credible performance and did not deserve to lose by three goals. During the first half there was little to separate the teams in terms of performance but Arsenal were just too good in the second half for Blackburn. It was somehow especially satisfying for the home fans the fact that Arsenal had to

Gilberto (hidden) heads Arsenal's second as the ball deflects into the net off Cesc Fabregas' knee.

sweat for the points. This gave the victory a realistic edge, and, as the team returned to the top of the Premiership, there was reason for enormous optimism.

It's three goals in three games for José Antonio Reyes as his shot beats Blackburn keeper Brad Friedel.

AUGUST

FA Barclaycard Premiership
Saturday 28 August 2004 at Carrow Road, 5.15 p.m.
Attendance: 23,944 Referee: Graham Poll

W L W D L D [10 scored, 9 conceded]

NORWICH CITY 1
Huckerby 50 pen

W W W W W W [18 scored, 8 conceded]

4 ARSENAL
Reyes 22, Henry 36,
Pires 40, Bergkamp 90

Substitutes					Substitutes
Darren **WARD**	21	Robert **GREEN**	1	1	Jens **LEHMANN**	Manuel **ALMUNIA**	24

Substitutes		Robert **GREEN**	1	1	Jens **LEHMANN**	Substitutes
Darren **WARD**	21	Marc **EDWORTHY**	17	3	Ashley **COLE**	Manuel **ALMUNIA** 24
Thomas **HELVEG**	26	Simon **CHARLTON**	16	31	Justin **HOYTE***	Gael **CLICHY** ▶ 22
▶ Youssef **SAFRI** 15		Craig **FLEMING**	5	28	Kolo **TOURE**	(Pires, 84 mins) ◀
◀ (Johnson, 45 mins)		Adam **DRURY**	3	12	**LAUREN**	Dennis **BERGKAMP** ▶ 10
▶ Leon **McKENZIE** 14		Mattias **JONSON**	9	7	Robert **PIRES**	(Reyes, 73 mins) ◀
◀ (McVeigh, 63 mins)		Damien **FRANCIS**	20	8	Fredrik **LJUNGBERG**	**EDU** ▶ 17
▶ Matthias **SVENSSON** 19		Gary **HOLT**	8	15	Francesc **FABREGAS**	(Fabregas, 73 mins) ◀
◀ (Doherty, 82 mins)		Paul **McVEIGH**	18	19	**GILBERTO**	
		Gary **DOHERTY**	27	9	José Antonio **REYES**	* Pascal Cygan was injured in the warm-up and replaced by Justin Hoyte.
		Darren **HUCKERBY**	6	14	Thierry **HENRY**	

MATCH REPORT

Arsenal temporarily lost their place at the top of the Premiership table earlier in the afternoon after Chelsea beat Southampton, and during the pre-match warm-up they lost Pascal Cygan when the defender strained his calf and had to be replaced by the inexperienced Justin Hoyte at the last moment. Any hopes that Arsenal would be thrown off-course by this setback were quickly answered as three first-half goals effectively ended the contest before the interval. There was an ease to this Arsenal victory that showed the gulf in class between promoted Norwich City and the reigning champions of the Premiership.

The visitors dominated the early stages with Freddie Ljungberg and Robert Pires both coming close to breaking the deadlock. Cesc Fabregas continued to impress and it was his inspired, authoritative midfield play that was behind much of Arsenal's attacking. On 22 minutes, Henry crossed from the byline and found José Antonio Reyes who opened the scoring with ease.

Just after the half-hour mark, a clearance from City goalkeeper Robert Green saw Lauren racing to defend as Darren Huckerby raced towards the Arsenal penalty box. Lauren clearly connected with Huckerby as the pair collapsed outside the box. The home fans demanded a red card but Lauren was only

José Antonio Reyes wheels away in delight after scoring the first.

Thierry Henry rises above Marc Edworthy to head Arsenal into a two-goal lead.

A low drive from Robert Pires makes it 3–0 just before the half-time interval.

shown a yellow, seemingly due to Justin Hoyte's presence meaning Lauren was not the last man.

Within minutes, Arsenal doubled their lead when some exciting interplay between Ljungberg and Henry resulted in the latter heading the Swede's cross into the corner of the goal. Then, five minutes before the half-time break, Arsenal made it 3–0. An increasingly involved Ljungberg stole the ball from Adam Drury on the edge of the six-yard box and fed Pires who fired into the far corner of Green's goal.

During his half-time team talk, Norwich City manager Nigel Worthington must have told his team to attack. After a first half in which Arsenal were able to dominate with ease, they were tested far more vigorously during the second period. Jens Lehmann had to pull off spectacular saves to deny Darren Huckerby and Gary Holt. But the goalkeeper was helpless when he faced a penalty from Huckerby. After Hoyte had felled him, Huckerby tucked away his spot-kick, sending Lehmann the wrong way.

Encouraged by their goal, Norwich upped their game and Arsenal had to work hard not to concede further goals. Midway through the half, Wenger replaced Reyes and Fabregas with Dennis Bergkamp and Edu. These changes made Arsenal more solid and nullified Norwich's threat.

After 80 minutes, Ashley Cole darted into Norwich City's area only to hit a poor cross when a shot would surely have seen him on the scoresheet.

Bergkamp gave the Arsenal fans the final treat of the afternoon when he scored from inside the penalty area with the last kick of the match. Norwich City had worked hard, particularly in the second half, but in reality Arsenal were able to win this match with minimal trouble.

It's poetry in motion as Dennis Bergkamp rounds off the scoring with the last kick of the match.

Arsenal.com PLAYER OF THE MONTH
José Antonio REYES

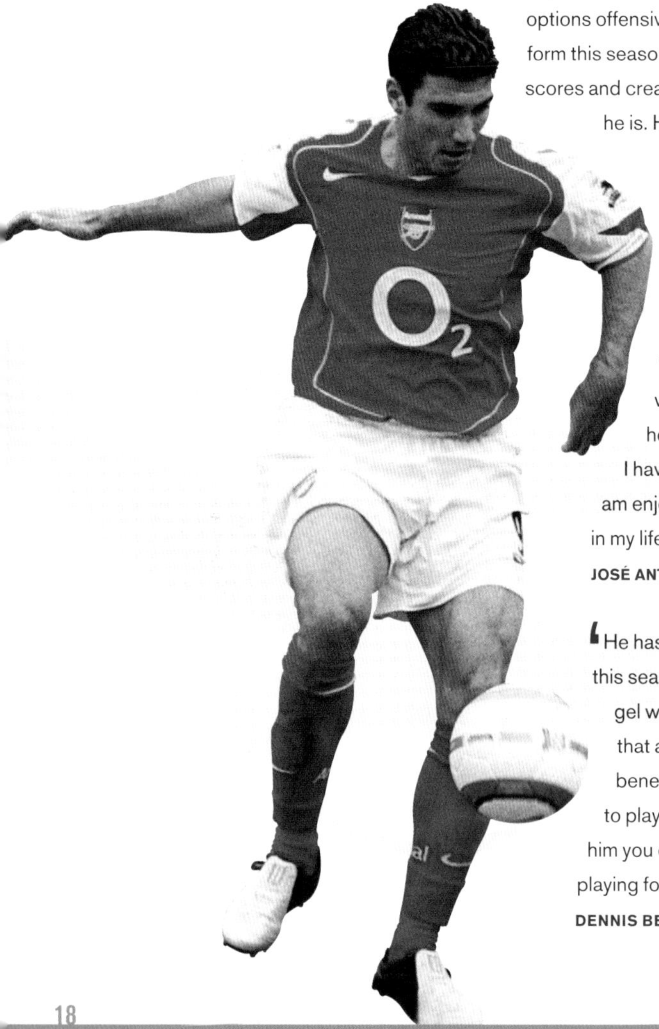

He has adapted and settled in quicker than I ever thought it would take him. He gives us different options offensively and I am delighted with his form this season. When you look at the goals he scores and creates, you can see how adaptable he is. He brings so much to the team and is now a vital player.

ARSÈNE WENGER

All seasons are important but particularly this one as it is my first full season for Arsenal. When I first came I was a bit weaker and I was surprised by how hard the English game was. I have the muscle now though and am enjoying my football more than ever in my life.

JOSÉ ANTONIO REYES

He has already taken the game by storm this season. He didn't need a period to gel with the team as he had done that already last season. So he has benefited from the start. It is a pleasure to play with José, I think when you watch him you can see how much he loves playing football.

DENNIS BERGKAMP

ARSENAL DIARY

Tuesday 10 August
- Francis Jeffers signs for Charlton Athletic. He scored eight goals in 39 appearances for Arsenal.

Friday 13 August
- Captain Patrick Vieira announces that he is to stay at Arsenal. 'My love for Arsenal and the ties I have here were too strong to break,' he tells arsenal.com.

Tuesday 24 August
- Vice-Chairman David Dein receives awards from the FA Premier League for Arsenal's team and supporters who both finished top of the Fair Play Tables for 2003/2004.

Tuesday 31 August
- Non-executive chairman Peter Hill-Wood announces record financial turnover results for the year 2003/2004.
- Sylvain Wiltord leaves Arsenal for Lyon.

THE WIDER WORLD

Friday 13 August
- Liverpool striker Michael Owen signs for Real Madrid.

Friday 20 August
- Newcastle United defender Jonathan Woodgate signs for Real Madrid.

Monday 23 August
- Southampton announce that manager Paul Sturrock is leaving the club by mutual consent.

Monday 30 August
- Sir Bobby Robson is sacked as manager by Newcastle United.

Tuesday 31 August
- Manchester United announce the signing of Wayne Rooney from Everton.

FA CARLING PREMIERSHIP

31 August 2004

	P	HOME					AWAY					Pts
		W	D	L	F	A	W	D	L	F	A	
ARSENAL	4	2	0	0	8	3	2	0	0	8	2	12
Chelsea	4	2	0	0	3	1	2	0	0	3	0	12
Bolton Wanderers	4	2	0	0	5	1	1	0	1	2	3	9
Tottenham Hotspur	4	1	1	0	2	1	1	1	0	2	1	8
Middlesbrough	4	1	1	0	4	3	1	0	1	5	5	7
Aston Villa	4	2	0	0	6	2	0	1	1	1	4	7
Everton	4	1	0	1	3	5	1	1	0	3	1	7
Charlton	4	2	0	0	5	1	0	0	2	1	8	6
Manchester United	4	1	1	0	2	1	0	1	1	1	2	5
Manchester City	4	1	1	0	5	1	0	0	2	1	3	4
Portsmouth	3	1	1	0	5	4	0	0	1	1	2	4
Liverpool	3	1	0	0	2	1	0	1	1	1	2	4
Fulham	4	1	0	1	2	2	0	1	1	4	5	4
Birmingham City	4	1	0	1	1	1	0	1	1	1	2	4
West Bromwich Albion	4	0	2	0	2	2	0	1	1	2	3	3
Southampton	4	1	0	1	4	4	0	0	2	1	4	3
Newcastle United	4	0	1	1	2	3	0	1	1	4	6	2
Norwich City	4	0	1	1	2	5	0	1	1	3	4	2
Blackburn Rovers	4	0	2	0	2	2	0	0	2	2	6	2
Crystal Palace	4	0	0	2	1	5	0	1	1	2	3	1

SEPTEMBER

FA Barclaycard Premiership
Saturday 11 September 2004 at Craven Cottage, 3.00 p.m.
Attendance: 21,681 Referee: Mark Halsey

L W D W L L [8 scored, 6 conceded]   W W W W W W [21 scored, 7 conceded]

FULHAM 0   3 ARSENAL

Ljungberg 62, Knight o.g. 65,
Reyes 71

Substitutes		Fulham			Arsenal		Substitutes
		Edwin **VAN DER SAR**	1	1	Jens **LEHMANN**		Substitutes
Mark **CROSSLEY**	12	Moritz **VOLTZ**	2	3	Ashley **COLE**	24	Manuel **ALMUNIA**
Billy **McKINLAY**	36	Carlos **BOCANEGRA**	3	18	Pascal **CYGAN**	22	Gael **CLICHY**
▸ Tomasz **RADZINSKI**	17	Sylvain **LEGWINSKI**	5	28	Kolo **TOURE**	15	Francesc **FABREGAS** ▸
◂ (Legwinski, 76 mins)		Zat **KNIGHT**	6	12	**LAUREN**		(Vieira, 75 mins) ◂
Alain **GOMA**	24	Mark **PEMBRIDGE**	7	8	Fredrik **LJUNGBERG**	21	Jermaine **PENNANT** ▸
▸ Brian **McBRIDE**	8	Andy **COLE**	9	4	Patrick **VIEIRA**		(Ljungberg, 73 mins) ◂
◂ (Boa Morte, 83 mins)		Luis **BOA MORTE**	11	19	**GILBERTO**	9	José Antonio **REYES** ▸
		Collins **JOHN**	15	7	Robert **PIRES**		(Pires, 61 mins) ◂
		Ian **PEARCE**	35	10	Dennis **BERGKAMP**		
		Papa Bouba **DIOP**	14	14	Thierry **HENRY**		

MATCH REPORT

Controversy over the performance of the referee should not be allowed to detract from another satisfying winning performance from Arsenal. Three second-half goals gave the Gunners their fifth straight win and their 45th game without defeat. To top off a fantastic afternoon for the travelling fans, captain Patrick Vieira was welcomed back after injury. What an inspiring sight for fans and players.

Dennis Bergkamp set up Freddie Ljungberg with two early chances but the Swede could not convert them. Former Gunner Luis Boa Morte (one of three former Arsenal players in the Fulham side, along with Andy Cole and Moritz Voltz) regularly tested Arsenal down the left wing and Mark Pembridge kept the Arsenal midfield busy.

Just after the half-hour mark, Andy Cole accelerated towards goal and was brought down by Ashley Cole. Referee Halsey pointed to the spot but after examining the body language of both sets of players, consulted his assistant referee and instead restarted the game with a drop ball. This prompted outrage among Fulham fans, players and the coaching team, but television replays later suggested that Halsey had, belatedly, come to the correct decision.

Freddie Ljungberg played a major part in this London derby victory, scoring one goal and forcing a defensive mistake for another.

As Fulham fans continued to voice their disapproval, Arsenal had a penalty appeal of their own turned down when Thierry Henry was brought down by Moritz Volz. Within minutes the referee was again the centre of attention when he disallowed a goal by Collins John.

If the first half was all about refereeing, the second was all about Arsenal's class. José Antonio Reyes replaced Robert Pires and, two minutes after his introduction, the Spaniard passed to Henry who expertly fed Ljungberg who shot home to give Arsenal the lead.

Two minutes later, Bergkamp and Henry showed once again what a fantastic strike partnership they are as they combined to send Ljungberg free. Zat Knight got in front of Ljungberg but sent the ball past his own goalkeeper to give Arsenal a two-goal lead.

Reyes had transformed the game and it was fitting that he was the scorer of Arsenal's third goal. Bergkamp, turning in a classy performance, sent him free and he fired a beautiful strike into the corner of Edwin van der Sar's net. Reyes had now scored in every Arsenal match since the start of the season.

Fulham's Zat Knight is helpless as he toe-pokes the ball past his own goalkeeper to put Arsenal 2–0 up.

The Gunners were good value for their win and though Fulham, looking for their first home win over Arsenal for nearly 39 years, will point to controversy over the referee, it was a fully deserved victory. Going into their first Champions League tie the following week with five straight Premiership wins under their belts was a huge boost.

After coming on as a substitute, José Antonio Reyes kept up his record of a goal a game since the start of the season.

SEPTEMBER

UEFA Champions League, Group Stage, Group E
Tuesday 14 September 2004 at Highbury, 7.45 p.m.
Attendance: 34,068 Referee: Domenico Messina, Italy

W W W W W W [22 scored, 6 conceded]   L W W W D W [20 scored, 7 conceded]

ARSENAL 1   0 PSV EINDHOVEN
Alex o.g. 41

	Substitutes						Substitutes	
	Manuel **ALMUNIA**	24	Jens **LEHMANN**	1	21	Edwin **ZOETEBIER**	Heurelho **GOMES**	1
	Gael **CLICHY**	22	Ashley **COLE**	3	2	André **OOIJER**	Theo **LUCIUS**	16
▶	Francesc **FABREGAS**	15	Pascal **CYGAN**	18	4	**ALEX**	Michael **LAMEY**	19
◀	(Vieira, 75 mins)		Kolo **TOURE**	28	5	Wilfred **BOUMA**	John **DE JONG** ▶	25
	▶ **EDU**	17	**LAUREN**	12	3	**LEE** Young-Pyo	(Cocu, 82 mins) ◀	
◀	(Reyes, 78 mins)		Robert **PIRES**	7	6	Mark **VAN BOMMEL**	Jan **VENNEGOOR OF**	9
	Jermaine **PENNANT**	21	Patrick **VIEIRA**	4	8	Phillip **COCU**	**HESSELINK** ▶	
	Justin **HOYTE**	45	**GILBERTO**	19	14	Johann **VOGEL**	(Sibon, 66 mins) ◀	
	Robin **VAN PERSIE**	11	José Antonio **REYES**	9	7	**PARK** Ji-Sung	Jefferson **FARFÁN** ▶	17
			Dennis **BERGKAMP**	10	35	Gerald **SIBON**	(Beasley, 59 mins) ◀	
			Thierry **HENRY**	14	11	Da Marcus **BEASLEY**	Csaba **FEHÉR**	22

MATCH REPORT

At the same point in last year's Champions League, Arsenal lost 3–0 at home to Inter Milan and were forced to play catch-up from then on. Thanks to a solid if unspectacular performance against PSV, the Gunners kicked off their European adventure this year with three points.

Arsenal started slowly and their caution was tangible in a quiet first half. José Antonio Reyes,

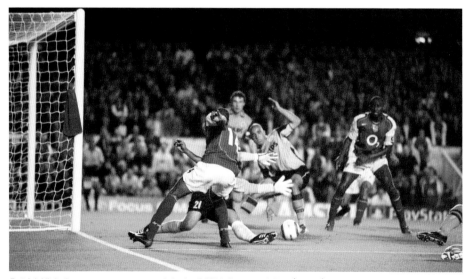

Patrick Vieira's presence causes panic in the PSV defence and Alex (centre) turns the ball into his own net.

The patience and professionalism of senior players like Thierry Henry showed that this Arsenal side have a real European pedigree.

coming in for the injured Freddie Ljungberg in the starting line-up, looked lively on the left flank but overall this was a quiet performance. Patrick Vieira and Robert Pires both wasted good opportunities to put Arsenal ahead before Pires had a headed effort ruled out for offside after Edwin Zoetebier could only parry Thierry Henry's shot.

Shortly before half-time, Mark van Bommel lost his footing and allowed Henry to pick up a loose ball on the left of the area and fired a dangerous ball into the box. As Vieira surged into the area, PSV defender Alex turned the ball into his own net. Arsenal were ahead and already the ghosts of last season's disappointment against Inter were being banished.

Any expectations that the second half would see the home side launching counter attacks in their search for an equaliser were not fulfilled. In their determination to win the Champions League, Arsenal are willing to play cautiously when the occasion requires it.

Park Ji-Sung gave the home fans a scare when he headed powerfully at Jens Lehmann's goal but he saw his effort go over the crossbar. Jan Vennegoor of Hesselink replaced Sibon and came close to securing the equaliser PSV craved. He sent a powerful shot across the face of Lehmann's goal which Pascal Cygan nearly deflected into his own net.

Arsenal had one further significant chance on 73 minutes when Dennis Bergkamp delivered a free-kick from the right, which Gilberto flicked on only to see Vieira just fail to connect with it. Cesc Fabregas and Edu were introduced in the second half, replacing Reyes and Vieira respectively. They showed the depth of the Arsenal squad and continued to control the central pastures.

After several seasons of coming close to European success, this Arsenal team are craving victory in the Champions League this campaign. A solid team effort brought them a winning start in Group E and gave the fans plenty to be confident about. The last time the song 'One-Nil to the Arsenal' reverberated around Highbury on European nights, Arsenal went on to win the European Cup-Winners' Cup. How everyone at Highbury would love to land the Champions League this year. Patient and professional, the performance of the Arsenal players in this tie showed a real European pedigree.

W W W W W W [20 scored, 5 conceded]   L W L W W D [9 scored, 8 conceded]

ARSENAL 2
Henry 31, Pires 66

2 BOLTON WANDERERS
Jaidi 63, Pedersen 85

Substitutes					Substitutes
Manuel **ALMUNIA**	24	Jens **LEHMANN**	1	22 Jussi **JAASKELAINEN**	Andy **OAKES** 13
▸ Gael **CLICHY**	22	Ashley **COLE** 3	18 Nicky **HUNT**	Anthony **BARNESS** 2
◂ (Pires, 82 mins)		Pascal **CYGAN** 18	5 Bruno **N'GOTTY**	Fernando **HIERRO** ▸ 20
Justin **HOYTE**	31	Kolo **TOURE** 28	15 Radhi **JAIDI**	(Campo, 75 mins) ◂
▸ Dennis **BERGKAMP**	10	▨ **LAUREN** 12	11 Ricardo **GARDENER** ▨	Les **FERDINAND** ▸ ▨ 23
◂ (Reyes, 70 mins)		Robert **PIRES** 7	16 Ivan **CAMPO** ▨	(Diouf, 55 mins) ◂
▸ **EDU**	17	Patrick **VIEIRA** 4	4 Kevin **NOLAN**	Henrik **PEDERSEN** ▸ 9
◂ (Gilberto, 67 mins)		**GILBERTO** 19	6 Gary **SPEED**	(Davies, 55 mins) ◂
		Fredrik **LJUNGBERG** 8	10 Jay-Jay **OKOCHA**	
		José Antonio **REYES** 9	21 El-Hadji **DIOUF**	
		Thierry **HENRY** 14	14 Kevin **DAVIES**	

MATCH REPORT

It is perhaps a mark of Arsenal's superb form that a 2–2 draw against the battling and technically astute Bolton Wanderers (who had recently beaten Liverpool and come within seconds of defeating Manchester United) was reported in some quarters as a disaster. For Arsenal fans, although it was disappointing to draw, there was satisfaction to be taken from this match. Although the 100 per cent start to the season was over, the unbeaten run was still intact.

During the opening half-hour of the match, few would have believed that Bolton Wanderers would go on to score twice. Indeed, it seemed that the Gunners were going to need patience in order to break down the visitors' defence. Scoring seemed low on Bolton's list of priorities as the visitors frustrated Arsenal by packing the midfield and defending in numbers. Arsenal had only one chance of note in the opening 30 minutes, when Thierry Henry was denied by Jussi Jaaskelainen.

Thierry Henry outpaces Bruno N'Gotty before putting Arsenal ahead.

On 31 minutes, Henry was fed by Patrick Vieira and with typical flourish outpaced Bruno N'Gotty to shoot into the far corner of Bolton's net. As the teams went in for the half-time break, it was hard to imagine what would occur in the second half. Jay-Jay Okocha had been largely anonymous during the opening half and Kevin Davies had been a forlorn and isolated figure.

Just past the hour mark, Jens Lehmann failed to collect the ball from a Jay-Jay Okocha corner, allowing Radhi Jaidi to head powerfully home. Within minutes Arsenal's lead was restored as Freddie Ljungberg picked up a crossfield pass from José Antonio Reyes and sprinted clear of Ricardo Gardener. He sent in a low cross which Pires poked home. Shortly afterwards, Wenger threw Dennis Bergkamp on to add to Arsenal's attacking options.

Far from being crushed by this swift response to their goal, Bolton seemed to be encouraged by it. Sam Allardyce sent on two substitute strikers, Henrik Pedersen and Les Ferdinand, and the pair combined to provide an equaliser five minutes from time. Ferdinand outjumped Kolo Toure to flick on an Okocha free-kick and Pedersen touched the ball past Lehmann.

While 2–2 was a disappointing final scoreline for Arsenal fans, it must be acknowledged that Bolton fully deserved their point. Allardyce was clever in his tactics, concentrating on a mixture of solid defending and bombarding the Arsenal defence from set pieces.

It is to the credit of the squad Arsène Wenger has assembled that they remain unbeaten this season during the absence through injury of Sol Campbell. However, the news that Campbell was close to returning to first-team action was particularly welcome. After the final whistle, Campbell was out on the Highbury turf being put through drills by the Arsenal physio. It was an inspiring sight for home fans. Once he's back in the team, who knows how much further this amazing unbeaten Premiership run could go?

Spurred on by Bolton's equaliser *Arsenal went ahead again three minutes later through Robert Pires.*

SEPTEMBER

FA Barclaycard Premiership
Saturday 25 September 2004 at the City of Manchester Stadium, 3.00 p.m.
Attendance: 47,015 Referee: Neale Barry

L L W L W W [13 scored, 6 conceded]   W W W W W D [18 scored, 6 conceded]

MANCHESTER 0 CITY

1 ARSENAL
Cole 14

Substitutes					Substitutes	
▸ Steve **McMANAMAN**	20	David **JAMES**	1	1 Jens **LEHMANN**		
◂ (Bosvelt, 76 mins)		Danny **MILLS**	18	3 Ashley **COLE**	Manuel **ALMUNIA**	24
Ronald **WATERREUS**	21	Richard **DUNNE**	22	23 Sol **CAMPBELL**	Francesc **FABREGAS** ▸	15
Stephen **JORDAN**	41	Sylvain **DISTIN**	5	28 Kolo **TOURE**	(Ljungberg, 88 mins) ◂	
Bradley		Sun **JIHAI**	17	12 **LAUREN**	Gael **CLICHY** ▸	22
WRIGHT-PHILLIPS	42	Shaun **WRIGHT-PHILLIPS**	29	8 Fredrik **LJUNGBERG**	(Reyes, 63 mins) ◂	
▸ Willo **FLOOD**	44	Joey **BARTON**	24	4 Patrick **VIEIRA**	Pascal **CYGAN**	18
◂ (Macken, 76 mins)		Paul **BOSVELT**	26	17 **EDU**	Robin **VAN PERSIE** ▸	11
		Antoine **SIBIERSKI**	10	9 José Antonio **REYES**	(Bergkamp 88 mins) ◂	
		Nicolas **ANELKA**	39	10 Dennis **BERGKAMP**		
		Jon **MACKEN**	11	14 Thierry **HENRY**		

MATCH REPORT

A cautious and professional performance saw Arsenal's unbeaten Premiership run extended to 47 matches and all three points returning to North London along with the Arsenal players and fans. The Gunners played as a side that had twice surrendered the lead in their previous Premiership match. Not that Arsenal did not attack; indeed they nearly went ahead in the first

With the City defence all standing off, Ashley Cole steals into the penalty area to put Arsenal ahead.

minute. Dennis Bergkamp sent a pass through the City defence and David James came flying off his line to intercept with a sliding save before Freddie Ljungberg could finish.

This scare seemed to focus the minds of the home team and some great work by Shaun Wright-Phillips (praised by Arsène Wenger in the run-up to this game) saw Paul Bosvelt play a deft through-ball for Jon Macken to test Jens Lehmann. Soon after this, Nicolas Anelka saw his first-time shot, delivered from outside the area, fly just wide of the post.

After 14 minutes, Arsenal were ahead. The impressive José Antonio Reyes played a clever pass into the box, and though Richard Dunne attempted to block the pass, the ball ended up with Ashley Cole after all. Cole coolly accepted the gift and beat David James with a composed finish.

The remainder of the first half saw plenty of hard work from Manchester City but to little effect. Indeed, the two best chances between Arsenal's opener and the break fell to Thierry Henry. On 30 minutes, James turned a low Henry shot round the post. Later, he parried an angled shot from Henry.

The second half saw a more cautious Arsenal with the team mindful of the need to not just retain the lead but to conserve their energies for a Champions League trip the following week. All the same, James and Jihai still had to combine to deny Ljungberg after an exciting run down the left by Henry.

Former Gunner Anelka was in a determined mood and the Frenchman had three chances to score in the second half. First, he narrowly failed to finish from a Macken cross. He then took two dangerous free-kicks, one of which only marginally missed the goal with Lehmann beaten.

Wenger made a defensive substitution just after the hour mark when he sent on Gael Clichy to replace Reyes. A few minutes later, Cole nearly doubled the visitors' lead when he smacked a shot against the post. Cole was in impressive form in

Thierry Henry shows perfect balance and poise as he heads toward the City goal.

all aspects of his game and he defended with tenacity just as he attacked with ability.

Kevin Keegan sent Steve McManaman and Willo Flood on for the last 14 minutes but though McManaman managed a long-range effort, City were by this point playing like a beaten side. Arsenal have not lost to City since the formation of the Premiership in 1992. But whatever records are being set or runs extended, the most important statistic remains the scoreline at the end of each game and another victory made this an enormously satisfying afternoon.

SEPTEMBER

UEFA Champions League, Group Stage, Group E
Wednesday 29 September 2004 at the Lerkendal Stadium, Trondheim, 8.45 p.m.
Attendance: 21,000 Referee: Florian Meyer, Germany

W W W L L L [12 scored, 9 conceded] W W W W D W [14 scored, 6 conceded]

ROSENBORG 1   1 ARSENAL
Strand 52   Ljungberg 6

Substitutes				Espen **JOHNSEN**	1	1	Jens **LEHMANN**		SUBSTITUTES
▶ Daniel **BRAATEN**	25			Christer **BASMA**	5	3	Ashley **COLE**	24	Manuel **ALMUNIA**
◀ (Brattbakk, 82 mins)				Vidar **RISETH**	10	23	Sol **CAMPBELL**	15	Francesc **FABREGAS**
Ivar **RONNINGEN**	30			Erik **HOFTUN**	3	28	Kolo **TOURE**	22	Gael **CLICHY**
Torjus **HANSEN**	16			Mikael **DORSIN**	33	12	**LAUREN**	18	Pascal **CYGAN**
Stale **STENSAAS**	21			Roar **STRAND**	6	8	Fredrik **LJUNGBERG**	21	Jermaine **PENNANT**
Thorstein **HELSTAD**	24			Jan Gunnar **SOLLI**	11	4	Patrick **VIEIRA**	16	Mathieu **FLAMINI**
▶ Christer **GEORGE**	18			Fredrik **WINSNES**	4	17	**EDU**	11	Robin **VAN PERSIE** ▶
◀ (Strand, 64 mins)				Harald **M BRATTBAKK**	22	7	Robert **PIRES**		(Pires, 82 mins) ◀
▶ Robbie **RUSSELL**	8			Oyvind **STORFLOR**	17	9	José Antonio **REYES**		
◀ (Basma, 74 mins)				Frode **JOHNSEN**	9	14	Thierry **HENRY**		

MATCH REPORT

A 1–1 draw on a chilly night in Norway kept Arsenal firmly on course for a place in the second round of the Champions League and meant the team remained unbeaten in the competition. Despite the disappointment of not winning, there was plenty to take from this tie which left Arsenal in a stronger position than they were at the equivalent point in last season's campaign.

Thierry Henry gave Rosenborg an early scare when he ran at their defence and Espen Johnsen did well to tip his shot against the post. From the resultant corner, taken by Henry, Erik Hoftun struggled to deal with the threat and Sol Campbell moved the ball into the path of Freddie Ljungberg who spun and finished decisively from six yards. This goal marked the first by an Arsenal player in this season's Champions League, the Gunners' other strike having come from an own goal.

Despite some hard work, Arsenal were unable to add to their lead in a frustrating first half. Henry set up his strike

After a number of early scares, Freddie Ljungberg puts the Gunners ahead.

Late in the second half, skipper Patrick Vieira came close to getting a winner for the Gunners.

partner José Antonio Reyes in the 16th minute but the Spaniard was unable to score as his first-touch let him down. Ljungberg had another chance to score but his cut-back pass to Robert Pires was easily dealt with by the Rosenborg defence. Had the Swede been more selfish, he would almost certainly have ended up scoring a second goal.

In the 39th minute, after some excellent work in the Rosenborg midfield, Christer Basma found himself in a threatening position and only some inspired work by Edu prevented him from delivering on that threat. This served notice of Rosenborg's determination to get back into the match.

After the half-time interval, the Norwegian team came out fighting. Three minutes after the restart, Ashley Cole had to block a shot by Strand after Campbell had surrendered possession with a misplaced clearance. On 52 minutes, a break from Storflor saw him pass the ball cleanly to Strand who sidefooted the ball past Jens Lehmann for the equaliser.

Soon after, Campbell released Cole with an inspired pass and the defender passed to Pires who dummied the ball only to see Ljungberg screw his shot well wide. It was a wonderful move from the Gunners and deserved a goal at the end of it. Reyes shot into the side-netting and both Henry and Patrick Vieira also came close to putting the Gunners back in the lead. As Arsenal's frustration built, Edu saw an effort sail just wide, and in injury time, Henry tested Johnsen in the Rosenborg goal.

Try as they did, Arsenal were unable to grab victory and had instead to settle for a point. In some quarters this 1–1 draw was portrayed as a disaster. But the Gunners had avoided defeat and there was no cause for alarm over the result. Every European tie is part of a learning curve and the Gunners seem set to bounce back even stronger in their next European outing.

SEPTEMBER 2004

Arsenal.com PLAYER OF THE MONTH
Thierry HENRY

He has tremendous spirit and, of course, exceptional ability. Many of his talents are now widely recognised but there are so many. He analyses what is happening around him and provides the right response. He also has enormous technical ability.

ARSÈNE WENGER

We are now producing the sort of performances and results that all teams want. We just go out in each game aiming for the top. I have improved since I arrived here but I always want to continue improving and working. I am never satisfied.

THIERRY HENRY

I am delighted for Thierry that he is such a success. He is a fantastic team-mate. I think you can see how exciting it is for fans when he gets the ball. He scores so many goals but also creates many goals and has so much all-round skill.

ASHLEY COLE

ARSENAL DIARY

Wednesday 1 September
- Sebastian Svard joins Brøndby IF on loan for the season.

Friday 10 September
- Arsène Wenger and José Antonio Reyes win the Barclays Manager of the Month and Player of the Month awards respectively for August.

Thursday 16 September
- Francesc Fabregas signs a long-term extension to his contract with Arsenal.

Monday 20 September
- Sol Campbell returns from injury to turn out in an Arsenal reserves match against Coventry City.

Friday 24 September
- Arsène Wenger announces that he plans to sign a new contract by the end of the year.

THE WIDER WORLD

Wednesday 8 September
- England beat Poland 2–1 to secure a vital World Cup qualifying victory.

Thursday 16 September
- Mark Hughes is appointed as the new manager of Blackburn Rovers replacing Graeme Souness who is moving on to manage Newcastle United.

Monday 20 September
- Brian Clough dies at the age of 69.
- Rio Ferdinand returns to the Manchester United first-team after an eight-month ban and celebrates as his team beat Liverpool 2–1.
- José Antonio Camacho quits as coach of Spanish giants Real Madrid.

FA CARLING PREMIERSHIP
30 September 2004

		HOME					AWAY					
	P	W	D	L	F	A	W	D	L	F	A	Pts
ARSENAL	7	2	1	0	10	5	4	0	0	12	2	19
Chelsea	7	2	1	0	3	1	3	1	0	4	0	17
Everton	7	2	0	1	4	5	3	1	0	5	1	16
Bolton Wanderers	7	2	2	0	8	4	1	1	1	4	5	12
Manchester United	7	2	1	0	4	2	1	2	1	4	4	12
Newcastle United	7	2	1	1	8	4	1	1	1	6	7	11
Charlton Athletic	7	3	1	0	6	1	0	1	2	2	9	11
Liverpool	6	3	0	0	8	1	0	1	2	2	4	10
Aston Villa	7	2	2	0	7	3	0	2	1	1	4	10
Tottenham Hotspur	7	1	2	1	2	2	1	2	0	2	1	10
Middlesbrough	7	2	1	1	6	5	1	9	2	5	6	10
Fulham	7	2	0	2	3	5	0	2	1	5	6	8
Manchester City	7	1	1	2	5	3	1	0	2	3	4	7
Portsmouth	6	2	1	1	8	6	0	0	2	1	3	7
Birmingham City	7	1	1	1	2	2	0	2	2	3	5	6
Blackburn Rovers	7	1	2	0	3	2	0	0	4	2	10	5
Southampton	7	1	0	2	5	6	0	1	3	1	5	4
West Bromwich Albion	7	0	3	0	3	3	0	1	3	3	9	4
Norwich City	7	0	2	1	2	5	0	2	2	3	7	4
Crystal Palace	7	0	0	3	2	7	0	2	2	4	7	2

W W W D W D [11 scored, 4 conceded]

W L D D W W [7 scored, 5 conceded]

ARSENAL 4

Ljungberg 33, Henry 48, 69,
Reyes 70

0 CHARLTON ATHLETIC

Substitutes						Substitutes
	Jens **LEHMANN**	1	1	Dean **KIELY**		
Manuel **ALMUNIA** 24	Gael **CLICHY**	22	2	Luke **YOUNG**	16	Stephan **ANDERSEN**
▸ Robin **VAN PERSIE** 11	Sol **CAMPBELL**	23	5	Chris **PERRY**	8	Matt **HOLLAND** ▸
◂ (Henry, 82 mins)	Kolo **TOURE**	28	24	Jonathan **FORTUNE**		(Stuart, 74 mins) ◂
▸ Jermaine **PENNANT** 21	**LAUREN**	12	12	Herman **HREIDARSSON**	20	Bryan **HUGHES**
◂ (Ljungberg, 49 mins)	Fredrik **LJUNGBERG**	8	13	Danny **MURPHY**	21	Jonatan **JOHANSSON** ▸
Pascal **CYGAN** 18	Patrick **VIEIRA**	4	15	Talal **EL KARKOURI**		(Euell, 66 mins) ◂
▸ Mathieu **FLAMINI** 16	Francesc **FABREGAS**	15	7	Radostin **KISHISHEV**	19	Dennis **ROMMEDAHL** ▸
◂ (Fabregas, 82 mins)	José Antonio **REYES**	9	4	Graham **STUART**		(Kishishev, 66 mins) ◂
	Dennis **BERGKAMP**	10	9	Jason **EUELL**		
	Thierry **HENRY**	14	10	Kevin **LISBIE**		

MATCH REPORT

In recent games, much of the focus had been on the emergence of young Francesc Fabregas, the breathtaking form of José Antonio Reyes and the welcome return of Patrick Vieira. But this match was, more than anything, about the excellence of Thierry Henry. After knocking down Charlton Athletic's resistance, Arsenal produced some exhilarating attacking football and much of it centred around the French striker.

Before showtime started, Charlton had the first opening when Danny Murphy tested Jens Lehmann. But for much of the opening half-hour, the visitors were concentrating on defence and the onus was on Arsenal to break them down. Dennis Bergkamp was set up by Henry but hit the post with his 20-yard effort. Soon after, Gael Clichy shot over the crossbar before Bergkamp tested Dean Kiely from 25 yards.

Charlton's brave resistance collapsed just after the half-hour mark. Jason Euell

Freddie Ljungberg points the way after scoring the first goal.

surrendered possession to Henry, who fed Bergkamp and the Dutchman's subsequent cross was calmly slotted home by Freddie Ljungberg.

Three minutes into the second half, a classy moment from Henry led to Arsenal doubling their lead. Receiving the ball on the corner of the six-yard box with his back to goal, the Frenchman, tightly marked, cheekily back-heeled the ball into the bottom corner of Kiely's net. As the home team's confidence rocketed, Reyes saw an attempt at goal blocked by Chris Perry and Henry fired a shot just over the bar.

The Frenchman was on irresistible form and after being fed by Reyes, he made it 3–0 when Kiely could only tip his shot onto the crossbar, which then sent the ball into the back of the net. One minute later, a by-now shell-shocked Charlton defence saw Henry return the compliment to Reyes. He fed the Spaniard who delivered a low shot into the far corner of the goal. Henry's outstanding performance was rewarded with a standing ovation as he left the pitch to be replaced by Robin van Persie after 82 minutes.

Both Reyes and captain Patrick Vieira had chances to add to the scoreline – Reyes with a right-foot shot and Vieira with a close-range effort – but the score remained 4–0 to Arsenal. Not that any of the home fans were complaining. When their heroes are in this sort of form, it reminds Arsenal fans of how lucky they are to be witnessing perhaps the greatest football ever played at Highbury.

At the end of 90 minutes the unbeaten run stood at 48 Premiership matches, and in this sort of form it is easy to see why the Gunners have not been shot down for so long. Again, this was a team effort but the magnificence of Henry was beyond question during a hugely enjoyable Premiership encounter.

Thierry Henry's cheeky back-heel makes it 2–0…

… then 3–0 as his right-foot shot goes in off the crossbar.

A low shot from José Antonio Reyes rounds off the scoring.

W W D W D W [12 scored, 3 conceded]   W D D W D D [12 scored, 8 conceded]

ARSENAL 3   1 ASTON VILLA

Pires 19 pen, 72, Henry 45   Hendrie 3

Substitutes				Substitutes
Stuart **TAYLOR** 13	Jens **LEHMANN** 1	13 Stefan **POSTMA**	Wayne **HENDERSON** 25	
Pascal **CYGAN** 18	Ashley **COLE** 3	2 Mark **DELANEY**	Noberto **SOLANO** 11	
▸ Mathieu **FLAMINI** 16	Sol **CAMPBELL** 23	4 Olof **MELLBERG**	Steven **DAVIS** 24 ▸	
◂ (Vieira, 66 mins)	Kolo **TOURE** 28	15 Ulises **DE LA CRUZ**	(Hitzlsperger, 45 mins) ◂	
▸ Jermaine **PENNANT** 21	**LAUREN** 12	3 JLloyd **SAMUEL**	Peter **WHITTINGHAM** 17 ▸	
◂ (Reyes, 76 mins)	Robert **PIRES** 7	8 Gavin **McCANN**	(Barry, 8 mins) ◂	
▸ Robin **VAN PERSIE** 11	Patrick **VIEIRA** 4	7 Lee **HENDRIE**	Juan Pablo **ANGEL** 9 ▸	
◂ (Pires, 84 mins)	Francesc **FABREGAS** 15	12 Thomas **HITZLSPERGER**	(Cole, 58 mins) ◂	
	José Antonio **REYES** 9	6 Gareth **BARRY**		
	Dennis **BERGKAMP** 10	18 Carlton **COLE**		
	Thierry **HENRY** 14	10 Darius **VASSELL**		

MATCH REPORT

An early goal from the visitors may have given Aston Villa hope that they would be the team to end Arsenal's unbeaten run. However, a stylish and gutsy fightback gave the Gunners victory. Indeed, only some wasteful finishing from Arsenal and superb goalkeeping from Stefan Postma prevented this from becoming a rout.

In the opening minutes, Arsenal won a corner that Sol Campbell rose to head, but he could only smash the ball against the bar. Aston Villa were relieved but within seconds they were overjoyed when, following great work from Carlton Cole during a Villa counter-attack, Lee Hendrie scored a powerful goal from the edge of the area.

An eventful opening saw Gareth Barry forced to leave the field through injury after six minutes and his replacement, Peter Whittingham, curled a shot narrowly wide. Although Villa could draw confidence from much of the opening period, they were soon to be on the receiving end of a determined assault on their goal.

Postma was soon being forced into save after save, denying José Antonio Reyes, Dennis Bergkamp, Cesc Fabregas and Patrick Vieira. While his performance in goal was increasingly heroic, the inevitable Arsenal goal came on 19 minutes. Thierry Henry outpaced Mark Delaney who fouled him inside the box. Robert Pires stepped up to score the penalty kick.

Robert Pires scores *Arsenal's first goal from the penalty spot.*

A curling shot from Thierry Henry beats Postma in the Villa goal to make it 2–1 on the stroke of half-time.

Just before half-time, Henry put the Champions further ahead with a right-footed shot after Reyes sent him free. A half that had begun so positively in many ways for Aston Villa ended with them 2–1 behind and Arsenal very much in the ascendancy in terms of the balance of play.

Postma and Jens Lehmann may have swapped ends but the same story applied in the second half – more heroics from Postma as Arsenal outran the Villa defence. Again, Arsenal eventually scoring past him despite his efforts seemed more and more inevitable.

Before then, the only low of the afternoon occurred when Patrick Vieira was forced to leave the field through injury. On a more positive note, his replacement Flamini looked impressive and was involved in the move that led to Arsenal's third goal. After 72 minutes Flamini carried the ball upfield and fed Henry, a deft touch from Henry gave Pires the ball unmarked in the penalty area. A right-footed shot from the midfielder beat Postma to nestle in the right-hand corner of the net.

With a Champions League trip to Greece on the horizon, Wenger withdrew Reyes and Pires to give them some rest. But Arsenal continued to control the game and kept the lead comfortably.

With the European trip and the chance to extend their unbeaten run to 50 at Old Trafford both in the week ahead, it was important that Arsenal could approach such an exciting seven days with the confidence that three points always brings. Villa had given them an early scare and Postma had heroically denied many of their attacks, but Arsenal had won in front of their loyal fans once again.

The Villa keeper lies prostrate as Robert Pires turns to celebrate: three goals and three points for the Gunners.

OCTOBER

UEFA Champions League, Group Stage, Group E
Wednesday 20 October 2004 at the Apostolos Nikolaidis, Athens, 7.45 p.m.
Attendance: 12,346 Referee: Valentin Ivanov, Russia

W W W L W D [9 scored, 2 conceded]   W D W D W W [12 scored, 4 conceded]

PANATHINAIKOS 2   2 ARSENAL

González 65, Olisadebe 81   Ljungberg 17, Henry 74

Substitutes		Konstantinos **CHALKIAS**	12	1	Jens **LEHMANN**	Substitutes	
Mario **GALINOVIC**	1	Nasief **MORRIS**	5	3	Ashley **COLE**	Stuart **TAYLOR**	13
René **HENRIKSEN**	2	Yannis **GOUMAS**	8	23	Sol **CAMPBELL**	Robin **VAN PERSIE**	11
Stephanos **KOTSOLIS**	33	Ezequiel **GONZÁLEZ**	9	28	Kolo **TOURE**	Pascal **CYGAN**	18
Silvio **MARIC**	4	Sotirios **KYRGIAKOS**	16	12	**LAUREN**	Jermaine **PENNANT**	21
▸ Joël **EPALLÉ**	10	Pantelis **KONSTANTINIDIS**	27	8	Fredrik **LJUNGBERG**	Mathieu **FLAMINI**	16
◂ (Mitu, 76 mins)		Angelos **BASINAS**	20	15	Francesc **FABREGAS**	Philippe **SENDEROS**	20
▸ Emanuel **OLISADEBE**	23	Dumitru **MITU**	21	17	**EDU**	Sebastian **LARSSON**	39
◂ (Konstantinou, 64 mins)		Loukas **VINTRA**	24	7	Robert **PIRES**		
▸ Miltos **SAPANIS**	22	Rudolf **SKÁCEL**	26	9	José Antonio **REYES**		
◂ (González, 90 mins)		Michalis **KONSTANTINOU**	19	14	Thierry **HENRY**		

MATCH REPORT

Arsenal returned from their trip to Greece still unbeaten in the Champions League but naturally disappointed that they didn't win against Panathinaikos. Cesc Fabregas came in for his first Champions League start to replace the injured Patrick Vieira. While the youngster performed with characteristic maturity, the captain's influence was missed.

The Gunners take the lead after 17 minutes as Freddie Ljungberg chips the keeper from inside the box.

A beautiful move involving Reyes, Robert Pires and Ashley Cole ends with Thierry Henry restoring Arsenal's lead.

Panathinaikos started the game with the most chances. Angelos Basinas had two great early opportunities to score, first shooting wide and then seeing a long-range effort impressively saved by Jens Lehmann.

But it was Arsenal who took the lead after 17 minutes. José Antonio Reyes cleverly opened up the home defence with a deft pass and Freddie Ljungberg scored from seven yards.

The Greek side tried hard to find an equaliser. González came close with a header after an impressive run into the Arsenal box; the increasingly effective Basinas had another long-range shot just after the half-hour mark; Sotirios Kyrgiakos headed wide and Basinas came close again. But Arsenal went in for the interval with their lead intact.

After 65 minutes, Sol Campbell appeared to be dealing with a long pass, but Lehmann, anxious to clear the danger himself, surged from his line to head clear. The ball went to González who chipped home from 35 yards.

Nine minutes later, Arsenal recaptured the lead. A mistake from Basinas was punished by a pacy Arsenal move involving Reyes, Robert Pires and Ashley Cole. Thierry Henry was the lucky recipient of this move and he scored to put Arsenal 2–1 ahead.

With a little over a quarter of an hour left, Arsenal seemed assured of victory. However, some uncertain defending meant they surrendered the lead. Olisadebe was challenged by Lehmann but the goalkeeper found himself stranded and the substitute striker equalised with nine minutes left.

During the closing minutes of the match Arsenal searched desperately for a winner. Chalkias made a dramatic double save as Reyes and Pires both had chances. But in the end the visitors shared the points with an impressive Panathinaikos team and remained in a better position in the Champions League compared to the corresponding point in last season's campaign.

W W W D D D [10 scored, 4 conceded]   D W D W W D [13 scored, 6 conceded]

MANCHESTER 2 UNITED   0 ARSENAL

van Nistelrooy 73 pen, Rooney 90

Substitutes					Substitutes
Tim **HOWARD**	1	Roy **CARROLL**	13	1 Jens **LEHMANN**	Stuart **TAYLOR** 13
Wes **BROWN**	6	⫴ Gary **NEVILLE**	2	3 Ashley **COLE** ⫴	Robert **PIRES** ▶ 7
Liam **MILLER**	17	Rio **FERDINAND**	5	23 Sol **CAMPBELL**	(Reyes, 70 mins) ◀
▶ Alan **SMITH**	14	Mikael **SILVESTRE**	27	28 Kolo **TOURE**	Robin **VAN PERSIE** 11
◀ (Ronaldo, 85 mins)		Gabriel **HEINZE**	4	12 **LAUREN**	Francesc **FABREGAS** 15
▶ Louis **SAHA**	8	Cristiano **RONALDO**	7	8 Fredrik **LJUNGBERG**	Pascal **CYGAN** 18
◀ (van Nistelrooy, 89 mins)		⫴ Phil **NEVILLE**	3	4 Patrick **VIEIRA** ⫴	
		Paul **SCHOLES**	18	17 **EDU** ⫴	
		Ryan **GIGGS**	11	9 José Antonio **REYES**	
		Wayne **ROONEY**	8	10 Dennis **BERGKAMP**	
		Ruud **VAN NISTELROOY**	10	14 Thierry **HENRY**	

MATCH REPORT

Although it's always disappointing to lose any match, Arsenal could take many positives from this defeat. The team started and finished an increasingly rainy afternoon at the top of the Premiership and are assured a place in the history books for a fantastic and unique 49-match unbeaten league run.

Patrick Vieira returned from injury to put in an assured performance in midfield, but the opening exchanges favoured the home team with Rooney going close twice. Then, Paul Scholes picked up the loose ball and returned it to Rooney who passed to the unmarked Ryan Giggs. The Welshman saw his shot blocked by the impressive Sol Campbell.

In the 18th minute, Dennis Bergkamp sent Freddie Ljungberg on a clear run to the United goal, the Swede fell under a challenge from Rio Ferdinand and the referee waved play on much to the consternation of the Arsenal fans.

Soon after, an impressive move saw José Antonio Reyes put Bergkamp into a great position in front of Roy Carroll's goal but the United goalkeeper rushed out to save at the Dutchman's

Freddie Ljungberg outpaces United's Wayne Rooney.

Ashley Cole slides in to dispossess flying winger Cristiano Ronaldo.

feet. This was followed by Thierry Henry running onto a fine pass from Edu, but seeing his effort blocked by Carroll.

Before half-time, an understandably tense match saw bookings for Ashley Cole and both Neville brothers. Arsenal were unhappy with a number of challenges on José Antonio Reyes during the opening 45 minutes which ended goalless and set the scene for an increasingly impressive, though ultimately disappointing performance from the visitors in the second half.

In the early stages of the second period, a Lauren cross was nearly turned into his own goal by Gary Neville. Then Ljungberg cut the ball back for Bergkamp who shot just wide, and an energetic Gabriel Heinze tested Jens Lehmann with a long-distance effort. At this point in the match Arsenal seemed to be in the ascendancy so the opening goal was a surprise when it came.

Rooney burst into the Arsenal area and tumbled when he was challenged by Campbell. The referee pointed instantly to the spot but the

surprise of the Arsenal players suggested he'd made the wrong decision. Ruud van Nistelrooy, who missed a penalty in the corresponding fixture last season, stepped up to take the spot-kick and stroked it home.

Arsenal responded in determined fashion and Edu set up Henry who once again saw his shot blocked. Then, in the dying moments of normal time, Cole shot fractionally over the bar.

During injury time, substitute Alan Smith set up Rooney with a simple chance, which the striker stuck away to cement the victory. The ecstatic scenes among the United players and fans at the final whistle were a huge compliment to Arsenal and confirmation of the respect and fear that all teams in the Premiership feel for Arsène Wenger's team. The unbeaten run was over, but no one at Highbury will ever forget those 49 incredible matches and the fantastic team that entertained us all as they made history.

OCTOBER

Carling Cup, 3rd Round
Wednesday 27 October 2004 at the City of Manchester Stadium, 7.45 p.m.
Attendance: 21,708 Referee: Peter Walton

W W L D W L [13 scored, 7 conceded]

W D W W D L [11 scored, 6 conceded]

MANCHESTER CITY 1

Fowler 90

2 ARSENAL

van Persie 78,
Karbassiyoon 90

Substitutes		Ronald **WATERREUS**	21	24	Manuel **ALMUNIA**		Substitutes
Kevin		Ben **THATCHER**	3	31	Justin **HOYTE**	13	Stuart **TAYLOR**
STUHR-ELLEGAARD	32	Sylvain **DISTIN**	5	18	Pascal **CYGAN**	34	Patrick **CREGG**
Patrick **McCARTHY**	43	Danny **MILLS**	18	20	Philippe **SENDEROS**	35	Johan **DJOUROU** ▸
▸ Bradley		Nedum **ONUOHA**	16	39	Sebastian **LARSSON**		(Pennant, 89 mins) ◂
WRIGHT-PHILIPS	42	Willo **FLOOD**	44	21	Jermaine **PENNANT**	42	Quincy
◂ (D'Laryea, 79 mins)		Jonathan **D'LARYEA**	31	15	Francesc **FABREGAS**		**OWUSU-ABEYIE** ▸
▸ Christian **NEGOUAI**	30	Antoine **SIBIERSKI**	10	16	Mathieu **FLAMINI**		(Smith, 61 mins) ◂
◂ (Sinclair, 69 mins)		Trevor **SINCLAIR**	28	47	Ryan **SMITH**	46	Daniel
▸ Stephen **JORDAN**	41	Shaun **WRIGHT-PHILIPS**	29	11	Robin **VAN PERSIE**		**KARBASSIYOON** ▸
◂ (Negouai, 83 mins)		Robbie **FOWLER**	8	40	Arturo **LUPOLI**		(Lupoli, 82 mins) ◂

MATCH REPORT

Three days on from the disappointment of losing at Old Trafford, Arsenal returned to Manchester to face City in the Carling Cup. Arsène Wenger made eleven changes to the side that started at Manchester United but as the travelling fans have come to expect, the same combination of determination, teamwork and skill runs through all Arsenal line-ups.

These evenings are enormously enjoyable for Arsenal fans as they catch a glimpse of the future by seeing the fruits of the hard work put in by Arsène Wenger and his staff in producing a superb group of youngsters. All the same, the opening 45 minutes were relatively uneventful.

Kevin Keegan fielded a City side that was almost full strength so the relatively inexperienced Arsenal eleven found it hard to create many chances during the first half. Willo Flood and Shaun Wright-Phillips tested Sebastian Larsson. Both Wright-Phillips and Robbie Fowler had chances to put City ahead but could not finish. Then, just before the interval, Antoine Sibierski forced Manuel Alumnia into a fine save with a powerful header.

Robin van Persie had attempted to chip Ronald Waterreus just after the half-hour mark and then during stoppage time in the first half, Cesc Fabregas fired a low shot which Waterreus stooped to save. This was the best chance Arsenal had during the 45 minutes.

After the interval, Arsenal were far more adventurous as confidence grew. Two minutes after the restart, Arturo Lupoli's low shot went just wide of the post. Shortly after, Jermaine Pennant also shot marginally wide of the post before Quincy Owusu-Abeyie set up van Persie who sent his shot high over the bar.

On 74 minutes, Fabregas sent a high ball to the increasingly effective van Persie on the edge of the area. He chested the ball down and his shot was parried by Waterreus. Lupoli fired the loose ball into the back of the net but the goal was disallowed for offside.

Four minutes later, an impressive Arsenal move saw Flamini set up van Persie who put the vistors ahead with a sliding finish, sparking joyous scenes of celebration. Arsenal had needed to be patient and received their reward.

Perfect balance allows Robin van Persie to open the scoring.

Right: Sebastian Larsson and Francesc Fabregas congratulate Daniel Karbassiyoon on cementing the Gunners' victory with his first goal for the Club.

In stoppage time, substitute Daniel Karbassiyoon doubled Arsenal's lead when he collected an exceptional pass from Fabregas and beat Waterreus with a sweet left-foot finish.

During the closing moments of the match, Manchester City were awarded a free-kick just outside the Arsenal area. Robbie Fowler slipped as he connected with the ball but still managed to score. This, however, was a mere consolation goal as Arsenal's impressive mixture of youngsters and reserves marched through to the next round of the Carling Cup. No wonder Arsène Wenger had such a smile on his face at the end of this tie. The defeat at Old Trafford had been disappointing but on the evidence of this match the future looks very rosy for Arsenal .

D W W D L W [12 scored, 6 conceded] W L D L D W [6 scored, 4 conceded]

ARSENAL 2 2 SOUTHAMPTON

Henry 67, van Persie 90 Delap 80, 85

Substitutes						Substitutes
Manuel **ALMUNIA**	24	Jens **LEHMANN**	1	1	Antti **NIEMI**	Alan **BLAYNEY**	28
Philippe **SENDEROS**	20	Ashley **COLE**	3	5	Claus **LUNDEKVAM**	Chris **BAIRD**	32
▸ Robert **PIRES**	7	Pascal **CYGAN**	18	6	Andreas **JAKOBSSON**	David **PRUTTON** ▸	20
◂ (Reyes, 61 mins)		Kolo **TOURE**	28	19	Danny **HIGGINBOTHAM**	(Svensson, 85 mins) ◂	
▸ Francesc **FABREGAS**	15	**LAUREN**	12	33	Paul **TELFER**	Neil **McCANN** ▸	10
◂ (Edu, 65 mins)		Fredrik **LJUNGBERG**	8	12	Anders **SVENSSON**	(Ormerod, 75 mins) ◂	
▸ Robin **VAN PERSIE**	11	Patrick **VIEIRA**	4	18	Rory **DELAP**	Leon **BEST** ▸	27
◂ (Ljungberg, 83 mins)		**EDU**	17	35	Mikael **NILSSON**	(Blackstock, 89 mins) ◂	
		José Antonio **REYES**	9	22	Darren **KENTON**		
		Dennis **BERGKAMP**	10	36	Brett **ORMEROD**		
		Thierry **HENRY**	14	24	Dexter **BLACKSTOCK**		

MATCH REPORT

After Manchester United had ended Arsenal's unbeaten Premiership run the previous weekend, everyone associated with the Club were keen to get back to Premier League action. Arsenal dominated a thoroughly eventful match but were forced to settle for a draw.

A knee injury to Sol Campbell forced him to miss the match with Pascal Cygan replacing him. But it was in attack that Arsenal made most impact. In the sixth minute, Thierry Henry rose to head a Dennis Bergkamp free-kick but his effort went wide. Nine minutes later, Henry's cross was parried by Antti Niemi and Andreas Jakobsson hacked the ball to safety.

On 20 minutes Southampton came close to taking the lead. When Danny Higginbotham crossed to the far post and Mikael Nilsson attempted to convert the chance, his shot hit the inside of the post and bounced back out of the goal.

On the half-hour, Bergkamp was fouled in the area and referee Matt Messias awarded a penalty. Thierry Henry sent Niemi the wrong way with his spot-kick but hit the post and José Antonio Reyes, picking up the rebound, fired wide. Soon

An elegant side-foot shot from Thierry Henry opens the scoring.

after, Bergkamp shot just wide after being set up by captain Patrick Vieira. Then, eight minutes before half-time, Henry's side-footed effort was saved by Niemi.

Just after the hour mark, Reyes was replaced by Robert Pires and Cesc Fabregas replaced Edu. These substitutions seemed to inject new life into Arsenal and when Bergkamp sent a long pass forward for Henry, the striker made no mistake to put the Gunners ahead. On 78 minutes, Arsenal almost made it two when Henry crossed for Ljungberg whose shot was saved by Niemi.

Southampton equalised in the 80th minute when a Neil McCann corner was headed into the back of Jens Lehmann's net by Rory Delap. They celebrated in front of their ecstatic fans and well they might have. Injury-hit and in a bad run of form, they had been given little hope by any pundits before kick-off.

Arsenal immediately came close to regaining the lead but Niemi was equal to Pires' shot. Then, Arsène Wenger sent on Robin van Persie to replace Ljungberg. The Dutchman had been full

of energy at the City of Manchester Stadium in midweek, could he make the difference here?

Before he could touch the ball, Arsenal were behind when McCann again set up a Delap header, this time from a free-kick. Again, the Southampton fans were delirious with joy. But the game had a final twist left in it.

In the dying moments of the match, van Persie fired home a spectacular equaliser. For his first goal at Highbury he picked up the ball in a crowded, chaotic penalty area and expertly fired it through the crowd into the top corner of Niemi's net. This goal sparked exuberant celebrations among the home fans who greeted it as if it were a winner.

In truth, Arsenal had created enough chances to comfortably win this match but in the circumstances, Gunners' fans were relieved to salvage a point so late in the game. The spirit Arsenal showed to secure a point and the impressive form of Robin van Persie also gave the home fans plenty of reason for celebration.

Robin van Persie looks pleased after opening his Highbury account...

... but Arsène Wenger looks even happier at the Gunners' last gasp equaliser.

OCTOBER 2004

Arsenal.com PLAYER OF THE MONTH
Thierry **HENRY**

❝I always say to myself that my target is to be consistent. People never notice that. They notice a player over two or three games, but you have to be there the whole season. You have to perform every weekend, every midweek, every weekend.❞

THIERRY HENRY

❝Thierry is intelligent and ambitious. A player with those two qualities can only get better. He'll continue to progress because he wants to improve all the time. Who can you compare him with? Nobody else up front can repeat week in, week out, the quality of what he is achieving. He was world champion at 20. Do I still think he's the best player in the world? Yes, I do.❞

ARSÈNE WENGER

❝I feel when you look at Thierry now you can see a player in the peak of his form. It is fantastic for us to have a guy like him playing for us. He might make it all look very simple but that is a mark of a special player. He is in such good form at the moment and perhaps he will get even better in the future?❞

ROBERT PIRES

ARSENAL DIARY

Tuesday 5 October
- Arsenal announce a lucrative sponsorship deal with Emirates Airlines, the largest of its kind in English football. The Club's new ground will be called the Emirates Stadium and the company will also become Arsenal's shirt sponsor for eight years from the 2006/2007 season.

Friday 22 October
- Manager Arsène Wenger celebrates his 55th birthday.

Wednesday 27 October
- Arsène Wenger signs a new contract that will keep him at Highbury until May 2008.

Friday 29 October
- Arsène Wenger and Club Director Ken Friar OBE are awarded the Freedom of the Borough of Islington.

THE WIDER WORLD

Saturday 9 October
- Goals from David Beckham and Frank Lampard secure England a 2–0 victory over Wales in a World Cup Qualifier. Meanwhile, the Republic of Ireland hold France to a 0–0 draw in Paris.

Wednesday 13 October
- England beat Azerbaijan 1–0 in a World Cup qualifier.

Tuesday 19 October
- Michael Owen scores his first goal in Spain to hand Real Madrid a 1–0 victory over Dynamo Kiev in the Champions League.

Tuesday 26 October
- West Bromwich Albion part company with their manager Gary Megson.

FA CARLING PREMIERSHIP

31 October 2004

			HOME				AWAY				
	P	W	D	L	F	A	W	D	L	F	A	Pts
ARSENAL	11	4	2	0	19	8	4	0	1	12	4	26
Chelsea	11	4	1	0	8	1	4	1	1	8	2	26
Everton	11	3	1	2	6	7	4	1	0	8	3	23
Bolton Wanderers	11	4	2	0	11	5	2	1	2	7	8	21
Middlesbrough	11	2	2	1	7	6	3	1	2	12	8	18
Liverpool	10	4	0	0	10	1	1	2	3	8	9	17
Manchester United	11	3	2	0	7	3	1	3	2	4	6	17
Newcastle United	11	3	1	1	12	7	1	3	2	10	12	16
Portsmouth	10	4	1	1	11	6	0	2	2	4	6	15
Aston Villa	11	3	2	0	9	3	0	4	2	5	10	15
Tottenham Hotspur	11	1	2	2	3	4	2	2	2	3	4	13
Charlton Athletic	11	3	2	1	8	4	0	1	4	2	15	12
Manchester City	10	2	1	2	6	3	1	1	3	6	8	11
Crystal Palace	11	2	0	3	7	7	1	2	3	5	8	11
Fulham	11	3	0	3	7	9	0	2	3	5	10	11
Birmingham City	11	1	3	2	4	5	0	3	2	3	5	9
West Bromwich Albion	11	1	4	1	6	8	0	1	4	3	12	8
Southampton	11	1	2	2	5	6	0	2	4	3	8	7
Blackburn Rovers	11	1	4	1	7	10	0	0	5	2	14	7
Norwich City	10	0	3	2	6	10	0	3	2	3	7	6

NOVEMBER

UEFA Champions League, Group Stage, Group E
Tuesday 2 November 2004 at Highbury, 7.45 p.m.
Attendance: 35,137 Referee: Luis Medina Canalejo, Spain

W W D L W D [13 scored, 8 conceded]　　　　W W D D L W [8 scored, 4 conceded]

ARSENAL 1　　1 PANATHINAIKOS

Henry 16 pen　　　　Cygan o.g. 75

Substitutes					Substitutes
	Jens **LEHMANN**	1	12	Konstantinos **CHALKIAS**	
Manuel **ALMUNIA** 24	Ashley **COLE**	3	2	René **HENRIKSEN**	Mario **GALINOVIC** 1
Mathieu **FLAMINI** 16	Pascal **CYGAN**	18	16	Sotirios **KYRGIAKOS**	Miltos **SAPANIS** 22
Philippe **SENDEROS** 20	Kolo **TOURE**	28	3	Elias **KOTSIOS**	Nasief **MORRIS** ▸ 5
Justin **HOYTE** 31	**LAUREN**	12	27	Pantelis **KONSTANTINIDIS** ▓	(Basinas, 89 mins) ◂
Johan **DJOUROU** 45	Fredrik **LJUNGBERG**	8	24	Loukas **VINTRA**	Emanuel **OLISADEBE** 23
▸ Robin **VAN PERSIE** 11	Patrick **VIEIRA**	4	20	Angelos **BASINAS**	Maciej **BYKOWSKI** 29
◂ (Ljungberg, 83 mins)	Francesc **FABREGAS**	15	4	Silvio **MARIC**	Michalis **KONSTANTINOU** ▸ 19
▸ José Antonio **REYES** 9	Robert **PIRES**	7	26	Rudolf **SKÁCEL** ▓	(González, 60 mins) ◂
◂ (Bergkamp, 72 mins)	Dennis **BERGKAMP**	10	9	Ezequiel **GONZÁLEZ** ▓	Dumitru **MITU** ▸ 21
	▓ Thierry **HENRY**	14	11	Dimitrios **PAPADOPOULOS**	(Papadopoulos, 62 mins) ◂

MATCH REPORT

On a chilly Tuesday evening, winter arrived in North London. The cold reality for Arsenal fans was that this draw with Panathinaikos – and PSV Eindhoven's victory over Rosenborg the same evening – left their team with much still to do to ensure qualification from Group E.

The game started in lively fashion and Dennis Bergkamp was the first to test Konstantinos

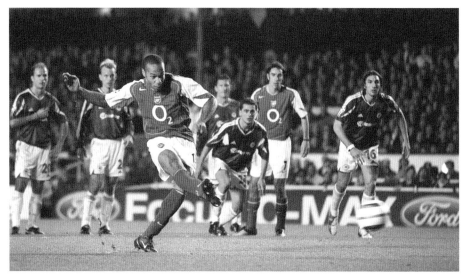

After missing a penalty *against Southampton, Thierry Henry makes no mistake with his spot-kick after 16 minutes.*

Dennis Bergkamp was a major threat to Panathinaikos throughout the match but was unable to get on the scoresheet.

Chalkias in the Panathinaikos goal with a long-range effort. After 16 minutes, the Dutchman was a key player as Arsenal took the lead. Bergkamp fired a free-kick into a crowded penalty area and Patrick Vieira tumbled to the ground during the ensuing melee. The referee awarded a penalty to the surprise of some spectators, but later replays showed that Sotirios Kyrgiakos had fouled Vieira.

Thierry Henry, who had missed from the spot during Arsenal's previous match, bravely and professionally stepped up to take the penalty and dispatched it in style. The Frenchman sent the goalkeeper the wrong way and fired the ball decisively into the left corner.

Having already surrendered the lead twice in this Champions League campaign, Arsenal were somewhat cautious following Henry's opener. That said, the Gunners did continue to create chances and a lively cross from Ashley Cole threatened to lead to a second goal before Cole was judged offside. Soon after, Vieira found himself in a threatening position but was unable to finish. As

half time came, there was ample reason for cautious optimism in the Arsenal ranks.

Eight minutes after the restart, a superb Arsenal move came near to doubling the home side's lead. The magnificent Robert Pires collected the ball on the halfway line and began a breathtaking run that saw him beat four opponents before releasing the ball to Henry. The striker turned, leaving his marker in his wake, and fired the ball into the net. But before the celebrations could begin, the assistant referee flagged Henry offside.

On 57 minutes, a Panathinaikos free-kick was headed into the danger zone by Elias Kotsios. Cole tangled with Dimitrios Papadopoulos and the referee awarded the visitors a penalty. After some delay, while the injured Papadopoulos was taken off, Angelos Basinas, one of Greece's heroes during their Euro 2004 victory, stepped up to take the spot-kick. He could not repeat his heroics of the summer, however, and shot high over the bar.

Having benefited from that, Arsenal's luck had well and truly run out for the night. On 74 minutes, Loukas Vintra launched a 25-yard shot at Jens Lehmann's goal and Pascal Cygan accidentally diverted it past his own goalkeeper. This was especially cruel on Cygan as he had been performing impressively all evening.

The home side's misfortune continued a minute later when substitute José Antonio Reyes saw his excellent volley blocked by Chalkias and the Spaniard's follow-up smashed against the bar. Arsène Wenger then brought Robin van Persie into the action in place of Freddie Ljungberg, but the winning goal did not arrive.

Although this draw, secured by a home side missing several injured players including Sol Campbell and Edu, was disappointing, it left Arsène Wenger one victory away from qualification for the knockout stages.

NOVEMBER

FA Barclaycard Premiership
Saturday 6 November 2004 at Selhurst Park, 5.15 p.m.
Attendance: 26,193 Referee: Mike Dean

D W L W W W [9 scored, 3 conceded]   W D L W D D [13 scored, 9 conceded]

CRYSTAL PALACE 1   1 ARSENAL
Riihilahti 65   Henry 63

Substitutes		Gabor **KIRALY**	28	1	Jens **LEHMANN**		Substitutes
Julian **SPERONI**	1	Emmerson **BOYCE**	21	3	Ashley **COLE**	24	Manuel **ALMUNIA**
Sandor **TORGHELLE**	10	Gonzalo **SORONDO**	26	18	Pascal **CYGAN**	16	Mathieu **FLAMINI** ▶
▶ Mikele **LEIGERTWOOD**	12	Tony **POPOVIC**	6	28	Kolo **TOURE**		(Fabregas, 81 mins) ◀
◀ (Sorondo, 24 mins)		Danny **GRANVILLE**	3	12	**LAUREN**	20	Philippe **SENDEROS**
▶ Vassilis **LAKIS**	32	Wayne **ROUTLEDGE**	7	8	Fredrik **LJUNGBERG**	11	Robin **VAN PERSIE** ▶
◀ (Routledge, 52 mins)		Aki **RIIHILAHTI**	15	4	Patrick **VIEIRA**		(Pires, 73 mins) ◀
▶ Dougie **FREEDMAN**	9	Michael **HUGHES**	17	15	Francesc **FABREGAS**	10	Dennis **BERGKAMP** ▶
◀ (Kolkka, 80 mins)		Ben **WATSON**	14	7	Robert **PIRES**		(Ljungberg, 73 mins) ◀
		Joonas **KOLKKA**	22	9	José Antonio **REYES**		
		Andrew **JOHNSON**	8	14	Thierry **HENRY**		

MATCH REPORT

On the face of it, this game may have seemed something of a mismatch. Crystal Palace have not enjoyed a home victory over Arsenal since 1979 and for much of the season the Eagles had seemed as out of their depth as Arsenal had appeared unbeatable. But just take a look at the two sides' form going into the match: Palace had lost just one of their previous five games while Arsenal had only won once during the same period.

The home side lived up to their impressive form during a lively opening period. After being forced to weather a few early attacks, Arsenal created their first chance after seven minutes when Patrick Vieira found José Antonio Reyes, starting in place of Dennis Bergkamp, in a threatening position but the Spaniard fired straight at Gabor Kiraly. Within seconds, Reyes fed Thierry Henry who shot just outside the post as Kiraly stood helpless.

Soon after, Henry turned provider as he fed Francesc Fabregas's well-timed burst into the box. The Spanish teenager collected the ball but his mis-hit shot was blocked. At this point, it

This match saw another fine midfield performance from Cesc Fabregas.

Despite desperate defending from Palace, Thierry Henry coolly bundles the ball home to put the Gunners ahead.

seemed only a matter of time before Arsenal found the net and Crystal Palace collapsed.

But time after time Palace survived Arsenal's attacks. Reyes saw a shot blocked by a defender, Henry fired a cross over the bar, Kolo Toure's long range effort was saved and Fredrik Ljungberg just failed to convert a Henry cross shortly before half-time.

After the interval, Palace were a different prospect. Andy Johnson had been an isolated figure in their attack during the first period but received increasing support from Joonas Kolkka and other team-mates in the second half.

Nonetheless it was Arsenal that finally broke the deadlock. Fabregas fed Ljungberg as he rampaged down the right and the Swede crossed to Henry who bundled the ball home from close range. If the script was that Palace would roll over at this point, Iain Dowie's men had not read it.

Two minutes after Henry's goal, Vassilis Lakis found himself in space on the right and his cross was met by Aki Riihilahti who shot past Jens Lehmann to equalise for Palace. If the visitors were stunned by this then matters could have taken a turn for the worse when seconds later only a magnificent last-ditch challenge by Toure stopped Riihilahti scoring a second goal. Then came a spectacular miss when Johnson's cross found Lakis three yards out with the goal at his mercy. He somehow fired over the bar to the relief of the visitors.

As Arsenal battled for a winner, Fabregas, Reyes and substitutes Robin van Persie and Dennis Bergkamp all came close. But Crystal Palace put everything they had into battling for a point and held on until the final whistle.

Having previously set the standard with a 49-match unbeaten run in the Premiership, Arsenal had now gone three matches without a league win.

NOVEMBER

Carling Cup, 4th Round
Tuesday 9 November 2004 at Highbury, 7.45 p.m.
Attendance: 27,791 Referee: Alan Wiley

D L W D D D [8 scored, 9 conceded]   L W W W D L [7 scored, 5 conceded]

ARSENAL 3   1 EVERTON

Owusu-Abeyie 25, Lupoli 52, 85   Gravesen 8

Substitutes					Substitutes
Michael **JORDAN**	38	Manuel **ALMUNIA** 24	1 Richard **WRIGHT**		
Jordan **FOWLER**	36	Justin **HOYTE** 31	22 Tony **HIBBERT**	5	David **WEIR**
‣ Sebastian **LARSSON**	39	Johan **DJOUROU** 35	20 Joseph **YOBO**	15	Gary **NAYSMITH**
◂ (Edu, 65 mins)		Philippe **SENDEROS** 20	4 Alan **STUBBS**	37	Ian **TURNER**
‣ Quincy		Daniel **KARBASSIYOON** 46	3 Alessandro **PISTONE**	21	Leon **OSMAN** ‣
OWUSU-ABEYIE	42	Jermaine **PENNANT** 21	2 Steve **WATSON**		(Watson, 71 mins) ◂
◂ (Smith, 21 mins)		▨ **EDU** 17	16 Thomas **GRAVESEN**	19	Nick **CHADWICK** ‣
‣ Patrick **CREGG**	34	Mathieu **FLAMINI** 16	17 Tim **CAHILL**		(Bent, 16 mins) ◂
◂ (Lupoli, 89 mins)		Ryan **SMITH** 47	14 Kevin **KILBANE** ▨		
		Arturo **LUPOLI** 40	11 James **McFADDEN**		
		Robin **VAN PERSIE** 11	7 Marcus **BENT**		

MATCH REPORT

Arsenal's only victory in their past five matches had come in the previous round of the Carling Cup and the home fans hoped that Arsène Wenger's impressive mixture of reserves and youngsters could help lift the disappointment of recent outings with another win. That they managed this, after going behind to a full-strength line-up from high-flying Everton and fielding a side with an average age of 19, made this one of the most satisfying results of the season.

Edu's inclusion was one of three changes from the last Carling Cup outing and the Brazilian took the captain's armband. But it was an in-form Everton, arriving on the back of an impressive performance against Chelsea at Stamford Bridge the previous Saturday, that looked good early on.

In the eighth minute, Thomas Gravesen's 20-yard free-kick deflected off the foot of Jermaine Pennant and goalkeeper Manuel Almunia could not readjust his positioning in time to prevent the goal. Soon after this, both sides were forced into changes, with

Joy unconfined for substitute Quincy Owusu-Abeyie who scored
four minutes after coming on for the injured Ryan Smith.

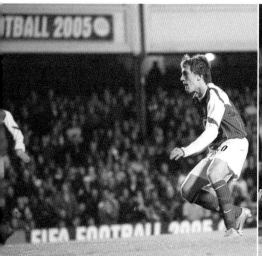

Arturo Lupoli becomes the first-ever Italian player to score for Arsenal.

Lupoli added a second five minutes from time with a shot from the edge of the area.

Nick Chadwick replacing Marcus Bent for the visitors and Owusu-Abeyie replacing Ryan Smith for Arsenal soon after.

Owuse-Abeyie made an immediate impression. Firstly, after a spectacular run, he forced Richard Wright to make a diving save. Minutes later, he received a pass from Pennant and cut inside Tony Hibbert before unleashing a shot into the corner of the net to restore parity.

For much of the remainder of the half, Arsenal looked most likely to take the lead. Arturo Lupoli received a neat pass from Robin van Persie and looked set to score until Joseph Yobo intervened. Then Owuse-Abeyie and van Persie both fired efforts just wide of Wright's goal.

Shortly after the break, Edu fired just wide but the home fans did not have long to wait until their team took the lead. Owusu-Abeyie burst forward leaving player after player in his wake. He found van Persie who shaped to shoot but instead found Lupoli who clipped the ball home to become the first Italian player ever to score for Arsenal. It was a remarkable move - and one that had Highbury in raptures.

Lupoli had another chance when he raced onto a pass from Pennant but Wright dived bravely at his feet to prevent a goal. However, five minutes from time, the young Italian was not to be denied again. Owusu-Abeyie was the architect of another impressive move that saw Lupoli score his second and Arsenal's third from the edge of the area.

Manuel Almunia still had a threat from Nick Chadwick and an effort from James McFadden to deal with but Arsenal marched comfortably into the last eight of the Carling Cup. Arsène Wenger's impressive second-string side had indeed given the home fans the perfect tonic. A superb team performance, with Owuse-Abeyie and Lupoli outstanding, had disposed of Everton, then sitting pretty in third place in the Premiership, and sent the Highbury faithful home with a spring in their steps. Could the first-team reciprocate on Saturday when they visited White Hart Lane for the North London derby?

NOVEMBER

FA Barclaycard Premiership
Saturday 13 November 2004 at White Hart Lane, 12.00 p.m.
Attendance: 36,095 Referee: Steve Bennett

L L W L L W [10 scored 11 conceded]   L W D D D W [9 scored, 8 conceded]

TOTTENHAM 4 HOTSPUR

Naybet 37, Defoe 61, King 74, Kanoute 88

5 ARSENAL

Henry 45, Lauren 55 pen,
Vieira 60, Ljungberg 69,
Pires 81

Substitutes						Substitutes
Marton **FULOP**	25	Paul **ROBINSON**	1	1	Jens **LEHMANN**	
Jamie **REDKNAPP**	15	Noe **PAMAROT**	17	3	Ashley **COLE**	Manuel **ALMUNIA**	24
▸ Simon **DAVIES**	7	Noureddine **NAYBET**	2	18	Pascal **CYGAN**	Mathieu **FLAMINI**	16
◂ (Mendes, 68 mins)		Ledley **KING**	26	28	Kolo **TOURE**	Robert **PIRES** ▸	7
▸ Frederic **KANOUTE**	9	Erik **EDMAN**	14	12	**LAUREN**	(Reyes, 68 mins) ◂	
◂ (Brown, 76 mins)		Pedro **MENDES**	8	8	Fredrik **LJUNGBERG**	Justin **HOYTE**	31
▸ Anthony **GARDENER**	30	Michael **BROWN**	11	4	Patrick **VIEIRA**	Robin **VAN PERSIE** ▸	11
◂ (Keane, 90 mins)		Michael **CARRICK**	23	15	Francesc **FABREGAS**	(Bergkamp, 82 mins) ◂	
		Reto **ZIEGLER**	16	9	José Antonio **REYES**		
		Robbie **KEANE**	10	10	Dennis **BERGKAMP**		
		Jermain **DEFOE**	18	14	Thierry **HENRY**		

MATCH REPORT

Perhaps the most thrilling North London derby of all time resulted in Arsenal returning to the top of the Premiership table after emerging triumphant from an astonishing and exhilarating match. This game will live long in the memory of all who witnessed it but none of those could have predicted the goal-fest to come during a relatively tame opening half-hour.

Jens Lehmann saved twice from Jermain Defoe but was helpless in the 36th minute when Noureddine Naybet converted a Michael Carrick free-kick to give Spurs the lead. Seconds later, Lehmann prevented a second goal when he stopped a Patrick Vieira header from entering his own net.

Deep into injury time at the end of the first half, Lauren picked out Thierry Henry with a fine pass

It's 1–1 as a low shot from Thierry Henry levels the scores deep in first-half injury time.

Ten minutes later it's 2–1 and Henry celebrates again, this time with Lauren whose penalty gave the Gunners the lead.

and, after outfoxing his marker, the Frenchman coolly slotted home.

In the first minute of the second half, Arsenal almost struck again when José Antonio Reyes just failed to convert from Freddie Ljungberg's pass. In the 55th minute, Ljungberg was hauled down in the area and Lauren confidently converted the resulting penalty. Five minutes later, Vieira made it three for Arsenal after he surged forward from midfield and clipped the ball over Paul Robinson and into the net.

Game over? Not so fast. Just 60 seconds later, Defoe collected a throw-in on the left and ran through the Arsenal defence to curl a shot into the top corner of Lehmann's goal. In the 69th minute, Francesc Fabregas exchanged passes with Henry before releasing a breathtaking reverse pass to Ljungberg who fired past Robinson to restore Arsenal's two-goal lead.

Even then the goalscoring was not over. Ledley King nodded in another Carrick free-kick. But Arsenal responded immediately when Robert Pires, who had replaced Reyes, burst onto a cute pass from Henry to tuck the ball home at the near post. Robin van Persie then replaced Dennis Bergkamp. With three minutes remaining, Tottenham substitute Frederic Kanoute punished a mistake from Henry and slotted the ball past Lehmann.

Arsenal held onto their lead to emerge triumphant from this extraordinary, see-saw encounter. Arsenal's return to the top of the table only lasted a few hours and Arsène Wenger will have been concerned to see his team concede four goals. But as the referee blew the final whistle to bring the derby thriller to an end the Arsenal players, coaching staff and fans were able to savour a spectacular victory over their local rivals.

From 'One-Nil to the Arsenal' to 'One-Nil Down, Two-One Up', scorelines have often featured in the chants of the Highbury faithful. As the triumphant, if somewhat stunned, Arsenal fans returned home from this match, they could add 'Five-Four to the Arsenal' to their repertoire.

On the hour mark Patrick Vieira makes it 3–1 as he clips the ball over Spurs' keeper Paul Robinson.

Now it's 4–2 as Freddie Ljungberg converts Thierry Henry's magnificent through ball.

Almost done as Robert Pires beats Robinson to make it 5–3 with nine minutes left.

W D D D W W [14 scored, 10 conceded]   W D L L D L [6 scored, 12 conceded]

ARSENAL 1
Pires 54

1 WEST BROMWICH ALBION
Earnshaw 79

Substitutes					Substitutes
Manuel **ALMUNIA**	24	Jens **LEHMANN** 1	1 Russell **HOULT**		
Philippe **SENDEROS**	20	**LAUREN** 12	2 Riccardo **SCIMECA**	29	Tomasz **KUSZCZAK**
Justin **HOYTE**	31	Kolo **TOURE** 28	5 Darren **MOORE**	22	Bernt **HAAS**
▶ José Antonio **REYES**	9	Pascal **CYGAN** 18	6 Darren **PURSE**	34	Robert **EARNSHAW** ▶
◀ (Fabregas, 81 mins)		Ashley **COLE** 3	19 Neil **CLEMENT**		(Contra, 75 mins) ◀
▶ Robin **VAN PERSIE**	11	Fredrik **LJUNGBERG** 8	16 Cosmin **CONTRA**	4	Thomas **GAARDSOE** ▶
◀ (Bergkamp, 88 mins)		Patrick **VIEIRA** 4	8 Jonathan **GREENING**		(Sakiri, 84 mins) ◀
		Francesc **FABREGAS** 15	10 Andy **JOHNSON**	9	Geoff **HORSFIELD** ▶
		Robert **PIRES** 7	20 Artim **SAKIRI**		(Kanu, 75 mins) ◀
		Dennis **BERGKAMP** 10	11 Zoltan **GERA**		
		Thierry **HENRY** 14	25 Nwankwo **KANU**		

MATCH REPORT

Substitute Robert Earnshaw's late equaliser was agonising for Arsenal who had dominated proceedings and thoroughly deserved victory on a wet afternoon at Highbury. The visitors went into the game without an away win all season and Earnshaw's goal was one of only two chances they created all afternoon. So there was frustration and disappointment among the home fans that they had not witnessed another Arsenal victory.

The Gunners dominated possession during a lively opening half and peppered the visitors' penalty area with a number of tasty crosses. Then Thierry Henry played a one-two with Patrick Vieira before firing a powerful shot at goal that was blocked by Darren Moore. Vieira himself also came close with a header.

In the 28th minute, Andy Johnson almost scored just two yards out from Jens Lehmann's goal and Zoltan Gera came close seconds later. At the other end, Francesc Fabregas almost caught out Hoult with a neat shot that the visiting goalkeeper had to scramble back to collect.

A thunderous drive from Robert Pires seemed to be covered by Baggies' keeper Russell Hoult but somehow he let the ball slip through his hands to give Arsenal the lead.

A rampaging Thierry Henry kept the West Bromwich defence on its toes throughout the match with a series of accurate crosses, shots and free-kicks. Despite this the Gunners were unable to find a winner.

After 38 minutes, Robert Pires sent in a dangerous free-kick and Pascal Cygan headed it towards goal only to see it blocked on the line. Four minutes later, Arsenal were awarded another free-kick when Robert Pires was felled just outside the area. Henry curled the ball dangerously and Hoult had to palm it aside to prevent a goal.

Arsenal's inventiveness continued after the half-time interval. In the 48th minute, a rampaging Henry crossed from the left-wing and Pires let rip at goal. The Frenchman's shot was blocked and when the ball arrived at Dennis Bergkamp's feet at the far post, the Dutchman sent the ball over the crossbar.

Refusing to be buckled by frustration at their bad luck, the Gunners continued to press and were rewarded by some good fortune in the 54th minute. Pires collected the ball, ran at the Albion defence and curled a shot that Hoult seemed to have controlled after a full-length dive. Somehow

though, he let the ball slip through his hands and Arsenal were ahead.

The Gunners worked tirelessly to try and build on the lead with Ljungberg firing in a number of dangerous crosses, Henry having a shot and Cygan again came close with a header. West Bromwich then produced an equaliser when Jonathan Greening surged down the wing and crossed for substitute Earnshaw to score.

Arsène Wenger sent on José Antonio Reyes and Robin van Persie to try and concoct a winner. But apart from a Vieira header, there were no more chances and Arsenal had to settle for a draw from a game they had dominated. Albion had worked hard for their point but, given Arsenal's superior possession and the amount of chances the home side fashioned, it was disappointing that they did not win.

NOVEMBER

UEFA Champions League, Group Stage, Group B
Wednesday 24 November 2004 at the Philips-Stadion, Eindhoven, 7.45 p.m.
Attendance: 35,200 Referee: Herbert Fandel, Germany

W D W W W W [9 scored, 0 conceded]　　　D D D W W D [13 scored, 10 conceded]

PSV EINDHOVEN 1　1 ARSENAL

Ooijer 8　　　Henry 31

Substitutes		Heurelho **GOMES**	1	1	Jens **LEHMANN**		Substitutes
Edwin **ZOETEBIER**	21	André **OOIJER**	2	12	**LAUREN**	24	Manuel **ALMUNIA**
Johann **VONLANTHEN**	15	**ALEX**	4	28	Kolo **TOURE**	20	Philippe **SENDEROS**
Theo **LUCIUS**	16	Wilfred **BOUMA**	5	23	Sol **CAMPBELL**	18	Pascal **CYGAN**
▸ DaMarcus **BEASLEY**	11	**LEE** Yong-Pyo	3	3	Ashley **COLE**	21	Jermaine **PENNANT**
◂ (Vogel, 65 mins)		Mark **VAN BOMMEL**	6	8	Fredrik **LJUNGBERG**	31	Justin **HOYTE** ▸
Eric **ADDO**	18	Johann **VOGEL**	14	4	Patrick **VIEIRA**		(Pires, 69 mins) ◂
Csaba **FEHÉR**	22	Phillip **COCU**	8	15	Francesc **FABREGAS**	11	Robin **VAN PERSIE** ▸
		PARK Ji-Sung	7	7	Robert **PIRES**		(Reyes, 63 mins) ◂
		Jefferson **FARFÁN**	17	9	José Antonio **REYES**	16	Mathieu **FLAMINI** ▸
		Gerald **SIBON**	35	1	Thierry **HENRY**		(Van Persie, 81 mins) ◂

MATCH REPORT

Arsenal were behind after just eight minutes but recovered to snatch an equaliser and then bravely held out for a point after being reduced to nine men in the second half of an eventful evening's

football in Holland. This was the Gunners' fourth 1–1 draw in six matches.

A bright start to the match saw Thierry Henry come close after pouncing on Francesc Fabregas's

Freddie Ljungberg's back-heel falls perfectly for Thierry Henry to fire home Arsenal's equaliser.

flick. But the visitors were soon behind. In the eighth minute, Jefferson Farfán's shot was blocked and from the resultant Mark van Bommel corner, André Ooijer surged between Henry and Patrick Vieira to nod home at the near post.

With confidence so key in the Champions League, particularly away from home, going behind so early on was a blow to Arsenal. Nevertheless, Arsène Wenger's men quickly recovered their composure and continued to attack. Henry came agonisingly close to creating an equaliser when he robbed Wilfred Bouma of the ball. The Frenchman then faced the goal from a tight angle and as Heurelho Gomes bore down on him, Henry could only find the side-netting.

Again the Gunners continued to probe and were given their reward on the half-hour mark. Henry cut inside from the right-wing and played a one-two with Fredrik Ljungberg while holding off Bouma. Ljungberg's cute back-heel fell perfectly into the Frenchman's path and he fired home from 12 yards.

Henry's determination and flair epitomised an impressive first-half performance from Arsenal and the visitors almost went ahead soon after the restart. On 50 minutes, José Antonio Reyes fired a long-range drive at goal which Gomes somehow managed to block. Then, a Robert Pires free-kick was almost turned into a goal when Sol Campbell came agonisingly close to connecting with it in a dangerous position.

By this point PSV were largely playing on the counter-attack. In the 62nd minute, van Bommel ran past Ashley Cole but saw his near-post effort saved by Jens Lehmann. Two minutes later, Arsenal were reduced to ten men when Lauren, who had already been cautioned, received his second yellow card of the night.

The determined Henry almost snatched a winner straight after Lauren's dismissal. He sped down the left and beat his marker in the area. Unfortunately, his goal-bound effort was saved by Gomes. Justin Hoyte then replaced Robert Pires as Arsenal reverted to a back-four again. Van Persie had already been thrown into the action

Despite being down to nine men, following the dismissals of Lauren (above) and Patrick Vieira, Arsenal battled bravely to secure a point in Eindhoven.

and he came close with a chip before Ljungberg fired a Henry cross straight at Gomes.

With 12 minutes left, Arsenal were reduced to nine men when Vieira received his second yellow card of the evening. Then van Persie had to be stretchered off after injuring himself in a challenge with Gerald Sibon. Brazilian Alex and Park Ji-Sung both had further chances but Arsenal courageously held on to save the point.

At the final whistle, the PSV fans celebrated joyously as their side guaranteed qualification from Group E. For the Arsenal fans, who had seen Henry score his 14th goal in 20 games this season, there was relief that their heroes' Champions League fate remained in their own hands.

W L W W L L [6 scored, 6 conceded]   D D W W D D [12 scored, 9 conceded]

LIVERPOOL 2   1 ARSENAL
Alonso 41, Mellor 90   Vieira 57

Substitutes				Substitutes	
	Chris **KIRKLAND**	22	1	Jens **LEHMANN**	
Jerzy **DUDEK** 1	Steve **FINNAN**	3	12	**LAUREN**	24 Manuel **ALMUNIA**
Salif **DIAO** 15	Sami **HYYPIA**	4	28	Kolo **TOURE**	20 Philippe **SENDEROS**
Igor **BISCAN** 25	Jamie **CARRAGHER**	23	23	Sol **CAMPBELL**	16 Mathieu **FLAMINI**
▸ Antonio **NUNEZ** 12	John Arne **RIISE**	6	3	Ashley **COLE**	31 Justin **HOYTE**
◂ (Pongolle, 69 mins)	Steven **GERRARD**	8	8	Fredrik **LJUNGBERG**	11 Robin **VAN PERSIE** ▸
Stephen **WARNOCK** 28	Xabi **ALONSO**	14	4	Patrick **VIEIRA** 〽	(Reyes, 67 mins) ◂
	Dietmar **HAMANN**	16	15	Francesc **FABREGAS**	
	Harry **KEWELL**	7	7	Robert **PIRES**	
	Neil **MELLOR**	33	9	José Antonio **REYES**	
	Florent Sinama **PONGOLLE**	24	14	Thierry **HENRY** 〽	

MATCH REPORT

Neil Mellor's spectacular late goal consigned Arsenal not just to defeat but to their third game without victory, and maintained the five-point gap Chelsea had opened at the top of the table the previous day. To compound a disappointing afternoon for the Gunners, Patrick Vieira was booked and will now miss the forthcoming match against Chelsea.

Although Arsenal's familiar flowing style was in evidence at times, in truth the visitors were unable to assert themselves enough to create many chances. Instead, an injury-struck Liverpool side produced a fluent and energetic performance that probably merited the three points they took from the game.

In the third minute, Steven Gerrard – in determined mood and playing his first game at Anfield since returning from injury – burst into the Arsenal penalty area. Kolo Toure appeared to stick a leg out as Gerrard raced past him but

Following great work from Henry and Pires, captain Patrick Vieira steals into the Liverpool penalty area to equalise.

Ashley Cole beats Dietmar Hamann down Liverpool's right flank but his cross was cut out before it reached Freddie Ljungberg.

referee Alan Wiley waved play on as the Liverpool man tumbled.

Liverpool were fired up by this and Xabi Alonso soon unleashed a long-range shot that went wide, Neil Mellor hit the crossbar and Harry Kewell forced a great save from Jens Lehmann. Then on 32 minutes, Vieira sent Ashley Cole surging forward on the left but the defender's cross was collected by Kirkland before it reached Fredrik Ljungberg.

But it was Liverpool who broke the deadlock. Five minutes before the interval, Gerrard sent an accurate pass to Alonoso who buried a 20-yard shot past the helpless Lehmann.

Despite having the lead, Liverpool continued to press immediately after the break. Gerrard was again in the thick of the action as a chance was created for the unmarked Florent Sinama-Pongolle. Dietmar Hamman also had a chance but his low drive was saved by Lehmann.

Arsenal professionally weathered this storm and equalised in the 57th minute. Thierry Henry and Robert Pires played some sublime passes

between each other and released Vieira who steamed into the area and coolly clipped his shot over the advancing Kirkland.

Robin van Persie replaced José Antonio Reyes on 67 minutes and the Dutchman injected new vigour into proceedings. Again however, most clear-cut chances were created by the home side. Gerrard was producing lots of problems for Toure who had to make a last-gasp tackle and then an acrobatic clearance from chances created by the Englishman. Gerrard then fired a stinging cross-shot which Lehmann impressively saved.

There was little the goalkeeper could do, though, when Liverpool took the lead. With only seconds remaining, Mellor collected the ball and paced forward before unleashing a powerful drive from 25 yards to win the points for Liverpool.

In recent years, Anfield has been a happy hunting ground for Arsenal so this was a disappointing result. It was the Gunners' final game of what had proved to be a difficult November. The Arsenal faithful left Merseyside hoping the next month would bring better fortune.

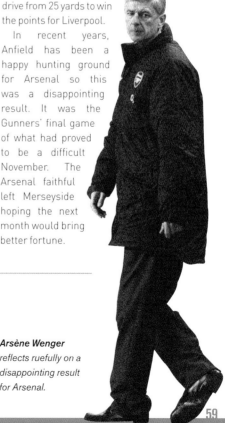

Arsène Wenger reflects ruefully on a disappointing result for Arsenal.

Arsenal.com PLAYER OF THE MONTH
Fredrik LJUNGBERG

‘He has been outstanding. The main three goalscorers so far this season have been Ljungberg, Pires and Henry. It is important to have at least three players in your team who can score.’

ARSÈNE WENGER

‘Fredrik is playing really well for us at the moment. He's making great runs, which are hard for teams to contain, and these lead to goals.’

PATRICK VIEIRA

‘I work on those runs in training and it is important for me to get them right in the match situation. So far I am quite proud of my contribution this season but that doesn't mean I am going to stop working. Winning is a good thing, obviously, because it gives you self-belief and puts you in a positive mind.’

FREDRIK LJUNGBERG

ARSENAL DIARY

Tuesday 9 November
- Patrick Vieira and Thierry Henry attend the UK launch of Diambars, the Senegalese charity co-launched by Vieira which, aims to motivate youngsters to become educated through football.

Wednesday 10 November
- Arsenal draw Manchester United in the Quarter-finals of the Carling Cup.

Tuesday 16 November
- Fredrik Ljungberg is named Sweden's Midfielder of the Year.

Thursday 18 November
- Goalkeeper Stuart Taylor joins Championship side Leicester City on a one-month loan deal.

Monday 29 November
- Thierry Henry is shortlisted for 2004's FIFA World Player of the Year.

THE WIDER WORLD

Tuesday 9 November
- West Bromwich Albion name Bryan Robson as their new manager.

Wednesday 17 November
- Spain beat England 1–0 in a friendly international.

Wednesday 23 November
- Harry Redknapp resigns as Portsmouth manager.

Sunday 28 November
- Both David Beckham and Michael Owen are on target for Real Madrid as the Spanish giants thrash Levante 5–0.

FA CARLING PREMIERSHIP

30 November 2004

	P	HOME					AWAY					Pts
		W	D	L	F	A	W	D	L	F	A	
Chelsea	15	5	2	0	11	3	6	1	1	16	3	36
ARSENAL	**15**	**4**	**3**	**0**	**20**	**9**	**5**	**1**	**2**	**19**	**11**	**31**
Everton	15	4	1	2	7	7	5	2	1	10	5	30
Manchester United	15	4	3	0	9	3	3	3	2	10	7	27
Middlesbrough	15	3	3	1	10	7	4	1	3	14	11	25
Aston Villa	15	5	2	0	13	3	1	4	3	7	13	24
Liverpool	14	6	0	1	15	5	1	2	4	8	11	23
Bolton Wanderers	15	4	2	2	12	8	2	3	2	10	11	23
Manchester City	15	3	3	2	10	5	2	2	3	9	9	20
Newcastle United	15	3	2	3	15	15	2	3	2	12	12	20
Portsmouth	14	4	1	2	12	9	1	2	4	6	11	18
Charlton Athletic	15	4	4	2	12	8	1	1	5	5	19	18
Tottenham Hotspur	15	2	2	4	11	12	2	2	3	3	5	16
Birmingham City	15	1	4	3	5	7	1	4	2	7	8	14
Fulham	15	3	0	5	8	15	1	2	4	9	12	14
Crystal Palace	15	2	1	4	8	10	1	3	4	9	13	13
Blackburn Rovers	15	1	5	1	10	13	1	2	5	6	16	13
Southampton	15	2	4	2	11	11	0	2	5	4	10	12
Norwich City	15	1	4	2	9	12	0	5	3	5	13	12
West Bromwich Albion	15	1	4	3	7	13	0	3	4	6	15	10

DECEMBER

D W W W W [12 scored, 2 conceded]   D W W D D W [13 scored, 9 conceded]

MANCHESTER 1 UNITED   0 ARSENAL

Bellion 1

Substitutes				Substitutes
RICARDO 34	Tim **HOWARD** 1	24 Manuel **ALMUNIA**		Chris **WRIGHT** 48
Gerard **PIQUE** 28	Phil **NEVILLE** 3	31 Justin **HOYTE**	48	Frankie **SIMEK** 34
Sylvan **EBANKS-BLAKE** 40	Wes **BROWN** 6	20 Philippe **SENDEROS**	34	Patrick **CREGG** ▸ 41
▸ Giuseppe **ROSSI** 42	John **O'SHEA** 22	35 Johan **DJOUROU**	41	(Larsson, 72 mins) ◂
◂ (Eagles, 79 mins)	Quinton **FORTUNE** 25	22 Gael **CLICHY**		Ryan **SMITH** ▸ 47
▸ David **JONES** 31	Chris **EAGLES** 33	21 Jermaine **PENNANT**	47	(Lupoli, 68 mins) ◂
◂ (Kleberson, 79 mins)	Eric **DJEMBA-DJEMBA** 19	16 Mathieu **FLAMINI**		Daniel 46
	Liam **MILLER** 17	39 Sebastian **LARSSON**		**KARBASSIYOON** ▸
	Kieran **RICHARDSON** 23	42 Quincy **OWUSU-ABEYIE**	46	(Clichy, 81 mins) ◂
	KLEBERSON 15	40 Aruro **LUPOLI**		
	David **BELLION** 12	11 Robin **VAN PERSIE**		

MATCH REPORT

Arsenal's brave and entertaining run in the Carling Cup came to an end at Old Trafford but there was still much reason for pride among the travelling Gunners' fans at the final whistle. Sir Alex Ferguson had fielded a far more experienced side – including eight full internationals – and Arsenal had responded positively to going behind so early.

Due to traffic congestion in the Manchester area, not all the fans had arrived when David Bellion put United ahead. Johan Djourou slipped in the first minute and gifted possession to Bellion whose weak shot was let in by Manuel Almunia. Just 20 seconds were on the clock and Arsenal now had a mountain to climb at Old Trafford.

With the Gunners somewhat stunned by this dramatic opening, United tried to finish off the game with more goals. Justin Hoyte came close to conceding a penalty when he fouled Kleberson just outside the penalty area. Goalscorer Bellion then set up Chris Eagles but Gael Clichy put the United youngster under pressure and forced him to shoot wide. John O'Shea also came close with a header.

High-flying Gael Clichy *gave a tremendous performance in the Arsenal rearguard at Old Trafford.*

Quincy Owusu-Abeyie shows the kind of concentration that was a feature of Arsenal's performances in this year's Carling Cup run.

In the 26th minute, Arsenal gave United a scare when, after receiving a backpass, Tim Howard tried to dribble the ball out of his area. The energetic Robin van Persie chased down on him and almost forced a dangerous error.

Almunia responded well to his earlier error making a fine block from Kieran Richardson's volley and he then rushed off his line to clear from Bellion. At the other end, Arturo Lupoli won a free-kick in the 40th minute and Jermaine Pennant's 20-yard strike forced Howard into a save.

The second period saw a somewhat improved performance from Arsenal. Pennant took another free-kick which was charged down by United and then Lupoli was blocked on the edge of the area as he bore down on goal. All the same, the superior experience in United's side continued to tell – especially in midfield. Bellion and Eagles again threatened to add to the scoreline but the Arsenal defence – and Gael Clichy most notably – continued to stand tall.

Arsenal's best chances in the closing stages came from van Persie. In the 75th minute he was blocked as he threatened to dribble into the area and then in the dying moments, he cut inside but saw his low shot go wide of Howard's post.

Arsène Wenger will take many positives from his team's Carling Cup run this season. His youngsters had beaten essentially full-strength sides, put out by Manchester City and Everton and reached the quarter-finals where they gave a strong Manchester United side a run for their money at Old Trafford. What a fantastic ray of light the likes of Lupoli and Owusu-Abeyie have proved to be during an impressive run in the Carling Cup. Here's to the future!

DECEMBER

FA Barclaycard Premiership
Saturday 4 December 2004 at Highbury, 3.00 p.m.
Attendance: 38,064 Referee: Dermot Gallagher

W W D D L L [11 scored, 10 conceded]   L L W L D D [5 scored, 7 conceded]

ARSENAL 3   0 BIRMINGHAM CITY

Pires 33, Henry 80, 86

Substitutes					Substitutes
	Manuel **ALMUNIA**	24	1	Maik **TAYLOR**	
Jens **LEHMANN** 1	**LAUREN**	12	29	Mario **MELCHIOT**	12 Ian **BENNETT**
Philippe **SENDEROS** 20	Kolo **TOURE**	28	4	Kenny **CUNNINGHAM**	15 Martin **TAYLOR** ▶
▶ Gael **CLICHY** 22	Sol **CAMPBELL**	23	5	Matthew **UPSON**	(Melchiot, 81 mins) ◀
◀ (Reyes, 68 mins)	Ashley **COLE**	3	3	Jamie **CLAPHAM**	7 Jesper **GRONKJAER** ▶
Quincy	Fredrik **LJUNGBERG**	8	22	Damien **JOHNSON**	(Anderton, 57 mins) ◀
OWUSU-ABEYIE 42	Patrick **VIEIRA**	4	8	Robbie **SAVAGE**	19 Clinton **MORRISON** ▶
▶ Mathieu **FLAMINI** 16	Francesc **FABREGAS**	15	32	Darren **ANDERTON**	(Dunn, 67 mins) ◀
◀ (Fabregas, 73 mins)	Robert **PIRES**	7	21	Julian **GRAY**	33 Dwight **YORKE**
	José Antonio **REYES**	9	10	David **DUNN**	
	Thierry **HENRY**	14	16	Emile **HESKEY**	

MATCH REPORT

It is no exaggeration to say that everyone associated with Arsenal was desperate for victory in this match. The team had lost to both Liverpool and Manchester United in the previous seven days and Chelsea's defeat of Newcastle United earlier in the day had seen the Blues open up an eight-point gap at the Premiership summit. The sense of determination was tangible in the air at Highbury.

There was only one change from the side that started at Anfield the previous weekend with Spanish keeper Manuel Almunia taking over from Jens Lehmann. But the goalkeeper had little to do in an opening 30 minutes that were marked more by nervous errors than clear-cut goalscoring chances.

Robert Pires saw his shot fly high over the bar after 10 minutes and then José Antonio Reyes and Henry combined magnificently but

the Frenchman's cross drifted harmlessly out of play. Similarly, Ljungberg released Henry but the striker lost control of the ball in the penalty area.

In the 33rd minute, Pires sent the ball into the penalty area from the left and then gratefully received Ljungberg's return pass. The Frenchman

After playing a one-two with Freddie Ljungberg, Robert Pires fires Arsenal into the lead just after the half-hour.

pounced on the ball and fired it neatly into the corner of the goal. With renewed confidence, Arsenal pushed to add to their lead. Francesc Fabregas had a shot saved by Maik Taylor and then in first-half injury-time, Henry sent a dangerous volley across the face of the goal.

The second half saw a penalty appeal from Ljungberg when he was felled in the area by a challenge from Jamie Clapham but the referee waved play on. Then Henry had a great chance to score but fired his header straight at Taylor. Would Arsenal be able to add to their lead?

Birmingham City boss Steve Bruce sent on Jesper Gronkjaer and Clinton Morrison to beef up their attack. With his first touch, Morrison received a pass from Robbie Savage and his first-time shot almost embarrassed Almunia when it crept through the goalkeeper's grasp but luckily he recovered in time. As the home fans' nerves recovered from that moment, Heskey also came dangerously close when he volleyed a shot just over the bar.

In the 80th minute, Henry received the ball from Gael Clichy and left two Birmingham City defenders in his wake before sidefooting the ball past Taylor. The sense of relief around Highbury was palpable. That relief turned to joy six minutes later when Ljungberg ran down the right wing and crossed for Henry to nod the ball home and make it 3–0 to Arsenal.

The final whistle heralded three points and a return to something approaching their finest form for Arsenal. Pires' goal – his 50th in an Arsenal shirt – and Henry's brace gave Arsenal a fine and thoroughly deserved victory that left them still breathing down the necks of Chelsea – their next league opponents – after an attempt to settle their Champions League fate against Rosenborg.

Ten minutes from time Thierry Henry sidefoots the ball past Birmingham keeper Maik Taylor to make it 2–0...

... then celebrates his second and Arsenal's third after heading home a cross from Freddie Ljungberg just four minutes from time.

DECEMBER

UEFA Champions League, Group Stage, Group E
Tuesday 7 December 2004 at Highbury, 7.45 p.m.
Attendance: 35,421 Referee: Stefano Farina, Italy

W D D L L W [11 scored, 9 conceded]   W L D L L D [8 scored, 10 conceded]

ARSENAL 5   1 ROSENBORG

Reyes 3, Henry 24, Fabregas 29,   Hoftun 38
Pires 41 pen, van Persie 84

Substitutes					Substitutes
Jens **LEHMANN**	1	Manuel **ALMUNIA**	24	1	Espen **JOHNSEN**	30	Ivar **RONNINGEN**
Philippe **SENDEROS**	20	Justin **HOYTE**	31	4	Fredrik **WINSNES**	8	Robbie **RUSSELL**
Fredrik **LJUNGBERG**	8	Kolo **TOURE**	28	16	Torjus **HANSEN**	15	Per Ciljan **SKJELBRED**
▸ Robin **VAN PERSIE**	11	Sol **CAMPBELL**	23	3	Erik **HOFTUN**	2	Odd Inge **OLSEN** ▸
◂ (Cole, 76 mins)		Ashley **COLE**	3	21	Stale **STENSAAS**		(Winsnes, 88 mins) ◂
▸ Gael **CLICHY**	22	José Antonio **REYES**	9	6	Roar **STRAND**	18	Christer **GEORGE** ▸
◂ (Bergkamp, 72 mins)		Mathieu **FLAMINI**	16	9	Frode **JOHNSEN**		(Strand, 62 mins) ◂
▸ Quincy **OWUSU-ABEYIE**	42	Francesc **FABREGAS**	15	11	Jan Gunnar **SOLLI**	17	Oyvind **STORFLOR** ▸
◂ (Pires, 88 mins)		Robert **PIRES**	7	25	Daniel **BRAATEN**		(Helstad, 78 mins) ◂
Sebastian **LARSSON**	39	Dennis **BERGKAMP**	10	24	Thorstein **HELSTAD**	19	Alexander **TETTEY**
		Thierry **HENRY**	14	22	Harald **M BRATTBAKK**		

MATCH REPORT

Arsenal made a mockery of the critics who predicted they would fail to qualify for the Champions League knockout stages by majestically sweeping aside Rosenborg and finishing top of Group E. This victory was all the more satisfying as it was achieved with a host of players – including Lauren, Vieira, Edu and Gilberto – unavailable due to suspension or injury.

The Gunners never looked back after José Antonio Reyes fired them into the lead in the third minute. Francesc Fabregas took a free-kick that Dennis Bergkamp eased into the path of Reyes. The Spaniard fired a shot that Espen Johnsen got a hand to but failed to stop completely.

In the 17th minute, Rosenborg striker Harald Brattbakk sent in a dangerous left-wing cross

José Antonio Reyes starts the goal fest after three minutes.

Thierry Henry's close-range lob makes it 2–0.

Cesc Fabregas became Arsenal's youngest-ever scorer in Europe when he fired in the third goal.

Just before half-time, Robert Pires scored Arsenal's fourth from the penalty spot.

that Almunia dealt with decisively. But it wasn't long before Arsenal added to their lead. Henry raced onto Mathieu Flamini's tackle-cum-pass and nipped between goalkeeper and defender to lob the ball home.

Arsenal were thoroughly in command by this point and five minutes later Fabregas became Arsenal's youngest ever scorer in Europe – and in some style. He received the ball from Pires and clipped it over Hoftun before turning to fire his shot into the corner of the goal. The Highbury faithful's growing admiration of Fabregas was seen by the roaring ovation that greeted his strike.

Rosenborg had injury problems of their own and were already out of the running for the knockout stages before kick-off but they were anything but a pushover. Seven minutes before half-time, Almunia saved a Brattbakk's free-kick only to see Hoftun score from the loose ball. Three minutes later Arsenal scored again when a challenge by Johnsen on Henry led to a penalty that Pires converted comfortably.

The second half was a more tame affair as Arsenal concentrated more on maintaining their lead rather than adding to it though Henry and Reyes both had chances. Robin van Persie replaced Ashley Cole with fifteen minutes to go and the Dutchman was his usual enthusiastic self. He sliced a shot just wide two minutes after his

introduction and seconds later he fired a shot straight at Johnsen. His determination was unflagging and he set up Reyes for a chance that came close to another goal.

Six minutes from the final whistle, van Persie's energy was amply rewarded. He ran onto a fine pass from Reyes and dinked the ball over Johnsen from six yards out. The 5–1 scoreline equalled Arsenal's best win in the Champions League and meant they finished the group stages unbeaten and sitting pretty at the top of Group E.

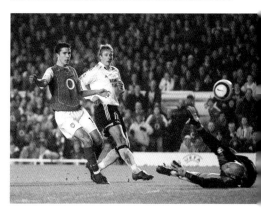

Robin van Persie's energetic appearance was rewarded with a fifth goal six minutes from time.

D D L L W W [11 scored, 6 conceded]   D D W W W L [13 scored, 5 conceded]

ARSENAL 2   2 CHELSEA

Henry 2, 29   Terry 17, Gudjohnsen 46

Substitutes					Substitutes
Jens **LEHMANN**	1	Manuel **ALMUNIA**	24	1	Petr **CECH**	23	Carlo **CUDICINI**
Philippe **SENDEROS**	20	**LAUREN**	12	20	Paulo **FERREIRA**	18	Wayne **BRIDGE** ▸
Justin **HOYTE**	31	Kolo **TOURE**	28	6	Ricardo **CARVALHO**		(Carvalho, 45 mins) ◂
▸ Gael **CLICHY**	22	Sol **CAMPBELL**	23	26	John **TERRY**	19	Scott **PARKER** ▸
◂ (Bergkamp, 82 mins)		Ashley **COLE**	3	13	William **GALLAS**		(Gudjohnsen, 77 mins) ◂
▸ Robin **VAN PERSIE**	11	Robert **PIRES**	7	11	Damien **DUFF**	9	Mateja **KEZMAN**
◂ (Reyes, 82 mins)		Mathieu **FLAMINI**	16	30	**TIAGO**	15	Didier **DROGBA** ▸
		Francesc **FABREGAS**	15	4	Claude **MAKELELE**		(Tiago, 45 mins) ◂
		José Antonio **REYES**	9	8	Frank **LAMPARD**		
		Dennis **BERGKAMP**	10	16	Arjen **ROBBEN**		
		Thierry **HENRY**	14	22	Eidur **GUDJOHNSEN**		

MATCH REPORT

In one of the most anticipated games of the season honours finished even after an enthralling 90 minutes of football. Two goals from Thierry Henry were not enough to secure a home victory against an enormously impressive Chelsea side who came from behind twice to win a point.

Kolo Toure and Sol Campbell congratulate Thierry Henry on his second-minute strike.

Lauren's return was the only change from the side that started against Rosenborg which meant that, owing to suspension, the Gunners had to face the league leaders without Patrick Vieira. But after 90 seconds, the home side were ahead when Thierry Henry headed a long Francesc Fabregas pass to José Antonio Reyes who immediately returned it to him. Henry turned and angled his strike past Petr Cech.

There was a real determination in Arsenal's step and they nearly added to the lead minutes later when Sol Campbell came within inches of converting a Dennis Bergkamp free-kick. But it was Chelsea who scored next. In the 17th minute, Manuel Almunia parried a Lampard shot over the bar. From the resulting corner, John Terry powered a header into the net.

Far from being crushed, Arsenal almost scored themselves seconds later when Ashley Cole's fine pass found Henry but the striker failed to hit the target. By now the game was end-to-end and Eidur Gudjohnsen saw a fine shot punched away by Almunia and Tiago blazed a chance high over the bar after some fine work from Arjen Robben.

Referee Graham Poll watches as Thierry Henry catches Chelsea keeper Petr Cech off-guard with his quickly taken free-kick to restore Arsenal's one-goal advantage.

In the 29th minute, Arsenal were awarded a free-kick and Henry took Chelsea by surprise by curling the ball home with Cech still trying to organise his wall. Despite bitter protests from Chelsea, the goal stood. Arsenal stayed composed and maintained their lead into the half-time break.

However, just 30 seconds into the second period the Gunners were caught out. Frank Lampard sent a free-kick to the far post and Willem Gallas nodded the ball back across the face of goal where Gudjohnsen scored with a header.

With the scoreline even once again, both sides pressed on gamely for the win. Chelsea had two great chances when Lampard headed over from just six yards out following a Damien Duff corner. Then the threatening Robben jinked past both Ashley Cole and Campbell but could only find the side-netting with his shot.

Arsenal's relief was surpassed in the Chelsea ranks when Henry missed a golden opportunity in the 76th minute. Fabregas and Pires were both involved in a glorious move that left Henry unmarked just six yards from goal. As Highbury prepared to celebrate, the Frenchman agonisingly missed.

The respect these two sides have for one another was clear from the professional way both teams approached the game and from the way the players heartily congratulated each other at the final whistle.

Robert Pires forces his way between the Chelsea midfielders Frank Lampard and Claude Makelele.

DECEMBER

FA Barclaycard Premiership
Sunday 19 December 2004 at Fratton Park, 4.05 p.m.
Attendance: 20,170 Referee: Howard Webb

L W L W D D [7 scored, 10 conceded]   D L L W W D [11 scored, 7 conceded]

PORTSMOUTH 0   1 ARSENAL
Campbell 75

Substitutes					Substitutes
Shaka **HISLOP**	1	Jamie **ASHDOWN**	30	24	Manuel **ALMUNIA**		
Nigel **QUASHIE**	11	Andy **GRIFFIN**	16	12	**LAUREN**	1	Jens **LEHMANN**
Aliou **CISSE**	18	Arjan **DE ZEEUW**	6	28	Kolo **TOURE**	15	Francesc **FABREGAS**
▸ Eyal **BERKOVIC**	10	Linvoy **PRIMUS**	2	23	Sol **CAMPBELL**	20	Philippe **SENDEROS**
◂ (Faye, 83 mins)		Matthew **TAYLOR**	14	3	Ashley **COLE**	31	Justin **HOYTE**
▸ Aiyegbeni **YAKUBU**	20	Steve **STONE**	8	7	Robert **PIRES**	10	Dennis **BERGKAMP** ▸
◂ (Fuller, 55 mins)		Gary **O'NEIL**	26	16	Mathieu **FLAMINI**		(Van Persie, 68 mins) ◂
		Amdy **FAYE**	15	4	Patrick **VIEIRA**		
		Patrik **BERGER**	23	22	Gael **CLICHY**		
		Lomano **LUA LUA**	32	11	Robin **VAN PERSIE**		
		Ricardo **FULLER**	19	14	Thierry **HENRY**		

MATCH REPORT

Arsenal's defence had faced criticism in some quarters since they conceded two goals at home to Chelsea. So how fitting that the back four not only kept a clean sheet in this game but that it was Sol Campbell who delivered the winning goal in this hard-fought meeting with an impressive Portsmouth side.

Robin van Persie made his first Premiership start and almost put Henry in on goal with a fine pass in the opening stages. After 10 minutes, Patrick Vieira – returning after suspension – was found by Henry's corner but fired his shot over the bar. Seven minutes later, Linvoy Primus slipped and Henry almost supplied van Persie with a fine chance but Jamie Ashdown intercepted the pass.

Arsenal were increasingly dominating the midfield and some fine interplay between

Mathieu Flamini and van Persie released Henry but Ashdown was equal to his shot. The Pompey keeper was less impressive on 28 minutes when he missed a punch from a corner, but Kolo Toure

It doesn't happen very often, but... Sol Campbell unleashes a 25-yarder that beats Jamie Ashdown in the Pompey goal and secures all three points for the Gunners.

There were entertaining duels all over the pitch in this hard-fought encounter and few better than the match up between Gael Clichy and Steve Stone.

headed just wide. After largely defending for 34 minutes, Portsmouth suddenly almost scored. Steve Stone passed to release Gary O'Neil but after shrugging off the attentions of Toure, the midfielder shot wide from 10 yards. Henry for Arsenal and Fuller for Portsmouth both had further chances to score during the closing stages of the first period.

Three minutes after the break, Fuller had a golden opportunity to score when Patrik Berger put him clear, but his first touch let him down. All the same, this incident heralded a second half that was going to be a lot tougher for Arsenal than the opening 45 minutes had been. Almunia was forced into a great save by Berger and his heroics were matched at the other end by Ashdown when he denied van Persie with Henry ready to pounce.

As the travelling fans wondered where an Arsenal goal was going to come from, up popped Sol Campbell. Collecting a pass from Vieira, he surged forward and walloped an unstoppable shot past Ashdown from 25 yards out. It was his first Arsenal goal for almost 16 months and was warmly welcomed by his team-mates and supporters alike.

The increasingly impressive Almunia was needed again when Stone's shot bounced off him and Lua Lua pounced on the rebound. He was also called into action by another fine effort from Berger during a nervous closing period.

This victory helped leave the disappointments of November behind. The Champions only won twice in November but this was their third victory in December and the Arsenal continued to put pressure on leaders Chelsea. The home fans gave Henry a standing ovation when he appeared for the warm-up but it was the travelling Arsenal fans who had cause for joy at the end having witnessed a determined and professional victory.

71

DECEMBER

L L W W D W [11 scored, 6 conceded]   L L L W D L [4 scored, 8 conceded]

ARSENAL 2   0 FULHAM

Henry 12, Pires 71

Manuel **ALMUNIA**	24	1	Edwin **VAN DER SAR**
LAUREN	12	2	Moritz **VOLZ**
Kolo **TOURE**	28	35	Ian **PEARCE**
Sol **CAMPBELL**	23	6	Zat **KNIGHT**
Gael **CLICHY**	22	3	Carlos **BOCANEGRA**
Robert **PIRES**	7	17	Tomasz **RADZINSKI**
Patrick **VIEIRA**	4	21	Zesh **REHMAN**
Francesc **FABREGAS**	15	14	Papa Bouba **DIOP**
Fredrik **LJUNGBERG**	8	7	Mark **PEMBRIDGE**
Dennis **BERGKAMP**	10	15	Collins **JOHN**
Thierry **HENRY**	14	9	Andrew **COLE**

Substitutes

Jens **LEHMANN** 1
Philippe **SENDEROS** 20
Jermaine **PENNANT** 21
▶ Mathieu **FLAMINI** 16
◀ (Ljungberg, 76 mins)
▶ Robin **VAN PERSIE** 11
◀ (Bergkamp 78 mins)

Substitutes

12 Mark **CROSSLEY**
5 Sylvain **LEGWINSKI**
28 Liam **FONTAINE**
8 Brian **McBRIDE** ▶
(Cole, 66 mins) ◀
4 Steed **MALBRANQUE** ▶
(Rehman, 81 mins) ◀

MATCH REPORT

Thierry Henry's opening goal was his 128th league strike for Arsenal, equalling the tally set by Highbury legend Ian Wright. But even the mercurial Frenchman would no doubt agree that most significant were the three points that his and Robert Pires' goals secured in the race to win the Premiership title.

On a crisp but sunny Boxing Day in North London, Arsenal's first chance arrived in the 11th minute when Pires robbed former Gunner Moritz Volz of the ball and tested Edwin van der Sar with a low shot. Within seconds, the Gunners were ahead. Ljungberg fed Henry who utterly bamboozled Ian Pearce before tucking an angled shot home. The festive cheers rang out among the home fans.

The rest of the first half really belonged to Arsenal. Francesc Fabregas found Henry

It's 128 and counting as Thierry Henry beats van der Sar to put Arsenal ahead.

on the edge of the penalty area and his flick came close to setting up Pires before Zat Knight intercepted. Ljungberg was buzzing around to great effect and both Pires and Dennis Bergkamp had shots blocked during the first period.

After the break, Fulham improved but the Gunners were still the dominant force in the game. Bergkamp floated a free-kick into the area and Kolo Toure came close to scoring from it. The Dutch master then chested the ball into the path of Pires and the Frenchman forced van der Sar into another save. Then Henry sent in a dangerous cross that Ljungberg came agonisingly close to converting.

Collins John was unlucky when his angled shot went just wide, and in the 65th minute Tomasz Radzinski charged into the box and tried to float the ball over Almunia who rose to save. However, Fulham's revival was short-lived and Henry soon hit the woodwork after exchanging neat passes with Pires. Then Bergkamp shot from six yards out forcing another fine save from his fellow Dutchman van der Sar.

In the 71st minute, the impressive Fabregas passed to Ljungberg inside the penalty area and Pires collected his pass after a fine dummy by Bergkamp. Pires left his marker for dead and bulldozed his shot past van der Sar.

Fulham were far more ambitious than they had been when they battled out a goalless draw at Highbury the previous season. Papa Bouba Diop in particular worked tirelessly to try and create chances for his team-mates but all too often his efforts were in vain. Had the impressive van der Sar not been in top form, the Gunners would have won by a far more handsome margin.

From the point of view of the Arsenal fans, this was another enjoyable performance to absorb leading to a most welcome victory. Something of the fluency of earlier in the season was back in evidence and the three points meant the Gunners remained well-placed in the league. The second half of the season promised much at this stage.

Easily outfoxing his marker, Ian Pearce, Robert Pires shoots past the keeper to secure all three points.

DECEMBER

FA Barclaycard Premiership
Wednesday 29 December 2004 at St James' Park, 8.00 p.m.
Attendance: 52,320 Referee: Steve Bennett

D L D D L D [6 scored, 12 conceded] L W W D W W [13 scored, 4 conceded]

NEWCASTLE 0 UNITED

1 ARSENAL
Vieira 45

Substitutes					Substitutes
Steve **HARPER**	12	Shay **GIVEN**	1	24	Manuel **ALMUNIA**		
James **MILNER**	16	Steven **TAYLOR**	27	12	**LAUREN** 〰	1	Jens **LEHMANN**
Martin **BRITTAIN**	39	Titus **BRAMBLE**	19	28	Kolo **TOURE**	20	Philippe **SENDEROS**
Peter **RAMAGE**	42	Aaron **HUGHES**	18	23	Sol **CAMPBELL**	22	Gael **CLICHY** ‣
‣ Charlie **N'ZOGBIA**	14	Olivier **BERNARD**	35	3	Ashley **COLE** 〰		(Van Persie, 76 mins) ◂
◂ (Bernard, 87 mins)		Kieron **DYER**	8	8	Fredrik **LJUNGBERG** 〰	15	Francesc **FABREGAS**
		Lee **BOWYER**	29	16	Mathieu **FLAMINI**	21	Jermaine **PENNANT**
		Jermaine **JENAS**	7	4	Patrick **VIEIRA**		
		Lauren **ROBERT**	32	7	Robert **PIRES**		
		Craig **BELLAMY**	10	11	Robin **VAN PERSIE** 〰		
		Shola **AMEOBI**	23	14	Thierry **HENRY**		

MATCH REPORT

Arsenal's final match of 2004 saw a highly professional performance resulting in a hard-fought 1–0 victory at St James' Park. However, an energetic and determined Newcastle United side made the Gunners work hard for the victory.

An eventful first half sprang into life in the second minute when Ashley Cole fed Robin van Persie and the Dutchman's snapshot smashed against goalkeeper Shay Given's face and bounced out for a corner. Newcastle failed to deal decisively with the corner but Sol Campbell fired wide from distance.

In the ninth minute, the home side had their first major chance when Shola Ameobi raced forward after Campbell had failed to deal with a long pass. Ameobi sent a powerful, bending shot goalwards which Manuel Almunia tipped wide.

At the other end, a testing corner from van Persie was headed towards goal by Campbell but cleared off the line by a Newcastle defender. A minute later, a Thierry Henry header rattled the post. Soon after this, the home side's appeals for a penalty were denied by the referee after Cole had handled in the box.

Fired up by a perception of injustice, Newcastle enjoyed their best period of the game in the

Mathieu Flamini closes down Aaron Hughes in the battle for midfield supremacy.

Skipper Patrick Vieira's shot deflects off Jermaine Jenas leaving Given stranded and putting Arsenal one-up just before the half-time interval.

closing stages of the first half with Lauren Robert testing Almunia. However, on the stroke of half-time, they went behind when the ball fell to Patrick Vieira's feet and the captain's dipping shot took a deflection that left Given no chance of saving it and gave Arsenal the lead.

The goal forced Newcastle to attack even more in the second half. Robert outpaced Lauren to the byline but overhit his cross with the Arsenal back-four on the ropes. Soon after, Newcastle were awarded a free-kick and the referee moved the set piece forward after adjudging that Ljungberg was delaying its taking. Robert was again at fault as he shot straight at the Arsenal wall to the disappointment of the vocal home supporters.

As Newcastle continued to attack, Wenger replaced van Persie with Gael Clichy. Soon after, another free-kick was awarded to Newcastle and again Robert wasted the chance by firing it straight at Almunia. The Arsenal goalkeeper was in fine form

dealing with some testing crosses and punching the ball out of danger on a number of occasions.

Although Henry was having a relatively quiet game, he created a great chance for himself late on but sent his shot just wide. In the closing stages, defender Steven Taylor fired a shot just over the bar and Lee Bowyer had an effort on goal saved by Almunia. Jermaine Jenas also weighed in with a chance that flew wide and there was time for another free-kick from Robert that went high and wide.

This was not the flowing, all-conquering Arsenal of August and September but to keep a clean-sheet – thanks mainly to tremendous performances by Toure and Campbell – and win away from home against a tough Newcastle side is the sort of achievement that great seasons are built on. After all the drama and joy of 2004, the Gunners ended the year as they spent so much of it – triumphant.

Arsenal.com PLAYER OF THE MONTH

Thierry HENRY

Perhaps people don't realise how many games I've played since I've been here, I rarely miss a game. When you play as a striker you always have to move, you always have to run, sprint, sprint, turn. I have set such high standards for myself in football.

THIERRY HENRY

What more can I say about Thierry? He is in spectacular form for us and is surely the greatest striker in the world at the moment. He is such a pleasure to play with both for France and for Arsenal.

PATRICK VIEIRA

I have played alongside many fantastic players in my career. Thierry is one of the best and we have struck up a good understanding on the field. It is such a good pleasure to play alongside him.

JOSÉ ANTONIO REYES

ARSENAL DIARY

Sunday 11 December
- Arsène Wenger is named Coach of the Year at the annual BBC Sports Awards ceremony.

Thursday 16 December
- Goalkeeper Stuart Taylor has his loan deal with Leicester City extended for another month.

Friday 17 December
- Arsenal are drawn against Bayern Munich in the first knockout round of the UEFA Champions League.

Monday 20 December
- Thierry Henry comes second behind Ronaldinho in the Fifa World Player of the Year Award for 2004.

Friday 31 December
- Arsenal are one of the 20 Premier League clubs to donate £50,000 to the Indian Ocean tsunami disaster relief fund.

THE WIDER WORLD

Thursday 2 December
- Former Rangers and Everton boss Walter Smith is confirmed as the new manager of Scotland.

Saturday 4 December
- England manager Sven-Goran Eriksson reveals he may like to manage Sweden or Brazil when his contract with the FA expires.

Tuesday 7 December
- Wolverhampton Wanderers appoint Glenn Hoddle as their new manager.

Wednesday 8 December
- Southampton appoint Harry Redknapp as their new manager.

Thursday 30 December
- Former Brazil coach Wanderley Luxemburgo replaces Mariano Garcia Remon as coach of Real Madrid.

FA CARLING PREMIERSHIP

31 December 2004

	P	HOME					AWAY					Pts
		W	D	L	F	A	W	D	L	F	A	
Chelsea	20	8	2	0	20	3	7	2	1	20	5	49
ARSENAL	20	6	4	0	27	11	7	1	2	21	11	44
Manchester United	20	7	3	0	19	5	4	4	2	12	8	40
Everton	20	7	1	2	13	10	5	3	2	10	7	40
Middlesbrough	20	6	3	1	18	9	4	2	4	16	15	35
Liverpool	20	8	1	1	20	7	2	3	5	14	13	34
Charlton Athletic	20	6	2	2	16	9	3	2	5	7	19	31
Tottenham Hotspur	20	3	3	4	17	14	5	2	3	7	5	29
Birmingham City	20	3	4	3	11	7	3	4	3	12	14	26
Portsmouth	20	5	1	4	15	14	2	4	4	9	13	26
Aston Villa	20	5	3	2	15	7	1	4	5	7	17	25
Manchester City	20	3	4	3	11	7	3	2	5	13	14	24
Bolton Wanderers	20	4	2	4	12	10	2	3	5	14	19	23
Newcastle United	20	3	3	4	16	17	2	4	4	15	21	22
Blackburn Rovers	20	1	7	2	12	16	2	3	5	7	16	19
Fulham	20	3	1	6	11	19	2	2	6	11	16	18
Crystal Palace	20	2	2	6	8	12	1	4	5	12	19	15
Norwich City	20	2	4	4	12	17	0	5	5	5	19	15
Southampton	20	2	6	2	13	13	0	2	8	5	19	14
West Bromwich Albion	20	1	4	5	7	19	0	4	6	9	23	11

L W W W D W [6 scored, 5 conceded]   W W D W W W [14 scored, 3 conceded]

CHARLTON 1 ATHLETIC
El Karkouri 45

3 ARSENAL
Ljungberg 35, 48, van Persie 67

Substitutes					Substitutes	
Stephan **ANDERSEN**	16	Dean **KIELY**	1	24	Manuel **ALMUNIA**	
Bryan **HUGHES**	20	Luke **YOUNG**	2	3	Ashley **COLE**	1
▸ Jason **EUELL**	9	Talal **EL KARKOURI**	15	23	Sol **CAMPBELL**	20
◂ (Thomas, 64 mins)		Jonathan **FORTUNE**	24	28	Kolo **TOURE**	(Campbell, 82 mins) ◂
▸ Paul **KONCHESKY**	18	Hermann **HREIDARSSON**	12	31	Justin **HOYTE**	39 Sebastian **LARSSON**
◂ (Kishishev, 64 mins)		Dennis **ROMMEDAHL**	19	8	Fredrik **LJUNGBERG**	21 Jermaine **PENNANT** ▸
▸ Jonatan **JOHANSSON**	21	Danny **MURPHY**	13	4	Patrick **VIEIRA**	(Ljungberg, 85 mins) ◂
◂ (Bartlett, 75 mins)		Radostin **KISHISHEV**	7	15	Francesc **FABREGAS**	7 Robert **PIRES** ▸
		Matt **HOLLAND**	8	22	Gael **CLICHY**	(van Persie, 71 mins) ◂
		Jerome **THOMAS**	14	11	Robin **VAN PERSIE**	
		Shaun **BARTLETT**	17	14	Thierry **HENRY**	

MATCH REPORT

Arsenal went into this match against in-form Charlton Athletic in the knowledge that Chelsea had secured all three points at Anfield hours earlier. The Gunners' first match of 2005 saw them take all three points in fine style in a competitive derby on a rainy day in South London.

The match exploded dramatically into life within seconds of the kick-off. Dennis Rommedahl burst through the Arsenal defence and tested Manuel Almunia with a low shot. Although Almunia was equal to it – diving to his left to collect comfortably – Charlton continued to dominate play in the opening minutes.

In the eighth minute, Arsenal had their first chance when Kolo Toure found Thierry Henry who spun and hooked in a shot that Dean Kiely did well to save. However, the home side continued to impress with Jonathan Fortune and Danny Murphy both

It's the Freddie Ljungberg show as he puts the Gunners ahead after 35 minutes with this right-foot shot...

... then, following Charlton's equaliser, he puts Arsenal ahead again with this cracking drive from a Fabregas pass.

Robin van Persie secures the three points by being first to Almunia's towering goal-kick and beating Kiely with this right-footer.

coming close to opening the scoring and Shaun Bartlett wasting a fine opportunity when he shot high over the bar.

Then, 10 minutes before the break, Arsenal took the lead. Robin van Persie released Patrick Vieira down the left and the captain's pass found Freddie Ljungberg. The Swede turned and fired an emphatic shot past Kiely. On the stroke of half-time, Charlton equalised when they were awarded a free-kick that Talal El Karkouri converted impressively from 30 yards. Honours were even at the end of an eventful first half.

The Gunners had not been at their best in the first 45 minutes but emerged much improved after the break. Three minutes into the second half, an on-form van Persie threaded the ball to Cesc Fabregas on the right. The youngster found Ljungberg with a breathtaking back-heel and the Swede advanced on goal and walloped a powerful drive past Kiely. While Charlton pounded the Arsenal backline with a series of long balls, Campbell and Toure stood tall to maintain the visitors' lead. On 60 minutes, it was

time for the Charlton defence to impress when Shaun Bartlett headed Henry's fine free-kick off the line.

Seven minutes later, Arsenal's lead was extended when Charlton failed to deal decisively with Almunia's powerful goal-kick. Van Persie, fully deserving of a goal in a fantastic performance, took advantage of a weak defensive header by Fortune and shot left-footed into the corner of the net.

Arsenal continued to try and add to the scoreline. Campbell came up for a corner and almost nodded in a fourth. Unfortunately, the defender landed awkwardly and injured his ankle. The sight of Campbell being substituted with the injury was the only down side of a fantastic result that gave Arsenal their fourth straight win against a Charlton side that went into the game on the back of a five-game unbeaten run.

W D W W W W [14 scored, 4 conceded]   L L W L D W [7 scored, 8 conceded]

ARSENAL 1
Ljungberg 75

1 MANCHESTER CITY
Shaun Wright-Phillips 31

Substitutes						Substitutes
Jens **LEHMANN**	1	Manuel **ALMUNIA**	24	1	David **JAMES**	Substitutes
Gael **CLICHY**	22	Ashley **COLE**	3	16	Nedum **ONUOHA**	David **SOMMEIL**	2
Sebastian **LARSSON**	39	Philippe **SENDEROS**	20	5	Sylvain **DISTIN**	Steve **McMANAMAN**	20
▸ Jermaine **PENNANT**	21	Kolo **TOURE**	28	22	Richard **DUNNE**	Ronald **WATERREUS**	21
◂ (Fabregas, 65 mins)		Justin **HOYTE**	31	3	Ben **THATCHER**	Bradley	42
Quincy		Fredrik **LJUNGBERG**	8	29	Shaun **WRIGHT-PHILLIPS**	**WRIGHT-PHILLIPS**
OWUSU-ABEYIE	42	Patrick **VIEIRA**	4	24	Joey **BARTON**	(Macken, 90 mins) ◂
		Francesc **FABREGAS**	15	26	Paul **BOSVELT**	Willo **FLOOD** ▸	44
		Robert **PIRES**	7	10	Antoine **SIBIERSKI**	(Barton, 77 mins) ◂
		Thierry **HENRY**	14	11	Jonathan **MACKEN**	
		Robin **VAN PERSIE**	11	8	Robbie **FOWLER**	

MATCH REPORT

Arsenal trailed Chelsea by seven points after a resolute Manchester City side held out under intense pressure for a 1–1 draw at Highbury. After beginning the match in somewhat slow style, an injury-hit Gunners side was unable to grab a winner.

Just 30 seconds after kick-off, Kevin Keegan's side threatened when a cross from Nedum

After anticipating Thierry Henry's overhead kick, Freddie Ljungberg dives to head Arsenal's equaliser 15 minutes from time.

Though under the cosh for most of the first half, Thierry Henry was unlucky not to get on the scoresheet during a second half that saw many chances go begging.

Onuoha was met with a powerful Robbie Fowler header that Manuel Almunia did well to save. City continued to look threatening and it was not until the eighth minute that Arsenal had their first chance. Robert Pires came agonisingly close to turning a Thierry Henry free-kick into the net and, seconds later, Justin Hoyte tested David James with a long-range shot.

Soon after, Ashley Cole sent in a high cross that Henry expertly controlled before spinning round and finding Robin van Persie. But the Dutchman's effort was fired straight into the arms of James who saved with ease.

Cole had so far been marshalling the threat of Shaun Wright-Phillips effectively but in the 31st minute he was helpless as the promising City youngster scored. Patrick Vieira was pressured by Joey Barton into making a mistake and Wright-Phillips helped himself to the loose ball. His curling right-foot shot gave Almunia no chance

and the visitors were ahead. Within minutes, City almost doubled their lead when Wright-Phillips found Fowler in space on the left. The striker looked set to continue his fine scoring record against Arsenal but the impressive Hoyte rushed back to rob him of the ball. This seemed to galvanise Arsenal and soon after a Robert Pires corner was powerfully met by the head of Vieira, only for the chance to go just wide.

The Gunners' new determination was not quelled by the half-time interval and within seconds of the restart, Cole's dangerous left-wing cross would only have needed the merest touch to be turned into a goal. Then van Persie picked out the left-back again, this time at the far post, but James saved his header.

By this point, Arsenal were laying siege to the City goal and van Persie was at the centre of much of their threat. The Dutchman was played in on the right only for the impressive Richard Dunne to deny him a shooting chance. Van Persie then picked up a Henry flick but his chance was saved by James. The goalkeeper was truly earning his wages and his next moment came when he tipped a dangerous long-range effort over the bar. Just as it seemed that James' goalkeeping was going to prove invincible, The Gunners got their equaliser. In the 75th minute, Dunne cleared a van Persie cross and Henry chased to retrieve the loose ball. His overhead kick had been anticipated by Freddie Ljungberg who sent his diving header into the corner.

By no means content with just drawing level, Arsenal probed for the winner. Van Persie hit the woodwork with a free-kick and Henry twice came close. But the winner would not come and Arsenal had to make do with just one point.

D W W W W D [10 scored, 4 conceded]   W W D L L L [2 scored, 3 conceded]

ARSENAL 2   1 STOKE CITY
Reyes 50, van Persie 70   Thomas 45

Substitutes					Substitutes
Manuel **ALMUNIA** 24	Jens **LEHMANN**	1	15	Steve **SIMONSEN**	Ed **DE GOEY**
▸ Justin **HOYTE** 31	Emmanuel **EBOUE**	27	2	Wayne **THOMAS** 1	Carl **ASABA** ▸
◂ (Eboue, 71 mins)	Kolo **TOURE**	28	32	Gerry **TAGGART** 7	(Greenacre, 77 mins) ◂
Pascal **CYGAN** 18	Philippe **SENDEROS**	20	22	Lewis **BUXTON**	Gifton **NOEL-WILLIAMS** 9
Sebastian **LARSSON** 39	Gael **CLICHY**	22	16	Marcus **HALL**	Karl **HENRY** ▸
Quincy	Francesc **FABREGAS**	15	19	Chris **GREENACRE**	(Halls, 52 mins) ◂
OWUSU-ABEYIE 42	Patrick **VIEIRA**	4	21	John **HALLS** 2	John **EUSTACE** ▸
	Robert **PIRES**	7	3	Clive **CLARKE**	(Clarke, 77 mins) ◂
	José Antonio **REYES**	9	10	Ade **AKINBIYI**	
	Robin **VAN PERSIE**	11	27	Jason **JARRETT**	

MATCH REPORT

Arsenal marched into the fourth round of the cup despite Stoke City taking a shock lead on the stroke of half-time at Highbury. With key players including Thierry Henry and Freddie Ljungberg rested, it was a youthful Arsenal side that denied a hard-working performance from the visitors.

Arsenal were in control in the opening stages and Robin van Persie had two long-range efforts in the first two minutes. Then José Antonio Reyes sent a right-footed shot towards goal but saw it blocked by Lewis Buxton. An action-packed opening period also saw Robert Pires and Jermaine Pennant creating openings as the visitors struggled to contain Arsenal. Van Persie sent a free-kick over the bar and then Patrick Vieira set him up for another chance which he sent marginally wide.

One shot each from Ade Akinbiyi and Chris Greenacre had been the extent of Stoke's attacking intent during the first half until deep into stoppage time. Then the returning Jens Lehmann blocked a header from Akinbiyi and Wayne Thomas slid in to smash the loose ball into the net. After Arsenal's control and dominance of the first half, this goal shook Highbury.

As the teams returned after the interval, it was clear that Arsenal, stung by Thomas's goal, were going to be dangerous and it took just five minutes for them to draw level. First, Cesc Fabregas set up van Persie and the Dutchman swivelled and shot, forcing a superb save from Stoke keeper Steve Simonsen. Then Kolo Toure crossed from the byline and the ball found Reyes on the edge of the area. The Spaniard volleyed the ball into the left-hand corner of the net and Highbury erupted.

Arsenal naturally continued to probe for the winner and Reyes set up van Persie with a good chance. Then Vieira came close from a corner. It would have been easy for Stoke to buckle under this pressure but they were not finished yet and Chris Greenacre's shot had to be scrambled off the line by Gael Clichy in the 61st minute.

As the contest became ever more enthralling, van Persie, Senderos and Fabregas all had chances to score but were unable to finish decisively. Then in the 67th minute, Akinbiyi, enjoying a thoroughly impressive afternoon of football, drilled a shot against the crossbar.

A superb volley from the edge of the box by José Antonio Reyes puts the Gunners back on level terms just after the break.

The two scorers celebrate as Robin van Persie puts Arsenal ahead after good work from Reyes and Jermaine Pennant.

That chance was another reminder for the Arsenal fans that they could not expect victory to come as a matter of course, but within three minutes their heroes were ahead. Reyes reached the byline and released the ball to Pennant who clipped it to van Persie who fired into the bottom corner.

Forced to press forward in search of an equaliser, Stoke City lost some of their organisation and were unable to threaten the Arsenal goal. However, the relief among the Arsenal fans at the final whistle was a great tribute to the visitors. In the final analysis though, Arsenal, who have dominated the competition in recent years, were safely into the Fourth Round of the FA Cup. Perhaps just as positive was a fantastic performance from a young Arsenal side, once again proving how hard and how effectively Arsène Wenger and his backroom team work.

JANUARY

FA Barclaycard Premiership
Saturday 15 January 2005 at The Reebok Stadium, 5.15 p.m.
Attendance: 27,514 Referee: Mike Clattenburg

L L W D W W [7 scored, 4 conceded]   W W W W D W [10 scored, 3 conceded]

BOLTON 1 WANDERERS   0 ARSENAL

Stelios 42

Substitutes						Substitutes
Kevin POOLE	1	Jussi JAASKELAINEN	22	24	Manuel ALMUNIA	
Ricardo VAZ TE	28	Nicky HUNT	18	3	Ashley COLE	Jens LEHMANN	1
Khalilou FADIGA	39	Tal Ben HAIM	26	23	Sol CAMPBELL	Philippe SENDEROS	20
▸ Henrik PEDERSEN	9	Bruno N'GOTTY	5	28	Kolo TOURE	Gael CLICHY	22
◂ (Okocha, 79 mins)		Ricardo GARDENER	11	31	Justin HOYTE	José Antonio REYES ▸	9
▸ Fernando HIERRO	20	Ivan CAMPO	16	8	Fredrik LJUNGBERG	(Fabregas, 66 mins) ◂
◂ (Nolan, 87 mins)		Jay-Jay OKOCHA	10	4	Patrick VIEIRA	Dennis BERGKAMP ▸	10
		Gary SPEED	6	15	Francesc FABREGAS	(van Persie, 66 mins) ◂
		Kevin NOLAN	4	7	Robert PIRES	
		El-Hadji DIOUF	21	11	Robin VAN PERSIE	
		Stelios GIANNAKOPOULOS	7	14	Thierry HENRY	

MATCH REPORT

Arsenal's first ever defeat at the Reebok Stadium profoundly damaged their chances of retaining the Championship leaving them 10 points behind league leaders Chelsea. A competitive match saw Arsenal leave the field bitterly disappointed and widely written out of the title race, though Arsène Wenger's men would not be giving up the chase in January.

The talented El-Hadji Diouf was Bolton Wanderers' lone striker but managed to be a thorn in the side of the Arsenal rearguard throughout the match. As early as the fifth minute, he sent in a dangerous cross that Justin Hoyte did well to clear. Diouf's subsequent crosses truly tested Arsenal.

In the ninth minute, it was an Arsenal cross that grabbed the attention. Ashley Cole sent in the ball from wide and Robin van Persie unleashed a fine, goal-bound shot that was blocked at the last moment

by Tal Ben Haim. A few minutes later, Patrick Vieira saw another chance sail over the bar.

After 20 minutes, Stelios sent in a teasing cross that Manuel Almunia punched only to see his

Despite several good chances the mercurial Thierry Henry was unable to get on the scoresheet at the Reebok.

Kolo Toure shows deft footwork to get past Bolton's Gary Speed.

clearance fall to Gary Speed. The Welshman reacted instantly by sending a fine effort that only just cleared the bar with Almunia grounded. Arsenal responded to this let-off by creating chances for both Cesc Fabregas and van Persie but neither was able to score.

The Gunners were seeming to wrestle control of the contest so it was a real blow when Bolton took the lead four minutes before half-time. Diouf found himself some space and sent in another testing cross that floated over Almunia and landed delightfully for Stelios at the far post. The Greek international duly converted with a header. Bolton almost doubled their lead just before the interval when Kevin Nolan took advantage of some indecision in the Arsenal back four but sent his effort fractionally wide.

A recharged and determined Arsenal side emerge for the second period. Within minutes of the restart, Kolo Toure found Thierry Henry who flicked the ball into the path of Ljungberg. Jussi Jaaskelainen prevented an almost certain goal by reaching the ball just ahead of the Swede. The goalkeeper then blocked a van Persie shot and was relieved when Robert Pires nodded the loose ball wide.

Arsenal were urgently seeking an equaliser and this inevitably left occasional gaps at the back on which Bolton tried to capitalise. Stelios latched onto a fine ball from Ricardo Gardener but fired his shot over the bar. Then Jay-Jay Okocha sent Stelios clear into a dangerous position but the midfielder fired wide to the relief of the travelling Arsenal fans.

By this stage, Bolton were regularly testing Arsenal with Speed, Ivan Campo and Diouf all coming close to scoring. Arsène Wenger replaced van Persie and Fabregas with Dennis Bergkamp and José Antonio Reyes in an attempt to galvanise his team. With 20 minutes left, Henry sent in a low shot and soon after he had another chance to score when he attempted unsuccessfully to turn in Ljungberg's cross. Arsenal were still probing for a goal when the final whistle brought a disappointing match to its end.

W W W D W L [9 scored, 4 conceded]   D W W D W W [9 scored, 4 conceded]

ARSENAL 1
Bergkamp 19

0 NEWCASTLE UNITED

Substitutes		Manuel **ALMUNIA**	24	1	Shay **GIVEN**		Substitutes	
Jens **LEHMANN**	1	Ashley **COLE**	3	27	Steven **TAYLOR**		12	Steve **HARPER**
Pascal **CYGAN**	18	Sol **CAMPBELL**	23	6	Jean-Alain **BOUMSONG**		18	Aaron **HUGHES** ▶
Emmanuel **EBOUE**	27	Kolo **TOURE**	28	19	Titus **BRAMBLE**			(Taylor, 45 mins) ◀
▶ Francesc **FABREGAS**	15	**LAUREN**	12	35	Olivier **BERNARD**		5	Andrew **O'BRIEN**
◀ (Reyes, 89 mins)		José Antonio **REYES**	9	8	Kieron **DYER**			(Boumsong, 67 mins) ◀
Robin **VAN PERSIE**	11	Patrick **VIEIRA**	4	29	Lee **BOWYER**		14	Charlie **N'ZOGBIA** ▶
		Mathieu **FLAMINI**	16	7	Jermaine **JENAS**			(Robert, 56 mins) ◀
		Robert **PIRES**	7	32	Lauren **ROBERT**		11	Patrick **KLUIVERT**
		Dennis **BERGKAMP**	10	23	Shola **AMEOBI**			
		Thierry **HENRY**	14	9	Alan **SHEARER**			

MATCH REPORT

Visiting goalkeepers fully expect a busy afternoon at Highbury and are only too aware they will need to be on top form to deny Arsenal. Ask Shay Given who produced the performance of a lifetime in goal for Newcastle United but still ended up on the losing side of this entertaining match.

In the first minute of the game a loose ball in the visitors' penalty area found Mathieu Flamini who twice tried to stab the ball home but Given denied him. In the 19th minute, Flamini sent a beautifully weighted pass into the path of the returning Dennis Bergkamp. In a moment of characteristic poise and skill, the Dutchman controlled the ball and steered it past Given for his first goal since August.

With renewed confidence and vigour, Arsenal hit irresistible form. Henry spun just outside the area and forced a save from Given. Then Bergkamp hit the side-netting with a fine effort. Before long, Robert Pires got in on the act with a curling shot that just shaved the outside of Given's post. Newcastle were exerting

Dennis Bergkamp shows ice-cool control on the edge of the Newcastle box before shooting the Gunners into a first-half lead.

most of their effort in merely containing Arsenal and Lee Bowyer wasted their only real chance of the first half, firing a right foot shot high into the North Bank.

The second half saw Given regularly tested. First, he saved a dangerous Henry free-kick, and after 60 minutes, when Vieira released Henry into the area, Given touched the striker's chance onto the post. The Irishman was relieved when the ball bounced back into his arms.

Kolo Toure came close from a corner and soon after Vieira fed the rampaging Reyes whose cross was met by a fine effort from Robert Pires. Given provoked gasps of astonishment when he managed to prevent what seemed a certain goal. Again and again Arsenal attacked only to be frustrated by Given. First Henry was denied a penalty after he seemed to be challenged by the goalkeeper in the area. Then Given managed to

distract both Henry and Cole enough to force errors from these normally cool finishers.

In the 75th minute came another moment of heroism from Given when he spectacularly turned in mid-air to save a fine effort from Henry. By this stage, it began to dawn on the home crowd that Arsenal may not add to their lead. Fortunately, the Gunners were able to defend it. In the 80th minute, Newcastle attempted to hit Arsenal on the break. Bowyer gifted himself some space and fired a shot that Manuel Almunia managed to smother.

At the final whistle, the points went to Arsenal but many of the plaudits went to Shay Given who had proven what a talented goalkeeper he was in the face of relentless attacks from an in-form Arsenal side.

Captain Patrick Vieira's commitment in midfield did much to secure this win over Newcastle in a tight but entertaining match.

W W D W L W [8 scored, 4 conceded]   D D L W W W [10 scored, 7 conceded]

ARSENAL 2
Vieira 53 pen, Ljungberg 82

0 WOLVERHAMPTON WANDERERS

Substitutes		Jens **LEHMANN**	1	1	Michael **OAKES**		Substitutes
Manuel **ALMUNIA**	24	Emmanuel **EBOUE**	27	5	Joleon **LESCOTT**	15	Kevin **COOPER**
Justin **HOYTE**	31	Sol **CAMPBELL**	23	6	Jody **CRADDOCK**	24	Keith **ANDREWS**
▸ Quincy		Pascal **CYGAN**	18	20	Joachim **BJORKLUND**	16	Kenny **MILLER** ▸
OWUSU-ABEYIE	42	Gael **CLICHY**	22	7	Shaun **NEWTON**		(Bjorklund, 61 mins) ◂
◂ (Ljungberg, 84 mins)		Fredrik **LJUNGBERG**	8	4	Seyi **OLOFINJANA**	33	Leon **CLARKE** ▸
▸ Francesc **FABREGAS**	15	Patrick **VIEIRA**	4	8	Paul **INCE** ▨		(Olofinajana, 76 mins) ◂
◂ (van Persie, 76 mins)		Mathieu **FLAMINI**	16	11	Mark **KENNEDY**	10	Colin **CAMERON** ▸
▸ Robert **PIRES**	7	José Antonio **REYES**	9	3	Lee **NAYLOR**		(Ince, 86 mins) ◂
◂ (Reyes, 70 mins)		Robin **VAN PERSIE**	11	19	Ki-Hyeon **SEOL** ▨		
		Thierry **HENRY**	14	27	Carl **CORT**		

MATCH REPORT

Arsenal's quest for another FA Cup Final appearance remained on course at the end of this Fourth Round tie in which Arsène Wenger's side comprehensively outgunned a spirited Wolverhampton Wanderers. Again, a visiting goalkeeper put in a fantastic performance at Highbury but left empty-handed.

Arsène Wenger made six changes from the side that beat Newcastle United but even with youngsters such as Emmanuel Eboue and Gael Clichy in the side, the Gunners were too good for a Wolves side driven on by midfield veteran Paul Ince.

Arsenal's dominance began in the fourth minute when Henry passed up a goalscoring opportunity to try and find a team-mate but saw his pass bobble away to safety. José Antonio Reyes twice tried his luck from distance and Robin van Persie bravely overcame two challenges but didn't manage to finish.

The Gunners had three penalty claims declined in the first half alone, and of the three, the trip on Eboue seemed beyond question to merit a spot-kick. Elsewhere, Reyes was twice denied by

After a number of penalty appeals had been turned down, *Patrick Vieira scores from the spot to give Arsenal a deserved lead just after half-time.*

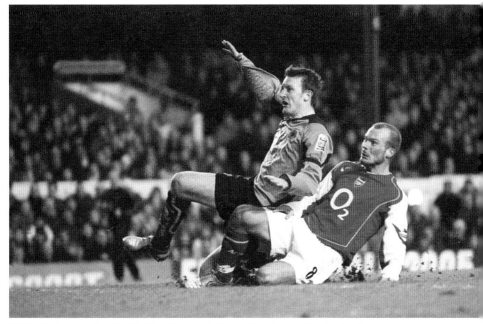

Eight minutes from time Freddie Ljungberg meets Thierry Henry's cross to volley the Gunners' second goal.

goalkeeper Michael Oakes and then Eboue hit the bar with a fine effort. Henry looked to have broken the deadlock when he intercepted a kick from Oakes and rolled the ball into an empty net but Mike Riley would not let the goal stand because he felt that Oakes had not let go of the ball.

After the break, Arsenal's dominance continued with Vieira heading a Henry corner towards goal only for Oakes to save again. A minute later, Reyes was bundled over in the box but Riley again waved away penalty appeals. However, within seconds, he pointed to the spot when Henry was brought down by Oakes.

Vieira took the spot-kick and fired it into the net to the joy of the home fans. For so long it had seemed that Arsenal might not capitalise on their dominance but they were now ahead.

Never satisfied with a mere one-goal lead, Arsenal continued to press and Oakes continued to impress. Van Persie's fine volley was saved and

he also managed to block Ljungberg's follow-up effort. Reyes and Eboue combined to set up Henry but the striker was unable to control the ball.

Henry was next to be set up, this time by van Persie, but he was again denied by the impressive Oakes. However hard the visiting goalkeeper worked, the home fans could sense that a second goal would come eventually and it duly did eight minutes from time. Henry reached the byline and sent in a powerful cross that Ljungberg volleyed home at the far post to confirm Arsenal's place in the Fifth Round.

The league campaign may have been proving a struggle at this point of the season, but another victory in the FA Cup gave great cheer to the Arsenal fans who once again left the ground looking forward to the draw for the next round of the competition.

Arsenal.com PLAYER OF THE MONTH
Fredrik LJUNGBERG

It is great to be recognised in this way. I am pleased with my form so far this season, though I always hope to improve. It is interesting that all my goals so far have come away from Highbury though I do not know why this may be.

FREDRIK LJUNGBERG

Of course, Freddie has shown many times in previous years that he is a central player for us and this season is no different. He can always make a difference to a game and that is the type of player you want in your team.

ARSÈNE WENGER

When Freddie is in a tight situation in the box, then I think he is one of the best players in the league for turning that chance into a goal. He is a great all-round player also.

PATRICK VIEIRA

ARSENAL DIARY

Wednesday 20 January
- Arsenal announce that a commemorative kit will be worn for the 2005/2006 campaign, the final season at Highbury.

Thursday 21 January
- Arsenal Football Club announces that Sol Campbell, Lauren and Justin Hoyte have agreed extensions to their current deals.
- Former Arsenal star Emmanuel Petit announces his retirement from professional football.

Thursday 27 January
- Jermaine Pennant joins Birmingham City on loan until the end of the season.

Monday 31 January
- Former Gunner Nicolas Anelka moves from Manchester City to Turkish side Fenerbahçe.

THE WIDER WORLD

Tuesday 4 January
- Controversy reigns as Tottenham Hotspur are denied a clear goal in the 0–0 draw at Old Trafford.
- Striker James Beattie joins Everton from Southampton.

Saturday 29 January
- The FA agrees in principle to support Sven-Goran Eriksson's appeal for a four-week break before the 2006 World Cup Finals.

Monday 31 January
- Unsettled striker Craig Bellamy leaves Newcastle United to spend the remainder of the season on loan at Celtic.

FA CARLING PREMIERSHIP

31 January 2005

		HOME					AWAY					
	P	W	D	L	F	A	W	D	L	F	A	Pts
Chelsea	24	10	2	0	25	3	9	2	1	23	5	61
ARSENAL	**24**	**7**	**5**	**0**	**29**	**12**	**8**	**1**	**3**	**24**	**13**	**51**
Manchester United	24	8	4	0	22	6	6	4	2	15	8	50
Everton	24	8	1	3	15	12	5	4	3	13	13	44
Liverpool	24	8	1	3	20	9	3	3	6	16	16	37
Middlesbrough	24	6	4	2	19	12	4	3	5	20	21	37
Charlton Athletic	24	7	2	3	20	13	4	3	5	20	21	37
Tottenham Hotspur	24	4	3	5	22	18	5	3	4	7	8	33
Bolton Wanderers	24	5	3	4	14	11	4	3	5	17	20	33
Manchester City	24	5	4	3	16	9	3	3	6	14	17	31
Aston Villa	24	7	3	2	19	7	1	4	7	8	22	31
Newcastle United	24	5	3	4	20	19	2	5	5	15	22	29
Fulham	24	5	1	6	15	20	3	3	6	16	20	28
Portsmouth	24	5	2	5	16	16	2	4	6	10	18	27
Birmingham City	24	3	4	5	13	11	3	4	5	14	19	26
Blackburn Rovers	24	2	7	3	13	17	3	3	6	8	17	25
Crystal Palace	24	4	2	6	13	12	1	4	7	14	25	21
Southampton	24	3	7	2	18	16	0	2	10	7	23	18
Norwich City	24	2	5	5	17	23	0	6	6	6	23	17
West Bromwich Albion	24	2	5	5	9	19	0	5	7	10	25	16

FEBRUARY

FA Barclaycard Premiership
Tuesday 1 February 2005 at Highbury, 8.00 p.m.
Attendance: 38,164 Referee: Graham Poll

D D W L W W [7 scored, 4 conceded]　　　　　　　　D W W W L W [10 scored, 3 conceded]

ARSENAL 2
Vieira 8, Bergkamp 36

4 MANCHESTER UNITED
Giggs 18, Ronaldo 54, 58, O'Shea 89

Substitutes					Substitutes
Jens **LEHMANN**	1	Manuel **ALMUNIA**	24	13 Roy **CARROLL**	Tim **HOWARD** 1
▸ Justin **HOYTE**	31	**LAUREN**	12	2 Gary **NEVILLE**	Phil **NEVILLE** 3
◂ (Campbell, 79 mins)		Sol **CAMPBELL**	23	5 Rio **FERDINAND**	John **O'SHEA** ▸ 22
▸ Francesc **FABREGAS**	15	Pascal **CYGAN**	18	27 Mikael **SILVESTRE** ■	(Fletcher, 61 mins) ◂
◂ (Lauren, 83 mins)		Ashley **COLE**	3	4 Gabriel **HEINZE**	Wes **BROWN** ▸ 6
▸ José Antonio **REYES**	9	Fredrik **LJUNGBERG**	8	24 Darren **FLETCHER**	(Ronaldo, 70 mins) ◂
◂ (Fabregas, 81 mins)		Patrick **VIEIRA**	4	16 Roy **KEANE**	Louis **SAHA** ▸ 9
Robin **VAN PERSIE**	11	Mathieu **FLAMINI**	16	18 Paul **SCHOLES**	(Giggs, 77 mins) ◂
		Robert **PIRES**	7	7 Cristiano **RONALDO**	
		Dennis **BERGKAMP**	10	8 Wayne **ROONEY**	
		Thierry **HENRY**	14	11 Ryan **GIGGS**	

MATCH REPORT

Arsenal's title hopes were dealt a huge blow by Manchester United after an eventful but ultimately bitterly disappointing evening's football at Highbury. This was the first league match Arsenal had lost at Highbury in 33 games but you would have to go back

even further for the last time such disappointment was felt among Gunners' fans at the end of a Premiership match.

Arsenal started brightest and Freddie Ljungberg tested the visitor's back four and goalkeeper twice

Highbury erupts as Patrick Vieira (hidden) heads home from a Thierry Henry corner to give Arsenal the lead.

in the opening eight minutes. Then, Thierry Henry earned and took a corner that Patrick Vieira rose to nod home sparking an explosion of joy among the home fans. Manchester United were hardly in the game for the opening 18 minutes but when they did get involved a goal was quick in coming. Paul Scholes fed Wayne Rooney on the right of the area and the England striker's pass found Giggs who scored with a fierce, deflected shot. With a goal under their belt, the visitors proceeded to take the game to Arsenal.

However, after weathering five minutes of sustained pressure from United, Arsenal went back into the lead. Henry rushed onto a long pass and released Dennis Bergkamp who surged forward and shot between Roy Carroll's legs. Shortly afterwards only a superb save by Aluminia from a Rooney effort kept Arsenal ahead at the break.

For Arsenal fans the second half was as frustrating as football can be. Eight minutes in, the increasingly dangerous Giggs found Ronaldo on the left of the area and despite the attentions of both Campbell and Almunia, the Portuguese winger found the back of the net. Soon after this, Rooney rattled the bar with a free-kick and then

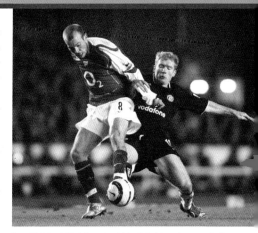

In a tight midfield contest *Freddie Ljungberg gets the better of United's Paul Scholes.*

came the blow of another goal from Ronaldo. Again Giggs was the architect and when he outfoxed Almunia, it was simple for Ronaldo to put away the Welshman's pass. Having taken the lead twice, Arsenal were now 3–2 behind.

In the 71st minute, Arsenal were given hope when Mikael Silvestre was dismissed for a foul on Ljungberg. Arsène Wenger replaced Flamini with José Antonio Reyes and Ljungberg and Henry both came close to scoring. But it was United who scored next when substitute John O'Shea exploited the space left by Arsenal's attacks to lob home.

Even facing such a bitter defeat, Arsenal continued to probe until the final whistle but the victory was to be United's. However, although this defeat left Arsenal with a great deal to do to retain the Championship, nobody at Highbury will be giving up until that is a mathematical impossibility. Arsenal fans have enjoyed many magical times down the years, perhaps it is the pain of evenings such as these that make the victories so sweet.

Arsenal celebrate retaking the lead *after Dennis Bergkamp's excellent strike on 36 minutes.*

FEBRUARY

FA Barclaycard Premiership
Saturday 5 February 2005 at Villa Park, 5.15 p.m.
Attendance: 42,593 Referee: Steve Bennett

W W L W L D [9 scored, 6 conceded]   D W L W W L [8 scored, 7 conceded]

ASTON VILLA 1   3 ARSENAL
Angel 74   Ljungberg 10, Henry 14,
                      Cole 28

Substitutes					Substitutes	
Stefan **POSTMA**	13	Thomas **SORENSEN**	1	1	Jens **LEHMANN**	
Martin **LAURSEN**	5	Ulises **DE LA CRUZ**	15	12	**LAUREN**	Manuel **ALMUNIA**	24
Carlton **COLE**	18	Olof **MELLBERG**	4	20	Phillipe **SENDEROS**	Justin **HOYTE**	31
▶ Thomas		Liam **RIDGEWELL**	19	18	Pascal **CYGAN**	Robert **PIRES** ▶	7
HITZLSPERGER	12	JLloyd **SAMUEL**	3	3	Ashley **COLE**	(Edu, 74 mins) ◀	
◀ (Samuel, 62 mins)		Nolberto **SOLANO**	11	8	Fredrik **LJUNGBERG**	Francesc **FABREGAS** ▶	15
▶ Mathieu **BERSON**	16	Eric **DJEMBA-DJEMBA**	14	4	Patrick **VIEIRA**	(Reyes, 82 mins) ◀	
◀ (Djemba-Djemba,		Steve **DAVIS**	24	17	**EDU**	Mathieu **FLAMINI** ▶	16
66 mins)		Gareth **BARRY**	6	9	José Antonio **REYES**	(Bergkamp, 74 mins) ◀	
		Juan Pablo **ANGEL**	9	10	Dennis **BERGKAMP**		
		Luke **MOORE**	31	14	Thierry **HENRY**		

MATCH REPORT

Arsenal reminded everyone that they are still Champions by beating Aston Villa in superb style. The 3-1 scoreline did no justice at all to the dominance enjoyed by the visitors who were simply breathtaking.

Jens Lehmann and Edu returned to the team and Arsenal were in control from the start of this game on a rainy day in the West Midlands. Dennis Bergkamp curled a fine shot that Thomas Sorensen could only fumble and Thierry Henry almost fired the loose ball home. Then Ashley Cole came close before Henry and Bergkamp combined to set up Patrick Vieira who fired just over the bar. Two minutes later, Arsenal were ahead. Edu fed Freddie Ljungberg who lifted the ball over Sorensen and into the net.

Villa had two chances both of which fell to Juan Pablo Angel but first Pascal Cygan and then Jens Lehmann denied the Colombian. Then José Antonio Reyes found Edu whose shot came off the post. Henry pounced onto the loose ball but shot

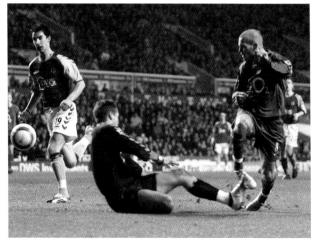

Freddie Ljungberg lifts the ball over Villa keeper Sorensen after good work from Edu to put Arsenal one-up after 10 minutes.

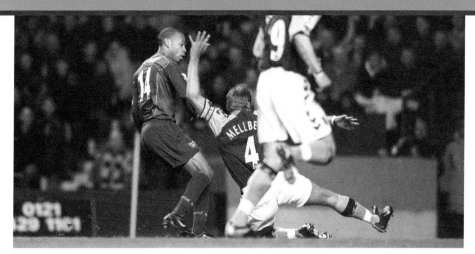

Four minutes later its 2–0 as Thierry Henry slides a left-foot shot into the Villa net.

over the bar. Minutes later, Vieira released Henry who scored his first goal for seven games, a rare barren patch for the Frenchman.

Just before the half-hour mark Arsenal underlined their dominance with a third goal. Bergkamp was putting in another fantastic performance and he picked out Cole's run with a perfectly weighted pass. The left-back confidently shot past Sorensen into the far corner of the goal. There was still time for Vieira and Henry to come close before the referee blew for half-time.

In comparison to the opening 45 minutes, the second half was a somewhat tame experience. Cygan continued to impress and the Frenchman prevented Villa from converting an early chance. The more that Villa came forward in search of a goal, the more openings there were at the back. Henry and Reyes swapped passes and the Frenchman came close to adding to the scoring.

In the 74th minute, Villa scored when Angel converted Mathieu Berson's fine cross. This goal gave the home side added belief and before long Angel, Hitzlsperger and Solano had all threatened to add to the scoring. Again, though, Arsenal stood firm in the face of pressure.

Substitute Robert Pires did get the ball in the net but his effort was ruled out for offside.

Hitzlsperger and Steven Davis each had chances to score but as the game wore on, it became clear that Arsenal were going to win deservedly.

This was a morale-boosting three points for Arsenal. Although they remained 10 points behind Chelsea, they had reminded the world and themselves that they are capable of controlling games and playing spectacular football. Reports of the Gunners' demise had been greatly exaggerated.

Ashley Cole wraps up the points meeting Dennis Bergkamp's pass with a superb left-foot volley.

W L W W L W [10 scored, 7 conceded]   W L L W D L [9 scored, 8 conceded]

ARSENAL 5   1 CRYSTAL PALACE

Bergkamp 32, Reyes 35,   Johnson 63 pen
Henry 39, 77, Vieira 54

Arsenal			Crystal Palace	
Substitutes		Jens **LEHMANN** 1	28 Gabor **KIRALY**	Substitutes
Manuel **ALMUNIA** 24		**LAUREN** 12	21 Emmerson **BOYCE**	1 Julian **SPERONI**
Philippe **SENDEROS** 20		Kolo **TOURE** 28	25 Fitz **HALL**	18 Gary **BORROWDALE**
▸ Francesc **FABREGAS** 15		Pascal **CYGAN** 18	26 Gonzalo **SORONDO**	32 Vassilis **LAKIS** ▸
◂ (Pires, 79 mins)		Gael **CLICHY** 22	3 Danny **GRANVILLE**	(Routledge, 64 mins) ◂
▸ Mathieu **FLAMINI** 16		Robert **PIRES** 7	7 Wayne **ROUTLEDGE**	12 Mikele
◂ (Edu, 62 mins)		Patrick **VIEIRA** 4	15 Aki **RIIHILAHTI**	**LEIGERTWOOD** ▸
▸ Robin **VAN PERSIE** 11		**EDU** 17	17 Michael **HUGHES**	(Riihilahti, 31 mins) ◂
◂ (Bergkamp, 79 mins)		José Antonio **REYES** 9	19 Tom **SOARES**	22 Joonas **KOLKKA** ▸
		Dennis **BERGKAMP** 10	8 Andrew **JOHNSON**	(Freedman, 64 mins) ◂
		Thierry **HENRY** 14	9 Dougie **FREEDMAN**	

MATCH REPORT

Arsenal surpassed their fine performance at Villa Park with a glorious victory over Crystal Palace. Breathtaking, fluent and deadly – this was Arsenal at their very best – and they were fully deserving of this 5–1 victory on Valentine's Day.

By full-time it was easy to forget that Crystal Palace started strongly with Dougie Freedman and Andy Johnson both testing Jens Lehmann. Then, Lehmann allowed Gael Clichy's backpass to slip under his foot and needed to rush back to avert a goal. Perhaps Palace hoped at this point that a shock victory might be on the cards for them. But then the tide turned.

Dennis Bergkamp set up Thierry Henry but the Frenchman's low shot went just wide. Then in the 32nd minute, Bergkamp put Arsenal ahead when he converted José Antonio Reyes' fine cross. Three minutes later, Henry had a shot cleared by Fitz Hall

Dennis Bergkamp starts a nine-minute goal rush, side-footing Reyes's superb cross past Palace keeper Kiraly.

Moments later José Antonio Reyes nets the second goal, meeting a loose ball with this magnificent left-foot volley.

*On his 200th league appearance, Thierry Henry
celebrates in style after putting Arsenal 3–0 up.*

*Captain Patrick Vieira makes it 4–0, making no
mistake from Henry's superb through ball.*

but the ball fell to Reyes on the edge of the area and the Spaniard shot into the far corner of the net. By now Arsenal were bombarding the Palace goal. Bergkamp and Henry both went close before the Frenchman – making his 200th league appearance for Arsenal – thumped a fine effort that no one could stop. In seven minutes, Arsenal had gone 3–0 ahead.

Nine minutes into the second half, Henry turned provider when his fine pass sent captain Patrick Vieira free and he made no mistake with his finish to make it 4–0.

Iain Dowie's men pulled one back in the 63rd minute. Andy Johnson tumbled in between Kolo Toure and Vieira in the penalty area and referee Rob Styles pointed to the spot. The Palace striker took the spot-kick and despatched it high in Lehmann's net. By now though, this was little more than a consolation.

Far from being deflated by this goal, Arsenal upped the ante and before long Bergkamp had stabbed just wide and Robert Pires hit the post. The Gunners were clearly not finished with goalscoring and in the 77th minute, Henry received a Bergkamp cross and rifled the ball home. This was his 174th goal for Arsenal, leaving him just 11 goals short of equalling Ian Wright's record.

Crystal Palace have proved interesting opposition for Arsenal in analysing Arsène Wenger's team's season. In November, a resolute Eagles side held Arsenal to a frustrating draw at Selhurst Park, while at Highbury Arsenal brushed them aside in a glorious 5–1 victory. There is no doubt which of the two performances was most enjoyable for Gunners' fans who welcomed the return of their heroes' finest form with a hearty ovation at the final whistle.

*Although Palace pulled one back, Thierry Henry
completes the scoring by crashing the ball home
from a Dennis Bergkamp cross.*

L W W L W W [13 scored, 7 conceded]   W L L D L D [8 scored, 6 conceded]

ARSENAL 1   1 SHEFFIELD UNITED

Pires 78

Gray 90 pen

Substitutes					Substitutes
Stuart **TAYLOR**	13	Manuel **ALMUNIA**	24	1	Paddy **KENNY**	12	Alan **QUINN**
Sebastian **LARSSON**	39	Emmanuel **EBOUE**	27	14	Jon **HARLEY**	10	Danny **CADAMARTERI**
Quincy		Kolo **TOURE**	28	4	Nick **MONTGOMERY**	21	Jonathan **FORTE** ▸
OWUSU-ABEYIE	42	Philippe **SENDEROS**	20	15	Paul **THIRLWELL**		(Montgomery, 82 mins) ◂
▸ Pascal **CYGAN**	18	Gael **CLICHY**	22	6	Phil **JAGIELKA**	30	Paul **SHAW** ▸
◂ (Reyes, 85 mins)		Fredrik **LJUNGBERG**	8	7	Andy **LIDDELL**		(Thirlwell, 45 mins) ◂
▸ Robert **PIRES**	7	Francesc **FABREGAS**	15	17	Leigh **BROMBY**	16	Simon **FRANCIS** ▸
◂ (van Persie, 65 mins)		Mathieu **FLAMINI**	16	18	Michael **TONGE**		(Liddell, 82 mins) ◂
		José Antonio **REYES**	9	32	Danny **CULLIP**		
		■ Dennis **BERGKAMP**	10	26	Derek **GEARY**		
		Robin **VAN PERSIE**	11	8	Andy **GRAY**		

MATCH REPORT

A ten-man Arsenal side looked set for a hard-earned victory in this FA Cup tie until a late penalty levelled the scoreline and forced a replay. In truth, Sheffield United probably deserved a second crack at the Gunners but that did not assuage a feeling of deep disappointment at the final whistle.

The visitors started the match strongly and Nick Montgomery looked set to score until Philippe Senderos raced back and forced a corner with his fine challenge. From the resultant set piece, Andy Gray sent in a dangerous header that the returning Manuel Almunia did very well to save. Gradually, Arsenal wrestled control of the game and Dennis Bergkamp almost gave them the lead with a fine curling shot that went just over the bar. Then Freddie Ljungberg set up Robin van Persie but the young Dutchman's strike was too weak to test Paddy Kenny. Cesc Fabregas was next up to try and score but he lifted his chance over the bar.

Leigh Bromby and Andy Liddell both came close to scoring for the visitors but the first blow to Arsenal's hopes of winning was not far away. Danny Cullip made a late challenge on Cesc Fabregas

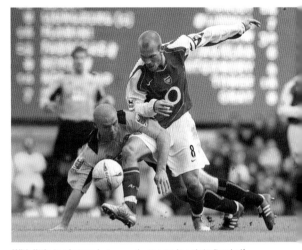

With little to choose between the teams in a tight first half, Freddie Ljungberg fights hard for midfield dominance with Sheffield's Danny Cullip.

With only 12 minutes remaining Robert Pires fires Arsenal ahead after Sheffield keeper Paddy Kenny had parried a shot from Cesc Fabregas.

sparking vociferous disagreements that led to Bergkamp being sent off. Just before half-time, Cullip thought he had given the visitors the lead but his back-heeled effort was disallowed.

The pace of the game increased in the second half with both sides sensing victory was within their grasp. Emmanuel Eboue exchanged passes with Mathieu Flamini and sent a vicious cross-shot that Kenny did well to control. José Antonio Reyes fired just over the bar after good work from Freddie Ljungberg. Then Kolo Toure and Reyes both took free-kicks that tested Kenny to the full.

Such was Arsenal's dominance that it was easy to forget that the home side were playing with ten men. On the hour, Lee Bromby's cross was scuffed by Montgomery and that was – almost – the only chance the visitors produced in the second half.

In the 78th minute, Arsenal looked to have fired themselves into the quarter-finals when Robert

Pires converted the loose ball after Kenny had parried Fabregas' shot. Moments later Fabregas came close to doubling Arsenal's lead but there was to be another twist in the tale.

In the 90th minute, Philippe Senderos was judged to have handled Cullip's hooked shot and the referee pointed to the spot, sparking wild celebrations among the travelling fans. Andy Gray stepped up to take the spot-kick and scored with aplomb. Arsenal had dominated the game but Sheffield United did well to limit Arsenal to just one goal and then take their chance to equalise in the final minute. With the Premiership run-in and Champions League commitments to come, a replay was the last thing Arsène Wenger needed but Arsenal's performance was convincing enough for them to travel to Sheffield with confidence.

FEBRUARY

UEFA Champions League, Eighth-Final, 1st Leg
Tuesday 22 February 2005 at Olympiastadion, Munich, 7.45 p.m.
Attendance: 59,000 Referee: Kim Milton Nielsen, Denmark

D W D W L W [13 scored, 5 conceded]   W W L W W D [14 scored, 7 conceded]

BAYERN MUNICH 3   1 ARSENAL
Pizarro 4, 58, Salihamidzic 65   Toure 88

Substitutes					Substitutes
	Oliver **KAHN**	1	1	Jens **LEHMANN**	
Michael **RENSING**	22 Willy **SAGNOL**	2	12	**LAUREN**	24 Manuel **ALMUNIA**
Jens **JEREMIES**	16 Robert **KOVAC**	5	28	Kolo **TOURE**	3 Ashley **COLE**
Thomas **LINKE**	25 **LUCIO**	3	18	Pascal **CYGAN**	(Clichy, 83 mins)
Bastian	Bixente **LIZARAZU**	69	22	Gael **CLICHY**	15 Francesc **FABREGAS**
SCHWEINSTEIGER	31 Martin **DEMICHELIS**	6	8	Fredrik **LJUNGBERG**	20 Philippe **SENDEROS**
▶ Owen **HARGREAVES**	23 Hasan **SALIHAMIDIZIC**	20	4	Patrick **VIEIRA**	39 Sebastian **LARSSON**
◀ (Salihamidzic, 74 mins)	Torsten **FRINGS**	8	17	**EDU**	16 Mathieu **FLAMINI**
▶ Mehmet **SCHOLL**	7 **ZÉ ROBERTO**	11	7	Robert **PIRES**	(Edu, 36 mins)
◀ (Roberto, 57 mins)	Roy **MAKAAY**	10	9	José Antonio **REYES**	11 Robin **VAN PERSIE**
▶ Paolo **GUERRERO**	33 Claudio **PIZARRO**	14	14	Thierry **HENRY**	(Ljungberg, 76 mins)
◀ (Pizarro, 68 mins)					

MATCH REPORT

Kolo Toure's 88th-minute goal gave Arsenal a sliver of hope after a devastating evening of football in Germany. With Sol Campbell and Dennis Bergkamp among the absentees and Ashley Cole only making the bench, Arsenal failed to wrestle control of the game on a bitterly cold night.

The Gunners went behind in the fourth minute. Bayern goalkeeper Oliver Kahn sent a fierce clearance upfield and Kolo Toure failed to deal with it decisively. His looped header gave Claudio Pizarro a great chance to score and he took it with aplomb. This was the worst possible start for Arsenal and they did not recover until the 13th minute when Thierry Henry set up Freddie Ljungberg only for the Swede to head weakly into Kahn's arms.

Henry and Ljungberg continued to combine well but the Bayern back-four prevented them from turning their understanding into clear-cut chances. Instead, Arsenal were reduced to hit and hope chances. Henry fired a free-kick wide and Gael Clichy's shot deflected off Henry and went wide of the post.

Showing perfect balance and concentration José Antonio Reyes *flies past Bayern's veteran French defender Bixente Lizarazu.*

Kolo Toure's 88th-minute strike gives Arsenal a lifeline as he fires home the loose ball after Patrick Vieira had hit the post.

Arsenal started the second half well and Reyes hit the side-netting with a shot before Ljungberg forced Kahn into a fine save at his near post. But Bayern were soon back in control when Ze Roberto's cross found Roy Makaay and the Dutchman forced a fine save from Lehmann. From the resultant corner, Salihamidzic headed into the side-netting.

In the 58th minute, Mehmet Scholl was sent on and he was the architect of Bayern's second goal. He sent in a free-kick from the left and Pizarro's header deflected off Toure into the net to make it 2–0 to the hosts. Six minutes later it was 3–0 when Torsten Frings sent in a high cross that Lehmann could only touch onto Salihamidzic who fired home at the far post. Soon after, Frings nearly made it 4–0 but sent his shot into the side-netting.

A shell-shocked Gunners side held its nerve and continued to probe. José Antonio Reyes came close to scoring with a free-kick but saw his effort sail narrowly over the bar. With time running out and with it Arsenal's Champions League hopes, the Gunners fashioned a goal that just kept them in touching distance of a place in the next round. Patrick Vieira hit the post from close-range and Toure fired home the loose ball.

Nothing could mask the disappointment felt by the Arsenal players, coaching staff and fans at full-time. Once again, an Arsenal team that dominates matches in the Premiership had failed on the European stage. But Toure's goal held out hope for the team. A 2–0 victory back at Highbury would be enough to see them through. Arsenal fans always keep the faith and would be there for the return leg to cheer their side on.

Jens Lehmann exhorts his team-mates to greater effort on a frustrating night in Munich.

FEBRUARY

FA Barclaycard Premiership
Saturday 26 February 2005 at St Mary's Stadium, 12.45 p.m.
Attendance: 31,815 Referee: Alan Wiley

W W L D D D [9 scored, 7 conceded]   W L W W D W [14 scored, 10 conceded]

SOUTHAMPTON 1   1 ARSENAL
Crouch 67   Ljungberg 45

Substitutes		Paul **SMITH**	13	1	Jens **LEHMANN**		Substitutes
Danny **HIGGINBOTHAM**	19	Rory **DELAP**	18	28	Kolo **TOURE**	13	Stuart **TAYLOR**
Michael **POKE**	25	Claus **LUNDEKVAM**	5	20	Philippe **SENDEROS**	12	**LAUREN**
Calum **DAVENPORT**	39	Andreas **JAKOBSSON**	6	18	Pascal **CYGAN**	30	Jeremie **ALIADIERE**
▸ Paul **TELFER**	33	Olivier **BERNARD**	23	3	Ashley **COLE**	27	Emmanuel **EBOUE** ▸
◂ (Le Saux, 72 mins)		■ David **PRUTTON**	20	8	Fredrik **LJUNGBERG**		(Toure, 75 mins) ◂
▸ Kevin **PHILLIPS**	7	Jamie **REDKNAPP**	38	4	Patrick **VIEIRA**	22	Gael **CLICHY** ▸
◂ (Camara, 85 mins)		Nigel **QUASHIE**	40	16	Mathieu **FLAMINI**		(Pires, 45 mins) ◂
		Graeme **LE SAUX**	3	7	Robert **PIRES**		
		Henri **CAMARA**	37	14	Thierry **HENRY**		
		Peter **CROUCH**	14	11	Robin **VAN PERSIE** ■		

MATCH REPORT

As befits a clash with a team staring relegation in the face, this was a match that began with more emphasis on commitment than beauty. It ended on a bitter note for Arsenal as Ashley Cole's late headed effort was disallowed by the referee. In between, the Gunners were not able to take an excellent opportunity to secure three points.

A lively opening saw Henri Camara certain to score until Pascal Cygan dispossessed him. Then, Mathieu Flamini and Thierry Henry combined in a fantastic break and Henry fed Robin van Persie. But the Dutchman sent his side-footed effort just wide. Soon after, the lively van Persie collected the ball from Flamini with his back to goal and spun free from his marker. His finish did not match the build-up and Paul Smith saved easily.

Rory Delap took a free-kick just past the half hour and Peter Crouch nodded it to Camara who forced a save from Jens Lehmann. But it was not until the 45th minute that the game truly sprang into life. David Prutton had already received one booking and

Southampton defenders *look down and out as Robin van Persie congratulates goalscorer Freddie Ljungberg.*

In the last minute of the match *Ashley Cole beat Southampton keeper Paul Smith with this diving header but the goal was ruled out for offside.*

when he caught Robert Pires on the touchline, he received his second yellow and was sent off while Pires was stretchered off.

Arsenal's numerical advantage told immediately and Henry weaved his way through a couple of challenges before passing to Ljungberg who gave the Gunners the lead with virtually the last kick of the half. Arsenal went into the second half a goal ahead and with an extra man but the game was far from over and there were a few twists to come.

The visitors' first chance of the second half came when Flamini threaded the ball to van Persie who cut inside and found Henry unmarked from five yards out. Smith was equal to Henry's effort and deflected the ball wide. Soon after this, the architect of that chance was dismissed. Already on a yellow card, van Persie received his second yellow after fouling Graeme Le Saux.

Even with the numbers equal, Arsenal continued to press and Henry set up both Ljungberg and Pascal Cygan. But the next goal

was scored by Southampton in the 62nd minute. Jamie Redknapp's corner evaded Lehmann and Crouch's header bounced over the line.

Arsenal endeavoured to reclaim the lead. Henry had a shot saved well by Smith and then the Frenchman took a free-kick that found its way to Ljungberg only for Smith to again block the goal-bound effort. Cole then drove forward but shot straight at Smith who was enjoying a heroic afternoon for Southampton.

With the final action of the match, Cole's header beat Smith but the referee chalked the 'goal' off for offside. It was just one of those days. With Chelsea not playing a league match that weekend and Manchester United not kicking off for some hours, this had been a chance for the Gunners to make up real ground on their rivals. The disappointment etched into the players' faces at the end of 90 minutes told the story.

Arsenal.com **PLAYER OF THE MONTH**

Fredrik **LJUNGBERG**

Of course, I am very much enjoying this season. Although not all the results have gone the way we would have wished, I still feel we are getting lots from our football. I will never stop working and striving to become a better player. The rest of the players are the same in that regard and that's why I love playing here!

FREDRIK LJUNGBERG

I am not surprised that Freddie won this award two months running as he is playing really well for the team at the moment. Opponents are finding him harder and harder to contain and I think he will get even better.

PATRICK VIEIRA

I enjoy playing with Freddie. We have combined on quite a few goals in our time and we continue to have a special understanding. He is deadly inside the box.

DENNIS BERGKAMP

ARSENAL DIARY

Monday 15 February
• Arsenal Football Club announces its support for London's bid to host the 2012 Olympic Games and Paralympic Games.

Friday 18 February
• Arsenal Holdings plc announcing interim results for the six months ending 30 November 2004 reveal that group operating profits before player trading increased to £10.2 million.

Sunday 20 February
• The Arsenal Ladies team reach the semi-finals of the Women's FA Cup.

Monday 21 February
• Arsenal Football Club hosts an LBC radio show in front of an exclusive audience at Highbury. The event raises over £3,000 for ChildLine, the Club's charity of the season.

THE WIDER WORLD

Thursday 3 February
• UEFA announces that clubs competing in the Champions League and the UEFA Cup will need to include four home-grown players in their 25-man squads from 2006.

Wednesday 9 February
• England draw 0–0 with Holland in a friendly match at Villa Park.

Tuesday 15 February
• Top players and coaches – including Thierry Henry and Arsène Wenger – appear as a World XI takes on a European XI at the Nou Camp in Barcelona to raise money for the tsunami relief fund.

Sunday 27 February
• Chelsea defeat Liverpool 3–2 to win the Carling Cup at the Millennium Stadium.

FA CARLING PREMIERSHIP

28 February 2005

		HOME					AWAY					
	P	W	D	L	F	A	W	D	L	F	A	Pts
Chelsea	27	10	3	0	25	3	11	2	1	25	5	68
Manchester United	28	10	4	0	26	7	8	4	2	21	10	62
ARSENAL	**28**	**8**	**5**	**1**	**36**	**17**	**9**	**2**	**3**	**28**	**15**	**58**
Everton	28	9	1	4	16	13	6	5	3	18	16	51
Liverpool	27	9	1	3	23	10	4	3	7	18	19	43
Middlesborough	28	7	5	2	22	14	4	4	6	21	23	42
Bolton Wanderers	28	6	4	4	17	12	5	3	6	19	22	40
Tottenham Hotspur	27	6	3	5	27	19	5	3	5	8	11	39
Charlton Athletic	27	7	2	4	21	15	4	4	6	11	23	39
Aston Villa	28	7	2	4	21	15	2	5	7	11	24	35
Newcastle United	27	6	4	4	23	21	2	6	5	16	23	34
Manchester City	27	5	5	4	17	12	3	4	6	14	17	33
Birmingham City	28	5	4	5	17	12	3	4	7	14	23	32
Portsmouth	28	6	2	6	19	19	2	4	8	12	23	30
Fulham	27	5	2	6	16	21	3	3	8	17	25	29
Blackburn Rovers	27	3	7	4	16	18	3	3	7	8	18	28
Crystal Palace	28	5	2	7	15	13	1	5	8	17	32	25
Southampton	28	3	9	2	21	19	0	3	11	8	25	21
Norwich City	27	3	5	5	20	25	0	6	8	6	27	20
West Bromwich Albion	27	2	7	5	11	21	0	5	8	12	28	18

L D L D L W [3 scored, 8 conceded]   L W W D L D [13 scored, 11 conceded]

SHEFFIELD 0   0 ARSENAL
UNITED

(after extra time)
ARSENAL won 4-2 on penalties

Substitutes		Paddy **KENNY**	1	24	Manuel **ALMUNIA**		Substitutes
Simon **FRANCIS**	16	Derek **GEARY**	26	12	**LAUREN**	13	Stuart **TAYLOR**
Steven **KABBA**	19	‖ Chris **MORGAN**	5	20	Philippe **SENDEROS**	28	Kolo **TOURE** ▸
Paul **SHAW**	30	Leigh **BROMBY**	17	18	Pascal **CYGAN**		(Fabregas, 90 mins) ◂
Danny **HAYSTEAD**	33	Jon **HARLEY**	14	3	Ashley **COLE**	27	Emmanuel **EBOUE**
▸ Alan **QUINN**	12	Andy **LIDDELL**	7	16	Mathieu **FLAMINI**	30	Jeremie **ALIADIERE** ▸
◂ (Tonge, 98 mins)		Nick **MONTGOMERY**	4	4	Patrick **VIEIRA**		(Flamini, 113 mins) ◂
		Phil **JAGIELKA**	6	15	Francesc **FABREGAS**	42	Quincy
		Paul **THIRLWELL**	15	22	Gael **CLICHY** ‖		**OWUSU-ABEYIE** ▸
		Michael **TONGE**	18	40	Arturo **LUPOLI**		(Lupoli, 45 mins) ◂
		Andy **GRAY**	8	8	Fredrik **LJUNGBERG**		

SHEFFIELD UNITED penalties:
Gray scored, **Jagielka** scored, Quinn saved, Harley saved
ARSENAL penalties:
Lauren scored, **Vieira** scored, **Ljungberg** scored, Cole scored

MATCH REPORT

Arsenal's goalkeepers have been criticised at times this season but it was a heroic penalty shoot-out performance from Manuel Almunia that underpinned their victory at Bramall Lane. The Spaniard saved twice to send Arsenal into the Sixth Round and keep alive dreams of another FA Cup Final appearance under Arsène Wenger.

The Gunners were short of first-choice firepower with Thierry Henry, Dennis Bergkamp and Robin van Persie all unavailable. Arsène Wenger chose to pair 17-year-old Arturo Lupoli with Freddie Ljungberg in attack. But it was the home side that mounted the first serious attack of the evening when Andy Gray crossed for Michael Tonge who blazed his shot over the bar. Arsenal's best chance during the first half fell to Ljungberg after great work from Cesc Fabregas and Lupoli, but the Swedish midfielder sliced his effort wide. Soon after, Patrick Vieira also shot wide. Then, in

the 39th minute, Vieira sent in a dangerous cross that Paddy Kenny struggled to control.

At half-time, Arsène Wenger replaced Lupoli with Quincy Owusu-Abeyie and the young Dutchman was immediately effective. First, he was sent clear by Mathieu Flamini but failed to beat Kenny. He then fired in a cross and Fabregas tested the Blades' keeper. The young Spaniard came close again when he hit the bar in the 62nd minute.

The Gunners continued to attack and Ljungberg was denied a fantastic scoring chance when Phil Jagielka tackled well. Then, in the 82nd minute, Fabregas produced a close-range effort that Kenny did well to save. However, as normal time came towards its end, Sheffield United almost took a shock lead. Derek Geary crossed and Jon Harley met the ball at the far-post with a fantastic diving header that Almunia saved in style.

After replacing Arturo Lupoli at half-time Quincy Owusu-Abeyie turned in a superb performance and consistently tested the Sheffield United back-four.

Right at the start of extra time Owusu-Abeyie, a thorn in the side of the Sheffield United back-four since his introduction, surged into the penalty area and came close to setting up a fine chance for Ljungberg. Pascal Cygan and substitute Jeremie Aliadiere wasted chances as extra-time progressed but ultimately, a penalty shoot-out was needed to separate the sides.

While it could be argued that Arsenal should have beaten Sheffield United with the chances they created but failed to convert during the game, there really is nothing quite so exciting as a penalty shoot-out. Lauren, Vieira, Ljungberg and Ashley Cole were all on target for Arsenal but it was Almunia's heroics in goal that shall linger longest in the memory. He saved from Alan Quinn and Jon Harley in a tense penalty shoot-out to spark wild celebrations among the travelling fans and Arsenal players. Thanks to injuries and suspensions, Arsène Wenger had been forced to field an inexperienced side with many players out of position and yet he was again on the winning side at the end of an FA Cup tie. What a hold this man has on the famous competition.

1–1   2–2   3–2   4–2

Man of the Match Manuel Almunia dives to save Alan Quinn's penalty.

Four perfect penalties: from Lauren, Vieira, Ljungberg, Cole, saw Arsenal safely into the quarter-finals.

W W D L D W [11 scored, 7 conceded]   W L W L W L [9 scored, 10 conceded]

ARSENAL 3   0 PORTSMOUTH
Henry 37, 53, 85

Substitutes		Jens **LEHMANN**	1	33	Kostas **CHALKIAS**		Substitutes
Manuel **ALMUNIA**	24	Kolo **TOURE**	28	16	Andy **GRIFFIN**	1	Shaka **HISLOP**
‹ **LAUREN**	12	Pascal **CYGAN**	18	3	Dejan **STEFANOVIC**	19	Ricardo **FULLER**
‹ (Cygan, 25 mins)		Philippe **SENDEROS**	20	6	Arjan **DE ZEEUW**	34	Valery **MEZAGUE**
Emmanuel **EBOUE**	27	Ashley **COLE**	3	14	Matthew **TAYLOR**	2	Linvoy **PRIMUS** ‹
‹ Fredrik **LJUNGBERG**	8	Francesc **FABREGAS**	15	26	Gary **O'NEIL**		(Griffin, 26 mins) ‹
‹ (Fabregas, 78 mins)		Patrick **VIEIRA**	4	8	Steve **STONE**	21	Diomansy **KAMARA** ‹
‹ Robin **VAN PERSIE**	11	Mathieu **FLAMINI**	16	11	Giannis **SKOPELITIS**		(Berger, 70 mins) ‹
‹ (Owusu-Abeyie,		Gael **CLICHY**	22	23	Patrik **BERGER**		
75 mins)		Thierry **HENRY**	14	32	Lomano **LUA LUA**		
		Quincy **OWUSU-ABEYIE**	42	20	Aiyegbeni **YAKUBU**		

MATCH REPORT

An Arsenal side hit by injuries and suspensions swept Portsmouth aside thanks to a hat-trick by Thierry Henry – his sixth for the Gunners. This victory was a helpful boost for the Champions as they prepared for the second-leg of their Champions League tie with Bayern Munich just days later. Arsène Wenger's reshuffling saw Kolo Toure play at right-back and Ashley Cole appear in left midfield.

Despite the unfamiliar line-up and positions, Arsenal were unstoppable in this match and there were encouraging performances from youngsters Philippe Senderos and Quincy Owusu-Abeyie. The young Dutchman, who linked up well with Henry, was lively from the start, dragging an early shot just wide after a pass from Patrick Vieira. Then on 12 minutes, he found Henry only for the Frenchman to drive wide. Although Portsmouth arrived with a defensive formation, Lomano Lua Lua twice tested Lehmann in this opening period.

After both sides were forced into early substitutions – Lauren replacing Pascal Cygan for the

New line-up, same old story as Thierry Henry scores a sixth hat-trick in his Arsenal career – here he celebrates his first just after the half-hour mark.

Gunners – Henry put Arsenal ahead. It was Lauren who sent in a dangerous cross in the 39th minute that Henry converted with aplomb. Vieira nearly made it 2–0 just before half-time but fired the ball over the bar. All the same, Arsenal were fully deserving of their half-time lead.

In the second half, Arsenal were more dominant and Cesc Fabregas – playing on the right-hand side of midfield – came close with a header, again set up by a cross from Lauren. In the 53rd minute, captain Vieira strode through midfield and passed to Henry who drew the goalkeeper and clipped the ball over him to double Arsenal's lead. It was a fine goal and prompted wild celebrations among the home fans.

Just after the hour mark, Henry almost completed his hat-trick when his cross nearly found its way into the back of the net. However, Portsmouth came close too when Steve Stone forced a fantastic save from Jens Lehmann. Then Aiyegbeni Yakubu fired just wide to the home fans' relief. All the same, the Gunners had been warned not to take their lead for granted.

With five minutes left, Henry finished what he had started. Arsenal were awarded a free-kick on the corner of the area. Henry, in bullish mood, took it and with his right foot curled the ball towards the

Eight minutes after the break he doubled the lead, lifting the ball over Chalkias after good work from Vieira.

top corner. Chalkias had it covered but in the end could only parry the ball into his own net. This goal left Henry just eight short of Ian Wright's all-time goalscoring record. But more importantly for the moment it secured Arsenal another three points and proved a good confidence boost ahead of a tricky Champions league tie.

Five minutes from the end it's hat-trick time as a curling free-kick beats the Portsmouth wall and finds the top corner.

MARCH

UEFA Champions League, Eighth-Final, 2nd Leg
Wednesday 9 March 2005 at Highbury, 7.45 p.m.
Attendance: 35,463 Referee: Massimo De Santis, Italy

W D L D D W [11 scored, 6 conceded]   L W W W W W [18 scored, 4 conceded]

ARSENAL 1   0 BAYERN MUNICH
Henry 66

Substitutes					Substitutes
Stuart **TAYLOR** 13	Jens **LEHMANN**	**1**	**1**	Oliver **KAHN**	
GILBERTO 19	**LAUREN**	**12**	**2**	Willy **SAGNOL**	Michael **RENSING** 22
Gael **CLICHY** 22	░ Kolo **TOURE**	**28**	**3**	**LUCIO**	Vahid **HASHEMIAN** 9
Quincy **OWUSU-ABEYIE** 42	Philippe **SENDEROS**	**20**	**5**	Robert **KOVAC**	Jens **JEREMIES** 16
▸ Francesc **FABREGAS** 15	Ashley **COLE**	**3**	**69**	Bixente **LIZARAZU** ░	Bastian **SCHWEINSTEIGER** 31
◂ (Flamini, 63 mins)	Fredrik **LJUNGBERG**	**8**	**6**	Martin **DEMICHELIS**	**ZÉ ROBERTO** ▸ 11
▸ Robert **PIRES** 7	Patrick **VIEIRA**	**4**	**20**	Hasan **SALIHAMIDZIC** ░	(Deisler, 73 mins) ◂
◂ (Reyes, 63 mins)	Mathieu **FLAMINI**	**16**	**26**	Sebasatian **DEISLER**	Thomas **LINKE** ▸ 25
▸ Robin **VAN PERSIE** 11	José Antonio **REYES**	**9**	**13**	Michael **BALLACK** ░	(Guerrero, 85 mins) ◂
◂ (Ljungberg, 80 mins)	░ Dennis **BERGKAMP**	**10**	**33**	Paolo **GUERRERO**	Owen **HARGREAVES** ▸ 23
	░ Thierry **HENRY**	**14**	**14**	Claudio **PIZARRO**	(Salihamidzic, 90 mins) ◂

MATCH REPORT

Only in the Champions League can a home victory cause such disappointment for a club. Thierry Henry's second-half goal gave Arsenal a win on the night but it was not enough to prevent their exit from the competition at the end of a tense evening. The beginnings of spring seemed to be in the air at Highbury and the home fans arrived full of hope that their heroes could overcome the deficit from the first leg and progress to the quarter-finals.

Arsenal struggled to take control of the game in the first half. After 18 minutes, Hasan Salihamidzic burst through towards goal but Dennis Bergkamp and Ashley Cole combined to stop him. Seven minutes later, Patrick Vieira found himself with a half-chance just five yards outside the area but his volley went marginally wide. Sebastian Deisler was a thorn in Arsenal's side throughout the first 45 minutes and when he and Paolo Guerrero swapped passes on the edge of the area, they worked a dangerous opening for the visitors which Mathieu Flamini did well to break up. Soon after Deisler swung in a testing corner that Lehmann

Despite the attentions of Lucio, Thierry Henry controls the ball before firing Arsenal ahead on 66 minutes.

Despite the huge efforts of players like Ashley Cole, victory on the night was not enough to see Arsenal through to the next round.

could only punch to Michael Ballack 10 yards out. Fortunately, Ballack's effort went just wide.

The Gunners had soaked up all this pressure – including another chance from Deisler – but then came close to taking the lead themselves in the 34th minute. Henry surged down the left and approached goal. However, the angle was very tight and his shot hit Kahn.

A rejuvenated Arsenal emerged for the second period and had Bayern pinned back for 10 minutes. Henry chipped a free-kick into the area and Vieira collected the ball but his volley went just inches wide of the post. Two minutes later, Ashley Cole received the ball from Bergkamp and fired over the bar. The pressure was mounting.

In the 64th minute, Arsène Wenger replaced Reyes and Flamini with Robert Pires and Cesc Fabregas. Soon after, Arsenal were ahead. Cole sent a long ball forward, Henry controlled it and sent an angled shot past Kahn into the net. Rather than celebrating, Henry rushed back to the centre circle. Arsenal needed to score again. All Bayern had to do was not concede another goal but they continued to press and Ballack was only denied by an acrobatic save from Lehmann. In the final 10 minutes, Arsenal pressed and pressed for the second decisive goal, but it would not come. Toure and Bergkamp came closest but as the tension racked up and the clock ticked down, it became clear that this was not to be Arsenal's night.

Another early exit from Europe left Arsenal's players, coaching team and fans disappointed. The Gunners had lost only one match during their whole Champions League campaign and went out victorious on the night. But these facts were no consolation at all.

W W D W L W [7 scored, 3 conceded]   D L D W W W [7 scored, 5 conceded]

BOLTON 0 1 ARSENAL
WANDERERS
Ljungberg 3

Substitutes		Bolton		Arsenal		Substitutes
		Jussi **KAASKELAINEN**	22	1	Jens **LEHMANN**	
Kevin **POOLE**	1	Nicky **HUNT**	18	12	**LAUREN**	3 Ashley **COLE**
Ivan **CAMPO**	16	Bruno **N'GOTTY**	5	28	Kolo **TOURE**	11 Robin **VAN PERSIE**
Radhi **JAIDI**	15	Tal Ben **HAIM**	26	20	Philippe **SENDEROS**	13 Stuart **TAYLOR**
(Hunt, 68)		Ricardo **GARDENER**	11	22	Gael **CLICHY**	15 Francesc **FABREGAS**
Henrik **PEDERSEN**	9	Kevin **NOLAN**	4	8	Fredrik **LJUNGBERG**	27 Emmanuel **EBOUE**
(Hierro, 81 mins)		Fernando **HIERRO**	20	4	Patrick **VIEIRA**	
Vincent **CANDELA**	23	Gary **SPEED**	6	16	Mathieu **FLAMINI**	
(Haim, 68 mins)		Stelios **GIANNAKOPOULOS**	7	7	Robert **PIRES**	
		El-Hadji **DIOUF**	21	9	José Antonio **REYES**	
		Kevin **DAVIES**	14	10	Dennis **BERGKAMP**	

MATCH REPORT

The Reebok Stadium has been the scene of some disappointments for Arsenal in recent seasons but this tie ended in victory and a place in the semi-finals of the FA Cup. An action-packed opening saw a goal and a sending off within the first eight minutes but the Gunners maintained their composure and emerged triumphant.

Arsenal came out of the traps playing some superb one-touch football and it was clear from the start that they meant business. After three minutes, Freddie Ljungberg raced onto a weighted pass from Robert Pires and guided the ball past the Bolton goalkeeper to give his team a dream start. Within minutes, the visitors nearly doubled their lead when a one-two between Dennis Bergkamp and José Antonio Reyes put the latter through on goal but Jaaskelainen saved the Spaniard's shot.

In the eighth minute, El-Hadji Diouf was dismissed after striking Jens Lehmann but even with 10 men and a goal behind, Bolton continued to work hard and made Arsenal work for their victory. Stelios twice came close with headers during the first half. The first

It's a dream start as Freddie Ljungberg gives Arsenal an early lead at the Reebok from a superbly weighted pass by Robert Pires.

went straight at Lehmann but the second forced the German to make a diving save.

While the sight of this Arsenal team in full-flowing goalscoring form is a wonder to behold, there is also great pleasure to be had from watching the team grind out a victory away from home against a tough side. The Gunners were magnificently professional in this game and no one more so than Philippe Senderos who put in perhaps his best performance so far in an Arsenal shirt .

There was still time before the interval for Reyes and Bergkamp to test Jaaskelainen. Although the Bolton keeper was once again equal to these shots, it was Arsenal that returned to the dressing room happiest.

Unsurprisingly, Bolton's priority during the second half was to bombard the Arsenal area with set pieces. Long throws, free-kicks and corners came firing in but the Arsenal rearguard was

equal to them all. In recent weeks, the Gunners had begun to look more solid at the back and this game was no different.

Not that it was all about Bolton attacking. In the 64th minute, Bergkamp released Reyes who outpaced his marker, cut inside and fully tested the Bolton keeper. Then it was Lehmann's turn to impress when he turned aside a fine header from Stelios Giannakopoulos.

Inevitably, the legs of 10-man Bolton began to tire first and both Ljungberg and Reyes had good chances as the second half wore on. In the final five minutes, Bergkamp twice tested the Bolton goalkeeper. In the last seconds of the match Ljungberg wasted a chance but it did not matter as the final whistle confirmed Arsenal's seventh FA Cup semi-final appearance in eight years.

Arsenal's defence had to work hard to keep Bolton out; here Lauren dispossesses striker Kevin Davies.

W D W W W D [7 scored, 1 conceded]   D L D W W W [7 scored, 5 conceded]

BLACKBURN 0
ROVERS

1 ARSENAL
van Persie 43

Substitutes						Substitutes
Peter **ENCKELMAN**	13	Brad **FRIEDEL**	1	1	Jens **LEHMANN**	
Jon **STEAD**	9	ⅷ Lucas **NEILL**	2	12	**LAUREN**	13 Stuart **TAYLOR**
▸ Kerimoglu **TUGAY**	8	Andy **TODD**	24	28	Kolo **TOURE**	8 Fredrik **LJUNGBERG**
◂ (Todd, 45 mins)		Ryan **NELSEN**	29	20	Philippe **SENDEROS**	42 Quincy
▸ Nils-Eric		Dominic **MATTEO**	22	22	Gael **CLICHY** ⅷ	**OWUSU-ABEYIE**
JOHANSSON	14	Aaron **MOKOENA**	15	15	Francesc **FABREGAS**	27 Emmanuel **EBOUE**
◂ (Matteo, 42 mins)		David **THOMPSON**	20	4	Patrick **VIEIRA**	18 Pascal **CYGAN**
▸ Brett **EMERTON**	7	Garry **FLITCROFT**	5	16	Mathieu **FLAMINI**	
◂ (Flitcroft, 60 mins)		ⅷ Steven **REID**	18	3	Ashley **COLE**	
		Morten Gamst **PEDERSEN**	12	11	Robin **VAN PERSIE**	
		ⅷ Paul **DICKOV**	10	9	José Antonio **REYES**	

MATCH REPORT

The media billed this tie as a dress rehearsal for the FA Cup semi-final but to the players and fans of both sides, the three points up for grabs meant much more on the day than the forthcoming cup tie. In the end, a moment of genius from a Dutchman won the points for Arsenal – and on

Robin van Persie makes it look simple as he takes the ball round Blackburn keeper Brad Friedel to score the only goal of the game.

Though he put in a superb personal performance, José Antonio Reyes was unable to get on the scoresheet despite several good chances.

this occasion that Dutchman was Robin van Persie. There was some happy irony for van Persie when he scored as he was not due to start the match until Freddie Ljungberg was injured during the warm-up at Ewood Park.

The first chance of the match went to Blackburn when David Thompson smashed an angled volley just wide. A relatively quiet first half did, however, see Arsenal create a number of chances. José Antonio Reyes chipped the ball and van Persie took up the charge to meet it only for Brad Friedel to intervene. After 19 minutes, Ashley Cole crossed and van Persie shot but saw his effort deflected to safety.

Towards the end of the half, the home side began to get back into the action. Morten Gamst Pedersen sent in a teasing cross that Jens Lehmann did well to deal with. Pedersen crossed again soon after but Steven Reid's header went straight into Lehmann's increasingly safe hands.

In the 43rd minute came van Persie's moment of inspiration. Cole passed to him on the edge of the area. He turned away from his marker, jinked around the advancing goalkeeper and completed the simple task of tapping into an empty net, sending the travelling Arsenal fans into raptures. The Gunners almost doubled the lead within minutes when Reyes tested Friedel with a pot-shot.

Within seconds of the start of the second half, the Champions again came close. The two Spaniards – Fabregas and Reyes – combined and Reyes' shot was only just dealt with by Friedel. This seemed to shake the home side back into life and before long, Pederson sent in a dangerous free-kick that Lehmann palmed aside before Garry Flitcroft nodded over the bar.

Cole, in a lively mood, then set up Mathieu Flamini but the young midfielder's hard shot was deflected by a Blackburn defender. With 20 minutes remaining, Reyes found van Persie who hit the bar with his shot. Reyes was first to the rebound but Friedel saved his low drive.

In the final 10 minutes, Blackburn pressed for a goal. Brett Emerton sent in a powerful shot from the right that fizzed just past the upright. Then Reid also found himself in a good position but his effort sailed wide.

Another three points for the Gunners put them in second-place, albeit only for a matter of hours. But the increased resilience apparent in Arsène Wenger's men bodes very well for the remainder of the season.

Arsenal.com PLAYER OF THE MONTH

Philippe SENDEROS

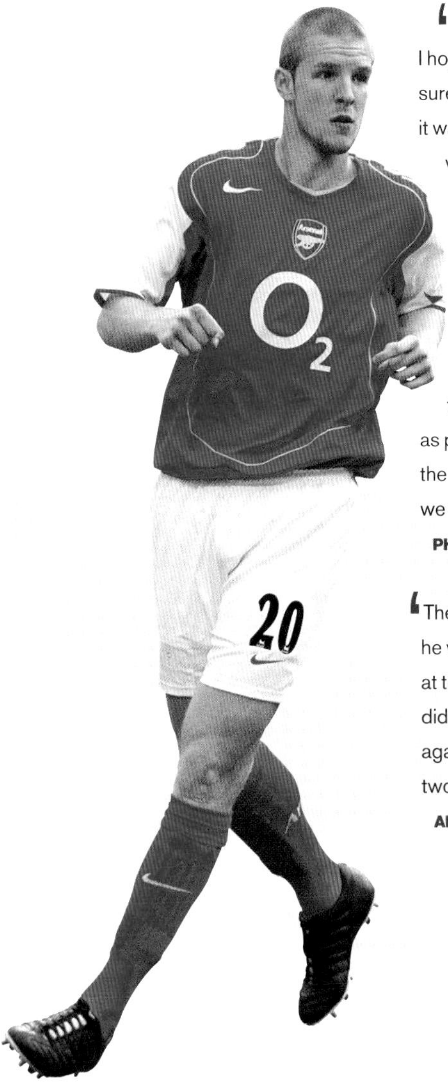

❝He's an aggressive defender and very strong. I hope he can play more and more games because I'm sure he'll keep getting better with every game. I know it was hard for him last season with his injury but we were all with him and all trying to help him. Now we've seen what he can do, he's fantastic. I'm very happy for him.❞

FRANCESC FABREGAS

❝I kept working hard and I got my chance. Now I feel really good. I am going to try my best to make sure that I can do well here for as long as possible. Us younger players want to be part of the future of Arsenal, that's why we are here, why we work so hard.❞

PHILIPPE SENDEROS

❝The month of March was a great one for him and he will never forget it. Not only did he make his debut at the top, top level [in the Champions League], he did well for Switzerland too. They had a good draw against France, won against Cyprus and kept two clean sheets.❞

ARSÈNE WENGER

ARSENAL DIARY

Wednesday 2 March
- Gilberto attends the Under-16s London Visually Impaired Football League Tournament at Highbury.

Sunday 6 March
- Arsenal Ladies lift their first silverware of the campaign after beating Charlton 3–0 in the League Cup Final.

Monday 14 March
- Arsenal are drawn with Blackburn Rovers in the semi-final of the FA Cup.

Saturday 26 March
- Patrick Vieira becomes Arsenal's most capped player when he wins his 78th cap for France against Switzerland.

THE WIDER WORLD

Wednesday 23 March
- The new England kit is unveiled at a ceremony in Manchester.
- Franz Beckenbauer announces that he will stand for the presidency of UEFA.

Friday 25 March
- The Executive Director of the FA, David Davies, announces he will quit his post after the 2006 World Cup.

Saturday 26 March
- England beat Northern Ireland 4–0 in a World Cup qualifier at Old Trafford.

FA CARLING PREMIERSHIP
31 March 2005

	P	HOME					AWAY					Pts
		W	D	L	F	A	W	D	L	F	A	
Chelsea	30	12	3	0	30	4	12	2	1	28	6	77
Manchester United	30	11	4	0	27	7	8	5	2	21	10	66
ARSENAL	30	9	5	1	39	17	10	2	3	29	15	64
Everton	30	9	1	5	16	14	6	5	4	19	18	51
Liverpool	30	10	2	3	25	11	4	3	8	18	20	47
Bolton Wanderers	30	7	4	4	18	12	6	3	6	20	22	46
Charlton Athletic	30	8	2	5	24	19	4	5	6	11	23	43
Tottenham Hotspur	30	7	3	5	29	20	5	3	7	8	14	42
Middlesbrough	30	7	5	3	23	17	4	4	7	21	25	42
Newcastle United	29	7	4	4	24	21	2	7	5	17	24	38
Aston Villa	30	8	3	4	23	13	2	5	8	11	26	38
Manchester City	30	5	5	5	17	13	4	4	7	18	21	36
Birmingham City	30	6	4	5	19	12	3	4	8	14	25	35
Blackburn Rovers	30	3	7	5	16	19	4	4	7	9	18	32
Portsmouth	30	6	3	6	20	20	2	4	9	12	26	31
Fulham	29	5	3	6	16	21	3	3	9	17	26	30
Southampton	30	4	9	2	22	19	1	3	11	11	26	27
Crystal Palace	30	5	3	7	15	13	1	5	9	18	36	26
West Bromwich Albion	30	3	7	5	13	21	1	5	9	16	30	24
Norwich City	30	3	5	7	23	31	0	6	9	6	28	20

D D W W W W [7 scored, 0 conceded]   W L L L L L [6 scored, 12 conceded]

ARSENAL 4   1 NORWICH CITY

Henry 19, 22, 66,   Huckerby 30
Ljungberg 50

Substitutes						Substitutes
	Jens **LEHMANN**	1	1	Robert **GREEN**		
Manuel **ALMUNIA** 24	**LAUREN**	12	17	Marc **EDWORTHY**	21	Darren **WARD**
Emmanuel **EBOUE** 27	Kolo **TOURE**	28	5	Craig **FLEMING**	27	Gary **DOHERTY**
▶ Francesc **FABREGAS** 15	Pascal **CYGAN**	18	24	Jason **SHACKELL**	26	Thomas **HELVEG** ▶
◀ (Flamini, 36 mins)	Ashley **COLE**	3	3	Adam **DRURY**		(Edworthy, 72 mins) ◀
▶ Gael **CLICHY** 22	Fredrik **LJUNGBERG**	8	4	Graham **STUART**	15	Youssef **SAFRI** ▶
◀ (Pires, 77 mins)	Mathieu **FLAMINI**	16	8	Gary **HOLT**		(Holt, 58 mins) ◀
▶ Robin **VAN PERSIE** 11	**GILBERTO**	19	20	Damien **FRANCIS**	19	Mathias **SVENSSON** ▶
◀ (Reyes, 70 mins)	Robert **PIRES**	7	6	Darren **HUCKERBY**		(McKenzie, 71 mins) ◀
	Thierry **HENRY**	14	36	Dean **ASHTON**		
	José Antonio **REYES**	9	14	Leon **McKENZIE**		

MATCH REPORT

Arsenal went second in the Premiership after a fantastic Thierry Henry hat-trick helped beat Norwich City. It was the Frenchman's second Premiership hat-trick in successive home matches and left him just four goals short of Ian Wright's record for the Gunners. Another notable aspect of the match was the warmly welcomed return of

Gilberto who started his first match since the home game with Bolton Wanderers in September. The Brazilian slotted back nicely into the centre of midfield and was a key influence in a match that the Gunners dominated from the start.

In the 10th minute, Henry received the ball and unleashed a hard, long-range shot that Robert

***Too hot to handle** – Norwich City's Jason Shackell is unable to stop Thierry Henry giving Arsenal the lead.*

***Three minutes later it's that man again**. Henry celebrates a magnificent solo goal.*

Green struggled to control. Five minutes later, Henry and Pires combined to send José Antonio Reyes clear but the Spaniard screwed his shot just wide. Then, in the 19th minute, Arsenal took a deserved lead. Mathieu Flamini passed to Pires who tapped the ball onto Henry. The Frenchman drifted to the right and fired a low shot into the corner of Green's net. The home fans had barely finished celebrating when, three minutes later, Henry made it 2–0. With the ball at his feet at the touchline, Henry took on a group of Norwich defenders and cut inside before firing home.

Freddie Ljungberg almost scored again soon after, but in the 30th minute Norwich struck back. Jens Lehmann punched a corner out and Graham Stuart collected the ball. His shot was off-target but Darren Huckerby sent an angled shot past Lehmann on the rebound. Though there were other chances, notably for substitute Cesc Fabregas – on for the injured Flamini – Henry and Ljungberg there were no more goals in the first half.

Second-half action started almost immediately as just four minutes after the break Reyes fed Ljungberg and the Swede's shot was cleared off the line by a Norwich defender. The visitors were helpless, however, when Ljungberg leapt to head home a Lauren cross seconds later.

With the game safe, the Gunners refused to stop buzzing and Henry was the busiest bee of them all.

Freddie Ljungberg leaps to head home Lauren's cross to make it 3–1 just after half-time.

In the 66th minute, he was set up by Reyes and tapped home from close range to complete his hat-trick. He received a standing ovation from the Highbury crowd. What a dream it is for Arsenal fans to experience first hand Thierry Henry on top form. This was his seventh hat-trick in Arsenal colours.

As Henry and the team trotted off the pitch at the end, the sense of optimism around Highbury was tangible. The sun was shining, and Arsenal were returning to the form that saw them dazzle all-comers at the start of the season.

Hat-trick hero Henry slides in his third goal – it was the Frenchman's seventh hat-trick in Arsenal colours.

APRIL

FA Barclaycard Premiership
Saturday 9 April 2005 at The Riverside Stadium, 3.00 p.m.
Attendance: 33,874 Referee: Phil Dowd

D L L L L W [6 scored, 11 conceded]   D W W W W W [10 scored, 1 conceded]

MIDDLESBROUGH 0   1 ARSENAL

Pires 73

Substitutes					Substitutes
Mark **SCHWARZER**	1	Bradley **JONES**	35	1	Jens **LEHMANN**	
▸ Ugo **EHIOGU**	4	Stuart **PARNABY**	21	12	**LAUREN**	24	Manuel **ALMUNIA**
◂ (Parlour, 90 mins)		Chris **RIGGOTT**	5	2	Kolo **TOURE**	18	Pascal **CYGAN**
▸ Danny **GRAHAM**	??	Gareth **SOUTHGATE**	6	20	Philippe **SENDEROS**	27	Emmanuel **EBOUE**
◂ (Doriva, 86 mins)		Franck **QUEUDRUE**	3	3	Ashley **COLE**	10	Dennis **BERGKAMP** ▸
Jason **KENNEDY**	??	Ray **PARLOUR**	15	15	Francesc **FABREGAS**		(Reyes, 45 mins) ◂
Colin **COOPER**	??	**DORIVA**	20	4	Patrick **VIEIRA**	11	Robin **VAN PERSIE**
		George **BOATENG**	7	19	**GILBERTO**		
		Stewart **DOWNING**	19	7	Robert **PIRES**		
		Szilard **NEMETH**	8	14	Thierry **HENRY**		
		Jimmy-Floyd		9	José Antonio **REYES**		
		HASSELBAINK	18				

MATCH REPORT

Arsenal strengthened their grip on second place and completed their fourth successive league 'double' over Middlesbrough in a tough match at the Riverside Stadium. This was not a swashbuckling victory; it was instead a hard-fought win but no less satisfying for that.

In an opening period, which the home team just shaded, Stewart Downing peppered the Arsenal box with a series of crosses from the left. Middlesbrough were in decent form and Gunners' old boy Ray Parlour surged forward from midfield and found Jimmy-Floyd Hasselbaink. The Dutchman fed Doriva, whose effort sailed over the bar. Minutes later, Hasselbaink had a shot himself but put it wide. In the 29th minute, Arsenal had their best chance yet when Patrick Vieira sent a cross into the penalty area, which found Reyes at the far post.

The Spaniard's shot was blocked by Bradley Jones. This earned the Gunners a corner, which found Gilberto, but the Brazilian shot wide.

In the closing minutes of the first half, both side had chances to open the scoring. Henry shot just

***Thierry Henry evades** the challenge of Middlesbrough's Doriva.*

two chances – one a header, the second a weak shot – but Lehmann was able to prevent a goal in both instances. The steel throughout the Arsenal side is not given as much praise or airtime as the flair side of the team, yet in this match, the steel was there for all to see as Arsenal professionally held onto their lead whatever Middlesbrough threw at them.

And so it was that Pires' goal – Arsenal's 100th goal of the season in their 500th Premiership game – was enough to win the points and increase Arsenal's chances of a second-place finish in the league and automatic qualification for the group stages of the Champions League. Next up was the FA Cup semi-final against a tough and challenging Blackburn Rovers side. Arsenal's performance at the Riverside suggested they would be more than capable of prevailing in Cardiff.

Gilberto starred in a dominant midfield performance marshalled by the superb Patrick Vieira.

over the bar and Kolo Toure headed just over from an Henry free-kick. For Middlesbrough, a Downing cross tested Lehmann to the full and Szilard Nemeth should have done better having been set up by Parlour.

In the second half, Arsenal dominated possession but were in the main unable to turn it into clear-cut chances. Thanks to a dominant performance from Vieira and the rest of the midfield, much of the action took place in the Middlesbrough half. However, it was not until the 73rd minute that the visitors took the lead. Fabregas found Vieira on the edge of the area and the captain attempted a one-two but his return pass was intercepted by Franck Queudreu. However, the loose ball fell nicely into the path of Robert Pires and the Frenchman scored from eight yards.

In the closing stages, Middlesbrough naturally pressed hard for an equaliser. Hasselbaink had

Ashley Cole is first on hand to congratulate goalscorer Robert Pires.

APRIL

FA Cup Semi-Final
Saturday 16 April 2005 at the Millennium Stadium, Cardiff, 12.15 p.m.
Attendance: 52,077 Referee: Steve Dunn

D W W W W W [10 scored, 1 conceded]   W W D L D W [5 scored, 1 conceded]

ARSENAL 3
Pires 42, van Persie 86, 90

0 BLACKBURN ROVERS

Substitutes			Jens **LEHMANN**	1	1	Brad **FRIEDEL**			Substitutes
Manuel **ALMUNIA**	24		**LAUREN**	12	2	Lucas **NEILL**		13	Peter **ENCKELMAN**
Pascal **CYGAN**	18		Kolo **TOURE**	28	24	Andy **TODD**		8	Kerimoglu **TUGAY**
▶ Francesc **FABREGAS**	15		Philippe **SENDEROS**	20	15	Aaron **MOKOENA**		9	Jon **STEAD** ▶
◀ (Ljungberg, 50 mins)			Ashley **COLE**	3	29	Ryan **NELSEN**			(Matteo, 83 mins) ◀
▶ Robin **VAN PERSIE**	11		Patrick **VIEIRA**	4	22	Dominic **MATTEO**		7	Brett **EMERTON** ▶
◀ (Bergkamp 82 mins)			**GILBERTO**	19	12	Morten Gamst **PEDERSEN**			(Flitcroft, 52 mins) ◀
▶ Jeremie **ALIADIERE**	30		Robert **PIRES**	7	5	Garry **FLITCROFT**		31	Robbie **SAVAGE** ▶
◀ (Reyes, 89 mins)			Fredrik **LJUNGBERG**	8	18	Steven **REID**			(Thompson, 63 mins) ◀
			José Antonio **REYES**	9	20	David **THOMPSON**			
			Dennis **BERGKAMP**	10	10	Paul **DICKOV**			

MATCH REPORT

Arsenal strode to their fourth FA Cup Final in five years with a well-earned victory over a physical and resolute Blackburn Rovers side. The Gunners – who were contesting their fifth successive FA Cup semi-final - were without Thierry Henry and Sol Campbell but still won comfortably in the end.

There were few chances in an opening half-hour that saw Rovers crowd the midfield with five men who contested every pass and fought tirelessly to frustrate Arsenal. Not that Rovers were without attacking ambition: Morten Gamst Pedersen fired a free-kick over the bar and Steven Reid tested Jens Lehmann with a fine effort.

In the 29th minute, Arsenal had their first serious chance when José Antonio Reyes hit a left-foot shot at goal. Nine minutes later, Dennis Bergkamp released Reyes but the Spaniard's low shot was blocked impressively by Brad Friedel. Robert Pires pounced to follow-up but his effort was also stopped. But three minutes before the break, Pires found the back of the net. Patrick Vieira

Yet another superb team performance was rewarded with a goal on half-time as Robert Pires tapped home after good work from Kolo Toure.

chipped a fine pass to Kolo Toure at the back post. The young defender outfoxed Ryan Nelson and calmly picked out Pires for the Frenchman to tap the ball home. Any attacker would have admired Toure's calm and precise assist for the goal.

The second half was naturally a more open affair with Rovers forced into the attack. This led to more openings for Arsenal, which were exploited with enthusiasm. Gilberto shot wide after being set up by his fellow central midfielder Vieira. Then substitute Cesc Fabregas created some space for himself and delivered a powerful shot that was blocked by a Rovers defender.

Arsenal were by now performing with the quality and assurance that one would expect from a team that have made such a success of themselves in the FA Cup for so many years. However, in the 63rd minute a wake-up call was delivered to any complacent Gunners fans when Brett Emerton cut inside from the left and sent a testing effort towards Lehmann. Buoyed by this effort, Rovers continued to press with a series of dangerous crosses but Toure and the excellent Philippe Senderos were equal to them all.

In the 80th minute, Fabregas looked set to settle the tie when he charged through midfield and sent a low shot towards the Blackburn goal. However, the impressive Friedel tipped the young Spaniard's effort wide. Soon after, Bergkamp sent in a free-kick from the right and Gilberto twice tested Friedel from close-range. As the Gunners got closer and closer, more goals seemed inevitable.

Robin van Persie replaced Bergkamp and the young Dutchman was soon on the scoresheet. Collecting a pass from Vieira, he bamboozled two defenders and place a well executed shot past Friedel. Then, in stoppage time, van Persie lashed a fantastic first-time shot past Friedel to finish off a magnificent substitute performance.

Whether the FA Cup's temporary move to the Millennium Stadium in Cardiff is to your liking or not, there is no doubting how well Arsenal have done in the competition in recent years and Gunners fans enjoyed yet another jubilant return home from the Welsh capital.

Robin van Persie takes on the Blackburn defence before slotting home his first goal four minutes before the final whistle.

But supersub van Persie was not content with that and lashed home his second in injury time to ensure Arsenal's place in the FA Cup Final.

APRIL

FA Barclaycard Premiership
Wednesday 20 April 2005 at Stamford Bridge, 8.00 p.m.
Attendance: 41,621 Referee: Steve Bennett

W W W W D W [15 scored, 8 conceded]   W W W W W W [11 scored, 1 conceded]

CHELSEA 0   0 ARSENAL

Substitutes						Substitutes
Carlo **CUDICINI**	23	Petr **CECH**	**1**	**1**	Jens **LEHMANN**	
Robert **HUTH**	29	Glen **JOHNSON**	**2**	**12**	**LAUREN**	
▸ **TIAGO**	30	John **TERRY**	**26**	**28**	Kolo **TOURE**	24 Manuel **ALMUNIA**
◂ (Cole, 79 mins)		William **GALLAS**	**13**	**20**	Philippe **SENDEROS**	23 Sol **CAMPBELL**
▸ Mateja **KEZMAN**	9	Ricardo **CARVALHO**	**6**	**3**	Ashley **COLE**	17 **EDU**
◂ (Duff, 85 mins)		Joe **COLE**	**10**	**15**	Francesc **FABREGAS**	30 Jeremie **ALIADIERE** ▸
▸ Jiri **JAROSIK**	27	Frank **LAMPARD**	**8**	**4**	Patrick **VIEIRA**	(Fabregas, 81 mins) ◂
◂ (Gudjohnsen, 89 mins)		Claude **MAKELELE**	**4**	**19**	**GILBERTO**	11 Robin **VAN PERSIE** ▸
		Damien **DUFF**	**11**	**7**	Robert **PIRES**	(Bergkamp, 79 mins) ◂
		Didier **DROGBA**	**15**	**10**	Dennis **BERGKAMP**	
		Eidur **GUDJOHNSEN**	**22**	**9**	José Antonio **REYES**	

MATCH REPORT

Although the point earned by Chelsea in this match took them to within touching distance of wrestling the Premiership title from Arsenal, there were positives to be taken from this game for the visitors. Arsène Wenger's men remain unbeaten by Chelsea this campaign and can be justly proud of another clean sheet against tough opposition. Perhaps most pleasing of all, however, was the spirit in which the tie was played.

Even against such accomplished opponents and with Thierry Henry missing through injury, Arsenal created chances from the start. In the third minute, Lauren delivered a dangerous cross, which José Antonio Reyes knocked into the path of Robert Pires. The Frenchman connected brilliantly and walloped a fierce, rising shot that came down off the underside of the bar and bounced away to safety. Frank Lampard tested Jens Lehmann soon after but at this stage, Arsenal were dictating the play and consequently enjoying the best chances. In the ninth minute, Pires played a corner to Dennis Bergkamp who played the ball back to the Frenchman. Pires then had the goal at his mercy but disappointingly sent his effort across goal and wide.

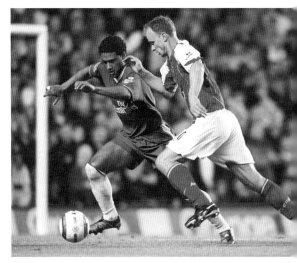

Dennis Bergkamp *takes on Chelsea's Glen Johnson but Arsenal failed to score during a dominant first-half performance.*

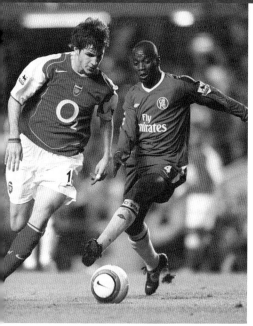

Cesc Fabregas eases his way past Chelsea's French midfielder Claude Makelele.

Frenchman prepared to pull the trigger, the tireless Lampard stole the ball.

Soon after the hour mark, Gallas' cross was dummied by Drogba and Lampard came racing onto the ball but to the relief of the travelling Arsenal fans, his shot went wide. Then, in the 78th minute came Arsenal's best chance of the second period when Pires fired straight at Cech. Fabregas also came close after weaving his way through a crowded area. In the final minutes, Wenger sent on both Robin van Persie and Jeremie Aliadiere but the extra firepower did not lead to a goal. Indeed, the only remaining action of note came when Drogba fired a free-kick over the bar.

Perhaps the most memorable moments of the evening came at the final whistle. Far from being an ill-tempered affair, the match had been played in fine spirit. That spirit continued after the match when both sets of players and coaching sides showed mutual respect for one another. Chelsea may have been on the brink of being crowned champions but their respect for Arsenal was clear to see.

Eidur Gudjohnsen came close with a header a few minutes later and this chance seemed to galvanise Chelsea. In the 30th minute, Damien Duff released Didier Drogba and the Ivorian forward found himself one-on-one with Jens Lehmann. The German goalkeeper confidently blocked the shot with his legs. Gilberto seemed to be in a great goalscoring position soon after but was intercepted by William Gallas. There remained time for two chances from Joe Cole before the half-time whistle was blown.

Whereas the first half was perhaps tipped slightly in Arsenal's favour, the second period saw Chelsea improve. In the 56th minute, Duff raced down the left and crossed for Drogba. The striker shot just wide of Lehmann's goal. Within seconds, Bergkamp found Pires at the other end but just as the

Gilberto's powerhouse performance in midfield did much to nullify the threat from Chelsea's expensive strike force.

125

D W W W W D [10 scored, 2 conceded]   L W D W D D [7 scored, 9 conceded]

ARSENAL 1 0 TOTTENHAM
Reyes 22 HOTSPUR

Substitutes					Substitutes
Manuel **ALMUNIA** 24	Jens **LEHMANN** 1	1 Paul **ROBINSON**	37 Radek **CERNY**
Sol **CAMPBELL** 23	**LAUREN** 12	34 Stephen **KELLY**	2 Noureddine **NAYBET**
▸ **EDU** 17	Kolo **TOURE** 28	20 Michael **DAWSON**	16 Reto **ZIEGLER**
◂ (Fabregas, 69 mins)	Philippe **SENDEROS** 20	26 Ledley **KING**	15 Ahmed Hossam **MIDO** ▸
▸ Jeremie **ALIADIERE** 30	Ashley **COLE** 3	14 Erik **EDMAN**	(Kanoute, 70 mins) ◂
◂ (Reyes, 88 mins)	Francesc **FABREGAS** 15	7 Simon **DAVIES**	10 Robbie **KEANE** ▸
▸ Dennis **BERGKAMP** 10	Patrick **VIEIRA** 4	4 Sean **DAVIS**	(Defoe, 78 mins) ◂
◂ (Van Persie, 69 mins)	**GILBERTO** 19	23 Michael **CARRICK**	
	Robert **PIRES** 7	19 Andy **REID**	
	Robin **VAN PERSIE** 11	9 Frederic **KANOUTE**	
	José Antonio **REYES** 9	18 Jermain **DEFOE**	

MATCH REPORT

Having seen their heroes secure the Premiership title against Tottenham Hotspur last season, Gunners fans were desperate that Arsenal should not surrender the Championship against their local rivals. Happily, a solid performance and fine goal from José Antonio Reyes ensured that the Premiership title race was kept alive for the time being at least.

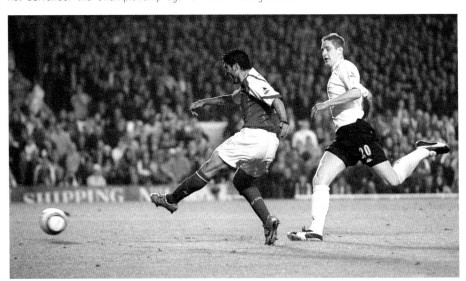

José Antonio Reyes outpaces Tottenham's Michael Dawson to give the Gunners the lead after 22 minutes.

Ashley Cole stretches to clear from Tottenham striker Frederic Kanoute.

In the 22nd minute, Reyes made up for his earlier miss. A majestic pass from Cesc Fabregas sent him free down the left wing. His crisp cross-shot beat Robinson and sent Highbury into raptures. The goalscorer pointed to the sky in celebration.

Roused by the goal, the Gunners piled forward to try and increase their lead. Patrick Vieira sent a far-post header just wide and also put in an unsuccessful claim for a penalty. Fabregas sent a long-distance shot just wide, and minutes later van Persie attempted to score from the same spot and also shot just wide. There was just time for Fabregas to shoot a Reyes cross straight at Erik Edman before half-time.

Tottenham enjoyed more possession in the second half but were unable to convert that possession into a goal or even into any chances of note. Meanwhile, the home team were limited to few clear-cut chances themselves. In the 68th minute, Philippe Senderos headed a Reyes free-kick just over the bar and soon after, Kolo Toure came close with another free-kick. But the longer the match went on, the more it seemed that 1–0 would remain the final score. After 74 minutes, Edu hit the post with a fine clipped shot from just outside the area and Gilberto then found Reyes only for the Spaniard to once again hit the side-netting.

In the 87th minute, Robbie Keane's header went just wide and Arsenal's first league double over Tottenham for 16 years was confirmed. Another solid performance, another clean sheet and another three points. The Gunners are in fine form at the moment. Although this was to be the last match that they played as Champions, there is plenty of evidence that Arsenal will be incredibly strong contenders in next season's title race.

Robin van Persie came in for Dennis Bergkamp but otherwise the team was the same as that which started the 0–0 draw at Stamford Bridge. The younger Dutchman played a killer ball to Reyes in the opening minute. The Spaniard rounded Paul Robinson and looked set to score until his mis-hit shot hit the side-netting.

Jermain Defoe then had two chances to score. First, he ran clear of Kolo Toure and sent in an unsuccessful chip from the edge of the area. Then, in the 16th minute, he again beat Toure and found himself in a great position to score. However, Jens Lehmann stood tall and prevented a goal.

Arsenal.com PLAYER OF THE MONTH

Philippe SENDEROS

> We don't really care about the others but you want to win every game until the end. I think it's a team effort, we did very well to keep a clean sheet again and we have to congratulate the other players. I don't think ahead, I think of the next game. We have to keep going.
>
> **PHILIPPE SENDEROS**

> Even though it's nice to hear comparisons with Tony Adams, it's still crazy. He accomplished so much in his career. He was a legend. But me? I'm just at the beginning of my journey.
>
> **PHILIPPE SENDEROS**

> Congratulations to Philippe. This season, so many fantastic young players have come through for us. Philippe has been most impressive and you can see how defensively stable he is. He and other players make me very optimistic for the future.
>
> **ARSÈNE WENGER**

ARSENAL DIARY

Thursday 14 April
- Thierry Henry is nominated for the PFA Player of the Year award.

Sunday 24 April
- Arsenal Ladies clinch their fourth Premiership title in five years with a 1–0 victory over Charlton Athletic.
- Ashley Cole and Thierry Henry are named in the PFA Team of the Year.

Monday 25 April
- Jermaine Pennant completes his move from Arsenal to Birmingham City following his successful loan spell at the club.

THE WIDER WORLD

Wednesday 13 April
- At least one English team is guaranteed a place in the UEFA Champions League Final as Chelsea and Liverpool reach the semi-finals.

Saturday 23 April
- Sunderland's 2–1 victory over Leicester City secures their promotion to the Premiership.

Sunday 24 April
- John Terry wins the 2005 PFA Player of the Year Award. The PFA Young Player of the Year Award goes to Wayne Rooney.

Saturday 30 April
- Chelsea secure the Premiership title with a 2–0 victory over Bolton Wanderers.

FA CARLING PREMIERSHIP
30 April 2005

		HOME					AWAY					
	P	W	D	L	F	A	W	D	L	F	A	Pts
Chelsea	35	13	5	0	34	6	14	2	1	33	7	88
ARSENAL	**34**	**11**	**5**	**1**	**44**	**18**	**11**	**3**	**3**	**30**	**15**	**74**
Manchester United	34	12	5	0	29	8	8	5	4	21	13	70
Everton	35	11	2	5	22	15	6	5	6	19	21	58
Liverpool	36	11	4	3	29	14	5	3	10	20	23	55
Bolton Wanderers	36	8	5	5	22	16	7	4	7	23	25	54
Middlesbrough	36	8	6	4	28	19	5	6	7	23	26	51
Manchester City	36	8	5	5	23	13	4	7	7	21	24	48
Tottenham Hotspur	35	8	4	5	31	21	5	5	8	11	18	48
Aston Villa	35	8	6	4	25	15	4	5	8	17	28	47
Charlton Athletic	35	8	3	6	27	23	4	6	8	13	28	45
Birmingham City	36	7	6	5	22	14	3	6	9	16	30	42
Blackburn Rovers	36	5	8	5	20	19	4	6	8	11	21	41
Newcastle United	35	7	6	5	24	24	2	7	8	19	29	40
Fulham	35	7	4	6	22	23	3	4	11	20	33	38
Portsmouth	36	8	3	7	29	25	2	5	11	13	31	38
Southampton	36	5	9	4	29	28	1	4	13	13	34	31
Crystal Palace	36	6	4	8	19	17	1	6	11	18	41	31
West Bromwich Albion	35	4	8	5	15	22	1	7	10	18	36	30
Norwich City	36	6	5	7	28	32	0	7	11	13	39	30

W W D D L D [8 scored, 4 conceded]   W W W W W W [10 scored, 1 conceded]

WEST BROMWICH 0 ALBION

2 ARSENAL
van Persie 66, Edu 90

Substitutes						Substitutes
Tomasz **KUSZCZAK**	29	Russell **HOULT**	1	1	Jens **LEHMANN**	
Riccardo **SCIMECA**	2	Thomas **GAARDSOE**	4	12	**LAUREN**	24	Manuel **ALMUNIA**
▶ Robert **EARNSHAW**	34	Darren **MOORE**	5	28	Kolo **TOURE**	23	Sol **CAMPBELL**
◀ (Albrechtsen, 80 mins)		Neil **CLEMENT**	19	20	Philippe **SENDEROS**	17	**EDU** ▶
▶ Nwankwo **KANU**	25	Martin **ALBRECHTSEN**	14	3	Ashley **COLE**		(van Persie, 74 mins) ◀
◀ (Gera, 80 mins)		Ronnie **WALLWORK**	24	15	Francesc **FABREGAS**	30	Jeremie **ALIADIERE**
▶ Geoff **HORSFIELD**	9	Kieran **RICHARDSON**	15	4	Patrick **VIEIRA**	10	Dennis **BERGKAMP** ▶
◀ (Campbell, 80 mins)		Paul **ROBINSON**	3	19	**GILBERTO**		(Fabregas, 74 mins) ◀
		Zoltan **GERA**	11	7	Robert **PIRES**		
		Kevin **CAMPBELL**	21	11	Robin **VAN PERSIE**		
		Jonathan **GREENING**	8	9	José Antonio **REYES**		

MATCH REPORT

With Arsenal's Premiership title officially surrendered and West Bromwich Albion still fighting for their lives at the bottom, some expected the Gunners to slip up here. However, Arsène Wenger's men do not know the meaning of anything but 100 per cent endeavour and were in any case still keen to secure second place. Little wonder then, that they emerged victorious at the end of a tough match.

West Brom began the match like a team fighting for their lives as the home crowd roared their every move. Kieran Richardson was particularly electric and his early corner was met by an overhead kick from Zoltan Gera, though the ball went wide of the post. As the home side continued to probe, it took fine performances from Kolo Toure and Philippe Senderos to repel them.

After half an hour, Arsenal sprang into life offensively. Lauren split the home defence open with an immense pass that Robin van Persie pounced upon, forcing a great save from Hoult. A couple of minutes later, Senderos sent a header just over the bar.

Although Arsenal were coming back into the match, in first-half injury time Gera released Ronnie Wallwork who hit the bar with his rising shot. It was a warning to Arsenal that they needed to raise their game in the second half if they wanted to take the points home with them.

The second half started in much the same way as the first with West Brom playing in lively fashion, roared on by passionate home support. In the opening minutes of the half, both Paul Robinson and Neil Clement came close to opening the scoring, the latter with a fine header that deflected off Gilberto.

As the half progressed, Arsenal came more into it with van Persie particularly effective. After seeing a free-kick blocked, the Dutchman did not need to wait long to give the visitors the lead. In the 66th minute, he received the ball from José Antonio Reyes on the edge of the area. The 21-year-old controlled it and beat Russell Hoult with a sublime left-foot shot. Six minutes later, the pair that combined for the first goal swapped roles with van Persie releasing Reyes. The Spaniard took the ball round Hoult and looked set to score until Clement raced back and cleared his shot off the goal-line.

Not that West Brom were rolling over – far from it. Richardson tested Jens Lehmann with a swerving

Arsenal take the lead *after 66 minutes with this magnificent left-foot shot from Robin van Persie.*

shot. Then, Bryan Robson sent on three substitutes, all of them strikers including Arsenal old boy Nwankwo Kanu. The Gunners needed to score again to make the win definite.

After some delightful keep-ball, Reyes and substitute Edu both came close to scoring that decisive second goal. Three minutes into injury time, the Brazilian went one better and made it 2–0. A pass from Arsenal's other substitute Dennis Bergkamp sent him through and his clipped shot deflected off Hoult into the net.

This victory took Arsenal one step closer to securing second place in the Premiership and with it, guaranteed Champions League football next season. It had been another tough battle for the Gunners but one again they were equal to that challenge and emerged not just with the points but also with another impressive clean-sheet.

After coming off the bench *Edu shows perfect poise to control Bergkamp's pass and score Arsenal's second.*

131

W W W D W W [11 scored, 1 conceded]　　　D W L D D W [6 scored, 5 conceded]

ARSENAL 3　1 LIVERPOOL

Pires 25, Reyes 29,　　Gerrard 51
Fabregas 90

Substitutes					Substitutes
Manuel **ALMUNIA**	24	Jens **LEHMANN**	**1**	**1** Jerzy **DUDEK**	
Sol **CAMPBELL**	23	**LAUREN**	**12**	**3** Steve **FINNAN**	20 Scott **CARSON**
▸ **EDU**	17	Kolo **TOURE**	**28**	**4** Sami **HYYPIA**	25 Igor **BISCAN**
◂ (Pires, 68 mins)		Philippe **SENDEROS**	**20**	**23** Jamie **CARRAGHER**	7 Harry **KEWELL** ▸
▸ Jeremie **ALIADIERE**	30	Ashley **COLE**	**3**	**21** Djimi **TRAORE**	(Riise, 45 mins) ◂
◂ (Reyes, 86 mins)		Francesc **FABREGAS**	**15**	**6** John Arne **RIISE**	11 Vladimir **SMICER**
▸ Dennis **BERGKAMP**	10	Patrick **VIEIRA**	**4**	**8** Steven **GERRARD**	9 Djibril **CISSE** ▸
◂ (van Persie, 68 mins)		**GILBERTO**	**19**	**14** Xabi **ALONSO**	(Baros, 45 mins) ◂
		Robert **PIRES**	**7**	**16** Dietmar **HAMANN**	
		Robin **VAN PERSIE**	**11**	**5** Milan **BAROS**	
		José Antonio **REYES**	**9**	**10** Javier Luis **GARCIA**	

MATCH REPORT

Arsenal were as good as guaranteed a top two finish after this enjoyable victory over Liverpool. Once again the Gunners found themselves up against a determined team with something to battle for – this time their opponents were desperately seeking a place in next season's Champions League.

In the 11th minute, the game exploded into action when Robin van Persie sent in a fine shot

Robert Pires picks his spot, firing this free-kick over the Liverpool wall and past Jerzy Dudek.

from the edge of the area that Jerzy Dudek could only parry. José Antonio Reyes picked up the loose ball and slotted home but he had strayed offside in the process. Within 60 seconds, Liverpool almost opened the scoring when Dietmar Hamann met a corner and sent John Arne Riise through. However, the Norwegian's effort was blocked by Jens Lehmann. Soon after, Milan Baros had the ball in the back of the net but the effort was ruled out for foul play during the build-up.

Robert Pires and Cesc Fabregas were by this point proving a thorn in Liverpool's side. The Spaniard sent a powerful shot just wide while the Frenchman came close himself twice and crossed for Lauren who hit the bar. In the 25th minute, his endeavour was rewarded. Patrick Vieira was fouled just outside the area and Pires side-footed the resultant free-kick over the Liverpool wall and into the top corner.

The Gunners were in merciless mood and within four minutes, the lead was doubled when Fabregas and Ashley Cole combined to set up Reyes. The Spaniard left his marker trailing and shot past Dudek into the far corner. Highbury was in buoyant mood and the crowd greeted Reyes' goal in style.

After the break, the previously cautious Liverpool added some teeth to their attack, bringing on Djibril Cisse and Harry Kewell. As they attacked with renewed vigour, a goal came six minutes into the second period. Steven Gerrard's free-kick from just outside the area was deflected off Fabregas past a helpless Lehmann.

On the hour mark, Gerrard was behind a move that almost drew Liverpool level. His inspired pass sent Luis Garcia through and only a wholehearted tracking run by Cole forced Garcia into sending his shot high over the bar. It was a moment typical of the exceptional defending that Arsenal had been producing in recent weeks. All the same, Gerrard and Garcia both had further chances.

In the 79th minute, Fabregas had the ball in the back of the net but his effort was disallowed.

Four minutes later José Antonio Reyes doubles the lead after good work from Fabregas and Cole.

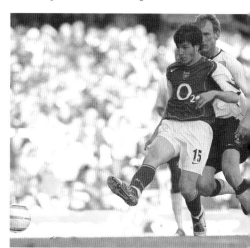

Francesc Fabregas wraps things up by slotting home Arsenal's third from another Dennis Bergkamp pass.

Then, at the death, the young Spaniard did score after Dennis Bergkamp slipped the ball through a tight defence. The only downside of a great afternoon was the knowledge that Pires, Gilberto and Vieira all picked up injuries. More happily, Arsenal had as good as secured second place and shown once again that they look a good bet to go one better next season.

W W D W W W [10 scored, 1 conceded]   L W W D L W [8 scored, 4 conceded]

ARSENAL 7   0 EVERTON

van Persie 8, Pires 12, 50,
Vieira 37, Edu 70 pen, Bergkamp 77,
Flamini 85

Substitutes		Jens **LEHMANN**	1	1	Richard **WRIGHT**		Substitutes
Manuel **ALMUNIA**	24	**LAUREN**	12	22	Tony **HIBBERT**	37	Iain **TURNER**
Kolo **TOURE**	28	Sol **CAMPBELL**	23	5	David **WEIR**	4	Alan **STUBBS**
▸ Francesc **FABREGAS**	15	Philippe **SENDEROS**	20	20	Joseph **YOBO**	24	Guillaume **PLESSIS**
◂ (Pires, 64 mins)		Ashley **COLE**	3	3	Alessandro **PISTONE**	10	Duncan **FERGUSON** ▸
▸ Mathieu **FLAMINI**	16	Patrick **VIEIRA**	4	26	Lee **CARSLEY**		(Arteta, 75 mins) ◂
◂ (Vieira, 45 mins)		**EDU**	17	11	James **McFADDEN**	7	Marcus **BENT** ▸
▸ Thierry **HENRY**	14	Robert **PIRES**	7	2	Steve **WATSON**		(Beattie, 65 mins) ◂
◂ (van Persie, 45 mins)		Dennis **BERGKAMP**	10	6	Mikel **ARTETA**		
		Robin **VAN PERSIE**	11	14	Kevin **KILBANE**		
		José Antonio **REYES**	9	8	James **BEATTIE**		

MATCH REPORT

What an evening. Arsenal simply destroyed Everton with a fantastic team performance that was personified by Dennis Bergkamp who set up three of the goals and scored one himself. The biggest Arsenal win ever under Arsène Wenger also saw Mathieu Flamini score his first goal for the Gunners, Edu stroke home a penalty in his final match at Highbury and Thierry Henry returned to action ahead of the FA Cup Final.

Ironically, in the second minute, Everton nearly took the lead when Mikel Arteta found himself unmarked but he shot straight at Jens Lehmann. However, six minutes later, the Arsenal goalscoring began when Bergkamp split the Everton defence and Robin van Persie shot past former Gunner Richard Wright.

Just four minutes later, it was 2–0. A superb pass from Bergkamp released José Antonio

Two up inside 12 minutes as first Robin van Persie (left) and Robert Pires (centre) get on the scoresheet. Captain Patrick Vieira (right) made it three just before half-time.

It was a magical night as another from Pires (top left), a penalty from Edu (top right), a goal from Man of the Match Dennis Bergkamp (above left) and finally seventh heaven as Matthieu Flamini nets his first ever Arsenal goal.

Reyes who crossed for Robert Pires. The Frenchman's shot was parried by Wright but he made no mistake with a follow-up header. Everton then had two chances to score through James Beattie and Arteta, but Arsenal were soon back on the attack. In the 38th minute, Patrick Vieira added a third, lifting the ball over Wright, sending Highbury into raptures. It was already tangible that something special was underway.

After the break, Wenger sent on Henry and Flamini for van Persie and Vieira. Five minutes later, Henry's pass inadvertently fell to Pires who slotted the ball home. Of course, Henry was not the only returning hero in fine form. In the 60th minute, substitute Marcus Bent raced through towards goal and the returning Sol Campbell was given his first real test. He passed with flying colours, raising a great roar from the home crowd.

In the 70th minute, Henry won Arsenal a penalty and Edu, in his final match at Highbury, was allowed to take the spot-kick. He made no mistake and celebrated in front of the Arsenal fans. Seven minutes later came the moment the home fans had really been hoping for as Bergkamp chased down a clearance and clipped the ball past Wright.

With the crowd and team both keen for another goal, the Gunners kept probing. The seventh came after Henry and Reyes combined to set up Mathieu Flamini. In an evening laden with significance, this was the young Frenchman's first Arsenal goal. Perhaps more significant was that this was Arsenal's final match at Highbury wearing a red and white kit. The longer this season goes on, the brighter Arsenal's future seems.

MAY

FA Barclaycard Premiership
Sunday 15 May 2005 at St Andrews, 3.00 p.m.
Attendance: 29,302 Referee: Dermot Gallagher

D D L D W L [4 scored, 7 conceded]   W D W W W W [16 scored, 1 conceded]

BIRMINGHAM 2 CITY

Pandiani 80, Heskey 90

1 ARSENAL

Bergkamp 88

Substitutes						Substitutes
	Maik **TAYLOR**	1	1	Jens **LEHMANN**		
Nico **VAESEN** 18	Mario **MELCHIOT**	29	28	Kolo **TOURE**	24	Manuel **ALMUNIA**
Robbie **BLAKE** 7	Kenny **CUNNINGHAM**	4	23	Sol **CAMPBELL**	30	Jeremie **ALIADIERE**
▶ Olivier **TEBILY** 2	Matthew **UPSON**	5	20	Philippe **SENDEROS**		(van Persie, 68 mins)
◀ (Melchiot, 78 mins)	Jamie **CLAPHAM**	3	3	Ashley **COLE**	16	Mathieu **FLAMINI**
▶ Clinton **MORRISON** 19	Jermaine **PENNANT**	8	15	Francesc **FABREGAS**		(Fabregas, 75 mins)
◀ (Carter, 62 mins)	Mehdi **NAFTI**	36	4	Patrick **VIEIRA**	17	**EDU**
▶ Martin **TAYLOR** 15	Darren **CARTER**	24	19	**GILBERTO**		(Ljungberg, 68 mins)
◀ (Pandiani, 90 mins)	Stephen **CLEMENCE**	25	8	Freddie **LJUNGBERG**	27	Emmanuel **EBOUE**
	⚅ Walter **PANDIANI**	9	10	Dennis **BERGKAMP**		
	Emile **HESKEY**	16	11	Robin **VAN PERSIE**		

MATCH REPORT

Following the emphatic victory over Everton, the final match of the Premiership was something of a disappointment for Arsenal fans. A most pleasing league campaign ended in defeat during a hot afternoon at St Andrews.

Birmingham City started the match the strongest, and in the 22nd minute Walter Pandiani released Stephen Clemence who raced into the area and sent in a hard shot that went over the bar. There followed some impressive moves from the hosts with Mario Melchiot and Mehdi Nafti sending some dangerous crosses and threatening passes.

Arsenal improved as the first half wore on. Kolo Toure, playing at right-back, was in determined mood and raced down the wing before sending in a fine cross for Robin van Persie. The Dutchman skilfully met the ball, flicked it up but his volleyed shot went wide.

Not that Toure was neglecting his defensive duties; quite the contrary, he saved the Gunners with a magnificent clearance from a Nafti cross as Darren Carter zoomed in ominously. Soon after this, Toure was again on the attack and once more

Substitute Jeremie Aliadiere beats Birmingham's Kenny Cunningham to the ball before sending in a dangerous cross.

sent in a testing cross that van Persie connected with but sent straight into the hands of the home goalkeeper, Maik Taylor. This was the last action of the half, but the visiting fans hoped it heralded a successful second period for Arsenal.

Dennis Bergkamp had starred in the demolition of Everton and the Dutchman was at the centre of many of Arsenal's attacks in the second half. Cesc Fabregas and van Persie combined well to release Bergkamp down the left. The elder Dutchman was just unable to lift the ball over Taylor and into the goal. Within minutes, the younger Dutchman had another fine chance to score. Although he shot from close range, he was unable to score.

In the 67th minute, the home side got back into the match as Clinton Morrison surged through on goal. Jens Lehmann rushed out and dealt authoritatively with the danger. However, it continued to be Arsenal who looked most likely to score. Substitute Jeremie Aliadiere broke into the area and twice tried to shoot past Taylor. Toure then bombed forward again but his shot hit the post.

But in the 80th minute, Birmingham City took the lead, somewhat against the run of play. Former Gunner Jermaine Pennant sent in a corner from the right flank and, following something of a scramble, Pandiani fired the ball in from close range. Eight minutes later, Arsenal equalised when captain Patrick Vieira sent a cute pass to Bergkamp and the Dutchman managed to bundle the ball home. A draw was the very least Arsenal deserved, but there was to be a final twist in the closing moments of the Premiership season.

A minute after Bergkamp's strike, Olivier Tebily fired a cross into the area and Sol Campbell's header inadvertently sent the ball into Emile Heskey's path and the big striker shot and scored from close range. Arsenal fans felt their team perhaps deserved more from the afternoon – but then many would say that the Gunners could have gone one better over the whole season.

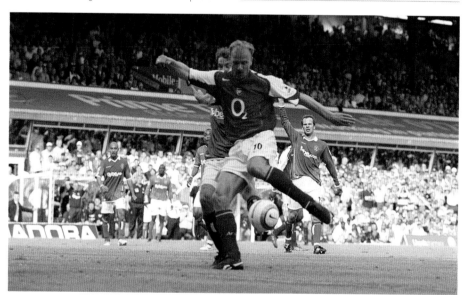

At the end of a season in which his contribution has been superb, it was fitting that Arsenal's last league goal should have been scored by the Dutch master Dennis Bergkamp. Unfortunately it was not the winner.

MAY

FA Cup Final
Saturday 21 May 2005 at the Millennium Stadium, Cardiff, 3.00 p.m.
Attendance: 71,876 Referee: Rob Styles

D W W W W W [16 scored, 2 conceded]   L W W D L W [10 scored, 7 conceded]

ARSENAL 0   0 MANCHESTER UNITED

(after extra time)
ARSENAL won 5-4 on penalties

Substitutes				Substitutes
Manuel ALMUNIA	24	Jens LEHMANN	1	13	Roy CARROLL	
Sol CAMPBELL	23	LAUREN	12	6	Wes BROWN	Tim HOWARD	1
▸ EDU	17	Kolo TOURE	28	5	Rio FERDINAND	Gary NEVILLE	2
◂ (Gilberto, 105 mins)		Philippe SENDEROS	20	27	Mikael SILVESTRE	Alan SMITH	14
▸ Robin VAN PERSIE	11	Ashley COLE	3	22	John O'SHEA	Quinton FORTUNE ▸	25
◂ (Fabregas, 86 mins)		Francesc FABREGAS	15	24	Darren FLETCHER	(O'Shea, 77 mins) ◂	
▸ Fredrik LJUNGBERG	8	Patrick VIEIRA	4	16	Roy KEANE	Ryan GIGGS ▸	11
◂ (Bergkamp, 65 mins)		GILBERTO	19	18	Paul SCHOLES	(Fletcher, 91 mins) ◂	
		Robert PIRES	7	7	Cristiano RONALDO		
		Dennis BERGKAMP	10	10	Ruud VAN NISTELROOY		
		José Antonio REYES	9	8	Wayne ROONEY		

ARSENAL penalties:
Lauren scored, Ljungberg scored, van Persie scored, Cole scored, Vieira scored
MANCHESTER UNITED penalties:
van Nistelrooy scored, Scholes saved, Ronaldo scored, Rooney scored, Keane scored

MATCH REPORT

Arsenal won the FA Cup for the tenth time and ended their season on a high after the first ever penalty shoot-out in an FA Cup Final. A gripping afternoon's football ended on the highest of notes for the Gunners' faithful when captain Patrick Vieira stroked home his spot-kick to land the cup for Arsenal.

This was Arsenal's fourth FA Cup Final in five years and the travelling fans have become accustomed to the Millennium Stadium during that time. However, in truth, Arsenal were in truth second-best for much of the tie but held out to win in the end.

Ronaldo's battle with Lauren was fascinating all afternoon and he created the first chance of the match when he crossed to Paul Scholes who could only head over the bar. Soon after, Arsenal threatened when a crossfield ball found José Antonio Reyes who drew Roy Carroll and passed to Cesc Fabregas. By now, United defenders had steamed back and the danger subsided accordingly.

Rio Ferdinand had the ball in the back of the net after 28 minutes but the effort was ruled out for offside. Then Wayne Rooney had two great chances with Lehmann saving the first and the second sailing over the bar.

In the second half, van Nistelrooy and Ronaldo both sent efforts over the bar, a Roy Keane effort was cleared by Patrick Vieira and soon after, Ljungberg nodded a van Nistelrooy header against the bar. By now, the nerves of all Gunners fans were on edge. Not that Arsenal were entirely without attacking moves. Robert Pires sent through a neat ball that Fabregas and Vieira were unable to exploit just before the hour. Minutes later, Bergkamp and Reyes combined but failed to threaten Carroll.

In extra time, substitute Robin van Persie won and took a free-kick just outside the area. He curled in a fine effort and Carroll did well to stop it. Rooney, Scholes and van Nistelrooy had further chances but with extra time running out the scoreline stayed at 0-0. Just before the final whistle of extra time was blown, the Gunners lost Reyes when he was dismissed after receiving a second red card.

Arsène Wenger's men negotiated the penalty shoot-out in textbook fashion. All five Arsenal players scored and Lehmann – who had starred all afternoon – did well to save from Scholes. When Vieira knocked the decisive spot-kick home, it rightly sparked jubilant celebrations among the Arsenal team.

Let those who would say Arsenal did not deserve to win say their worst. There have also been those who have doubted Patrick Vieira's commitment to the club or Jens Lehmann's ability, there can be no doubt on either front after the pair's performances in this match. The history books will show another fact: that Arsenal won the 2005 FA Cup.

Jens Lehmann saves from Scholes and sets up Arsenal's third FA Cup triumph in five years.

This is how you do it: Lauren (top left), Ljungberg (top right), van Persie (left) and Cole (right) all score...

... allowing captain Patrick Vieira the honour of striking the winning kick past Roy Carroll.

Arsenal.com PLAYER OF THE MONTH
Philippe SENDEROS

'There is always a good spirit here and we showed that during and after the FA Cup Final in Cardiff. It was great in the dressing room afterwards. We enjoyed every moment and that it is what you have to do when you win a trophy. For me it has been another fantastic and enjoyable month. I look forward very much to next season. We all want to build on our current successes and we believe we can. Belief is the key to success.'

PHILIPPE SENDEROS

'What a season it has been for Philippe, I am delighted for him. He has shown what everyone at the club have long known, that he is an accomplished defender already – and with the promise to become even better. I am sure Philippe has learned and improved during this season. I am also sure he will learn more next year.'

PATRICK VIEIRA

'This has been an important year for Philippe and his form in May reflects how well he has done throughout the season. He was a key part of a special defensive performance in the FA Cup Final and that summed up his year. He has taken some big steps for both Arsenal and Switzerland and he has always looked like he belongs where he is – at the top level.'

ARSÈNE WENGER

ARSENAL DIARY

Saturday 7 May
• Arsenal Ladies complete and incredible unbeaten league season beating Fulham 6–2.

Thursday 12 May
• Midfielder Edu announces that he is going to leave Arsenal after four years at the Club.

Tuesday 17 May
• It is announced that Arsenal have topped the Fair Play League for the second successive year.

Tuesday 31 May
• Thierry Henry is co-awarded the Golden Shoe as Europe's top marksman. Henry, the first player to win the award in consecutive years since it was relaunched in 1996, will share the award with Diego Forlan of Villarreal.

THE WIDER WORLD

Tuesday 3 May
• Liverpool beat Chelsea 1–0 to secure their place in the UEFA Champions League Final.

Sunday 8 May
• Wigan win promotion to the Premiership with their 3–1 victory over Reading.

Thursday 12 May
• US sports tycoon Malcolm Glazer wins control of Manchester United FC in a £740 million takeover bid.

Wednesday 18 May
• CSKA Moscow beat Sporting Lisbon 3–1 to win the UEFA Cup.

Wednesday 25 May
• Liverpool win Champions League beating AC Milan on penalties after a 3–3 draw in Istanbul.

FA CARLING PREMIERSHIP
15 May 2005

	P	HOME					AWAY					Pts
		W	D	L	F	A	W	D	L	F	A	
Chelsea	38	14	5	0	35	6	15	3	1	37	9	95
ARSENAL	**38**	**13**	**5**	**1**	**54**	**19**	**12**	**3**	**4**	**33**	**17**	**83**
Manchester United	38	12	6	1	31	12	10	5	4	27	14	77
Everton	38	12	2	5	24	15	6	5	8	21	31	61
Liverpool	38	12	4	3	31	15	5	3	11	21	31	61
Bolton Wanderers	38	9	5	5	25	18	7	5	7	24	26	58
Middlesbrough	38	9	6	4	29	19	5	7	7	24	27	55
Manchester City	38	8	6	5	24	14	5	7	7	23	25	52
Tottenham Hotspur	38	9	5	5	36	22	5	5	9	11	19	52
Aston Villa	38	8	6	5	26	17	4	5	10	19	35	47
Charlton Athletic	38	8	4	7	29	29	4	6	9	13	29	46
Birmingham City	38	8	6	5	24	15	3	6	10	16	31	45
Fulham	38	8	4	7	29	26	4	4	11	23	34	44
Newcastle United	38	7	7	5	25	25	3	7	9	22	32	44
Blackburn Rovers	38	5	8	6	21	22	4	7	8	11	21	42
Portsmouth	38	8	4	7	30	26	2	5	12	13	33	39
West Bromwich Albion	38	5	8	6	17	24	1	8	10	19	37	34
Crystal Palace	38	6	5	8	21	19	1	7	11	20	43	33
Norwich City	38	7	5	7	29	32	0	7	12	13	45	33
Southampton	38	5	9	5	30	30	1	5	13	15	36	32

THE SEASON IN REVIEW

A familiar sight! Arsenal players celebrate their third FA Cup victory in five years at the Millennium Stadium after victory in a penalty shoot-out against Manchester United.

WENGER'S REMARKABLE RECORD

An incredible season for Arsenal ended as it began – with victory over Manchester United at the Millennium Stadium. In between, Arsenal again treated spectators across Europe to some of the finest, flowing football they are ever likely to witness. Winning their fourth FA Cup under Arsène Wenger – the Club's tenth in total – was naturally an extremely gratifying end to the campaign for Arsenal supporters. Perhaps the season's greatest legacy though, was the emergence and gelling of a group of young talents who look set to star for some years to come. The form of the likes of Philippe Senderos and Francesc Fabregas shows how hard the club is working to maintain the success that Arsenal fans have become accustomed to in recent years.

Arsène Wenger's remarkable record in the FA Cup continued as Arsenal reached their fourth Final in five years. Along the way there were memorable performances: most notably the penalty shoot-out at Bramall Lane and hard-fought victories against Blackburn Rovers and Bolton Wanderers. The Final itself saw Arsenal at

their resilient best, with Jens Lehmann a particular hero throughout the match and most especially during the penalty shoot-out that Patrick Vieira concluded with the winning kick. An Arsenal captain, lifting a trophy in May – this is becoming a familiar sight.

The Gunners began the Premiership season still on the unbeaten run that was to see them make history after going a record 49 matches undefeated. Sweeping aside most opponents, they were in imperious form. However, defeat was always going to come in the end and when it was finally delivered by Manchester United, Arsenal took a while to get back on full form again. Of course, the surrendering of the Premiership title, following an extraordinarily strong challenge from Chelsea, was a disappointment. However, the closing stages of the campaign saw Arsenal in such strong form that the West London outfit will undoubtedly find it extremely hard to keep their grip on the trophy in the coming season. Likewise, Wenger's team looks set for a determined assault on the

2004/2005

Flamini and Jeremie Aliadiere, these players are pointing the way to a bright future.

As Arsenal Football Club enters its final season at Highbury, it is time for both reflection and anticipation. What superb memories we will all take from Highbury and how excited all Arsenal fans can be about the future at our new home, Emirates Stadium.

Despite his advancing years Dennis Bergkamp *put in some magisterial performances during the season, scoring 8 goals in 38 games.*

Champions League after qualifying for that competition for the eighth successive season.

As ever, it was very much a team effort from Arsenal but certain individuals stood out. Once again, Thierry Henry stunned onlookers with his breathtaking skill, he netted 30 goals during the campaign. Patrick Vieira continued to lead Arsenal in the style of a colossus and his magisterial performances in midfield emphatically silenced any critics who wrongly questioned his commitment to the Club. Robert Pires was as threatening as ever, netting a remarkable 17 goals, and Freddie Ljungberg was also in fine scoring form ending the season with 14 strikes to his name.

These star players are now household names across the globe but perhaps the most exciting performances came from younger players. Philippe Senderos was a rock in the heart of the defence, playing in the mould of Tony Adams; Francesc Fabregas was a revelation in midfield throughout the campaign; Robin van Persie showed skill, promise and passion in attack. Along with the likes of Gael Clichy, Kolo Toure, Mathieu

Pick of the Crop? The emergence of players like Philippe Senderos *points the way towards a bright future for the Club.*

Another fine season, another 30 goals as Thierry Henry *continued to stun football fans worldwide with his breathtaking skill.*

ENGLAND 2004/2005

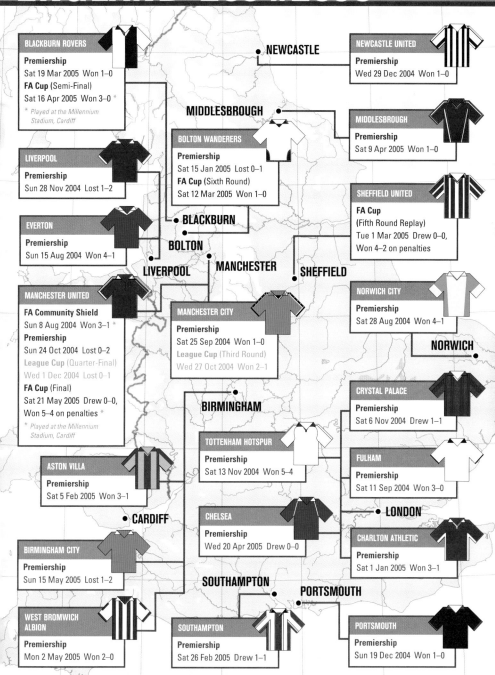

BLACKBURN ROVERS
Premiership
Sat 19 Mar 2005 Won 1–0
FA Cup (Semi-Final)
Sat 16 Apr 2005 Won 3–0 *
Played at the Millennium Stadium, Cardiff

LIVERPOOL
Premiership
Sun 28 Nov 2004 Lost 1–2

EVERTON
Premiership
Sun 15 Aug 2004 Won 4–1

MANCHESTER UNITED
FA Community Shield
Sun 8 Aug 2004 Won 3–1 *
Premiership
Sun 24 Oct 2004 Lost 0–2
League Cup (Quarter-Final)
Wed 1 Dec 2004 Lost 0–1
FA Cup (Final)
Sat 21 May 2005 Drew 0–0,
Won 5–4 on penalties *
Played at the Millennium Stadium, Cardiff

ASTON VILLA
Premiership
Sat 5 Feb 2005 Won 3–1

BIRMINGHAM CITY
Premiership
Sun 15 May 2005 Lost 1–2

WEST BROMWICH ALBION
Premiership
Mon 2 May 2005 Won 2–0

BOLTON WANDERERS
Premiership
Sat 15 Jan 2005 Lost 0–1
FA Cup (Sixth Round)
Sat 12 Mar 2005 Won 1–0

MANCHESTER CITY
Premiership
Sat 25 Sep 2004 Won 1–0
League Cup (Third Round)
Wed 27 Oct 2004 Won 2–1

TOTTENHAM HOTSPUR
Premiership
Sat 13 Nov 2004 Won 5–4

CHELSEA
Premiership
Wed 20 Apr 2005 Drew 0–0

SOUTHAMPTON
Premiership
Sat 26 Feb 2005 Drew 1–1

NEWCASTLE UNITED
Premiership
Wed 29 Dec 2004 Won 1–0

MIDDLESBROUGH
Premiership
Sat 9 Apr 2005 Won 1–0

SHEFFIELD UNITED
FA Cup
(Fifth Round Replay)
Tue 1 Mar 2005 Drew 0–0,
Won 4–2 on penalties

NORWICH CITY
Premiership
Sat 28 Aug 2004 Won 4–1

CRYSTAL PALACE
Premiership
Sat 6 Nov 2004 Drew 1–1

FULHAM
Premiership
Sat 11 Sep 2004 Won 3–0

CHARLTON ATHLETIC
Premiership
Sat 1 Jan 2005 Won 3–1

PORTSMOUTH
Premiership
Sun 19 Dec 2004 Won 1–0

NEWCASTLE
MIDDLESBROUGH
BLACKBURN
BOLTON
LIVERPOOL
MANCHESTER
SHEFFIELD
NORWICH
BIRMINGHAM
LONDON
CARDIFF
SOUTHAMPTON
PORTSMOUTH

PLAYER OF THE SEASON

CHAMPAGNE Lanson

Arsenal.com PLAYER OF THE SEASON
Thierry **HENRY**

"It is simply an honour to play for Arsenal Football Club, in front of such special supporters. I am happier than I have ever been and I believe that much is clear when you watch me play. But my form this season would not have been possible without my team-mates. I feel we have a very strong squad at the moment and we all look forward to an even better season next time."

THIERRY HENRY

"It is no surprise to me that Thierry has won the Player of the Season award. He has been incredible all season. He scores so many goals for us, including at important moments. But he also sets up goals too and works so hard for the team. Thierry is a strong character. You can see how much the Arsenal fans think of him. I can assure you that his team-mates feel the same way."

PATRICK VIEIRA

"Once again, Thierry has brought lots of pleasure to the Arsenal fans. There is no questioning what a star he is, or what he brings to the Arsenal team. In the end, you have to say that for all we can speak about Thierry, the important thing to do is to watch him play."

ARSENE WENGER

FA BARCLAYCARD PREMIERSHIP

Date	Opponents (Venue)	Score	League Position
Sun 15 Aug	Everton (A)	4–1	1
Sun 22 Aug	Middlesbrough (H)	5–3	1
Wed 25 Aug	Blackburn Rovers (H)	3–0	1
Sat 28 Aug	Norwich City (A)	4–1	1
Sat 11 Sept	Fulham (A)	3–0	1
Sat 18 Sept	Bolton Wanderers (H)	2–2	1
Sat 25 Sept	Manchester City (A)	1–0	1
Sat 2 Oct	Charlton Athletic (H)	4–0	1
Sat 16 Oct	Aston Villa (H)	3–1	1
Sun 24 Oct	Manchester United (A)	0–2	1
Sat 30 Oct	Southampton (H)	2–2	1
Sat 6 Nov	Crystal Palace (A)	1–1	2
Sat 13 Nov	Tottenham Hotspur (A)	5–4	2
Sat 20 Nov	West Bromwich Alb (H)	1–1	2
Sun 28 Nov	Liverpool (A)	1–2	2
Sat 4 Dec	Birmingham City (H)	3–0	2
Sun 12 Dec	Chelsea (H)	2–2	3
Sun 19 Dec	Portsmouth (A)	1–0	2
Sun 26 Dec	Fulham (H)	2–0	2
Wed 29 Dec	Newcastle United (A)	1–0	2
Sat 1 Jan	Charlton Athletic (A)	3–1	2
Tue 4 Jan	Manchester City (H)	1–1	2
Sat 15 Jan	Bolton Wanderers (A)	0–1	2
Sat 23 Jan	Newcastle United (H)	1–0	2
Tue 1 Feb	Manchester United (H)	2–4	3
Sat 5 Feb	Aston Villa (A)	3–1	3
Mon 14 Feb	Crystal Palace (H)	5–1	3
Sat 26 Feb	Southampton (A)	1–1	3
Sat 5 Mar	Portsmouth (H)	3–0	3
Sat 19 Mar	Blackburn Rovers (A)	1–0	3
Sat 2 Apr	Norwich City (H)	4–1	2
Sat 9 Apr	Middlesbrough (A)	1–0	2
Wed 20 Apr	Chelsea (A)	0–0	2
Mon 25 Apr	Tottenham Hotspur (H)	1–0	2
Mon 2 May	West Bromwich Alb (A)	2–0	2
Sun 8 May	Liverpool (H)	3–1	2
Wed 11 May	Everton (H)	7–0	2
Sun 15 May	Birmingham City (A)	1–2	2

UEFA CHAMPIONS LEAGUE

Date	Opponents (Venue)	Score
Tue 14 Sept	PSV Eindhoven (H) Gp E	1–0
Wed 29 Sept	Rosenborg (A) Gp E	1–1
Wed 20 Oct	Panathinaikos (A) Gp E	2–2
Tue 2 Nov	Panathinaikos (H) Gp E	1–1
Wed 24 Nov	PSV Eindhoven (A) Gp E	1–1
Tue 7 Dec	Rosenborg (H) Gp E	5–1
Tue 22 Feb	Bayern Munich (A) EF 1L	1–3
Wed 9 Mar	Bayern Munich (H) EF 2L	1–0

FA CUP

Date	Opponents (Venue)	Score
Sun 9 Jan	Stoke City (H) Rd 3	2–1
Sat 29 Jan	Wolverhampton W (H) Rd 4	1–0
Sat 19 Feb	Sheffield United (H) Rd 5	1–1
Tue 1 Mar	Sheffield United (A) Rd 5 R	0–0•
Sat 12 Mar	Bolton Wanderers (A) QF	1–0
Sat 16 Apr	Blackburn Rovers (*) SF	3–0
Sat 21 May	Manchester United (*) F	0–0†

• Arsenal won 4-2 on penalties

* played at Millennium Stadium, Cardiff

† Arsenal won 5-4 on penalties

CARLING CUP

Date	Opponents (Venue)	Score
Wed 27 Oct	Manchester City (A) Rd 3	2–1
Tue 9 Nov	Everton (H) Rd 4	3–1
Wed 1 Dec	Manchester United (A) QF	0–1

FA COMMUNITY SHIELD

Date	Opponents (Venue)	Score
Sun 8 Aug	Manchester United (*)	3–1

* played at Millennium Stadium, Cardiff

APPEARANCES (SUBS IN BRACKETS) AND GOALS

Player	Premiership Apps	Gls	FA Cup Apps	Gls	Carling Cup Apps	Gls	Champions League Apps	Gls	Community Shield Apps	Gls	Totals Apps	Gls
JEREMIE ALIADIERE	0 (4)	0	0 (2)	0	0	0	0	0	0 (1)	0	0 (7)	0
MANUEL ALMUNIA	10	0	2	0	3	0	1	0	0	0	16	0
DENNIS BERGKAMP	20 (9)	8	4	0	0	0	4	0	1	0	29 (9)	8
SOL CAMPBELL	16	1	1	0	0	0	4	0	0	0	21	1
GAEL CLICHY	7 (8)	0	5	0	1	0	1 (1)	0	0 (1)	0	14 (10)	0
ASHLEY COLE	35	2	3	0	0	0	7 (1)	0	1	0	46 (1)	2
PATRICK CREGG	0	0	0	0	0 (2)	0	0	0	0	0	0 (2)	0
PASCAL CYGAN	15	0	2 (1)	0	1	0	3	0	1	0	22 (1)	0
JOHAN DJOUROU	0	0	0	0	2 (1)	0	0	0	0	0	2 (1)	0
EMMANUEL EBOUE	0 (1)	0	3	0	0	0	0	0	0	0	3 (1)	0
EDU	6 (6)	2	0 (1)	0	1	0	3 (1)	0	0	0	10 (8)	2
FRANCESC FABREGAS	24 (9)	2	4 (2)	0	1	0	4 (1)	1	1	0	34 (12)	3
MATHIEU FLAMINI	9 (12)	1	4	0	3	0	2 (2)	0	0	0	18 (14)	1
GILBERTO	13	0	2	0	0	0	1	0	1	1	17	1
THIERRY HENRY	31 (1)	25	1	0	0	0	8	5	1	0	41 (1)	30
JUSTIN HOYTE	4 (1)	0	0 (1)	0	3	0	1 (1)	0	0 (1)	0	8 (4)	0
DANIEL KARBASSIYOON	0	0	0	0	1 (2)	1	0	0	0	0	1 (2)	1
SEBASTIAN LARSSON	0	0	0	0	2 (1)	0	0	0	0	0	2 (1)	0
LAUREN	32 (1)	1	4	0	0	0	7	0	1	0	44 (1)	1
JENS LEHMANN	28	0	5	0	0	0	7	0	1	0	41	0
FREDRIK LJUNGBERG	24 (2)	10	5 (1)	2	0	0	6	2	0	0	35 (3)	14
ARTURO LUPOLI	0	0	1	0	3	2	0	0	0	0	4	2
QUINCY OWUSU-ABEYIE	1	0	0 (2)	0	1 (2)	1	0 (1)	0	0	0	2 (5)	1
JERMAINE PENNANT	1 (6)	0	1	0	3	0	0	0	1	0	6 (6)	0
ROBERT PIRES	26 (7)	14	4 (2)	2	0	0	7 (1)	1	0	0	37 (10)	17
JOSÉ ANTONIO REYES	25 (5)	9	6	1	0	0	7 (1)	1	1	1	39 (6)	12
PHILIPPE SENDEROS	12 (1)	0	6	0	3	0	1	0	0	0	22 (1)	0
RYAN SMITH	0	0	0	0	2 (1)	0	0	0	0	0	2 (1)	0
SEBASTIAN SVARD	0	0	0	0	0	0	0	0	0 (1)	0	0 (1)	0
KOLO TOURE	35	0	5 (1)	0	0	0	8	1	1	0	49 (1)	1
ROBIN VAN PERSIE	12 (14)	5	3 (2)	3	3	1	0 (6)	1	0 (1)	0	18 (23)	10
PATRICK VIEIRA	32	6	6	1	0	0	6	0	0	0	44	7

Jeremie Aliadiere

Position forward **Squad number** 30
Born Rambouillet, France, 30 March 1983
Joined Arsenal as scholar in summer 1999, professional in March 2000
Senior Arsenal debut 27 November 2001 v Grimsby Town at Highbury
(League Cup, as substitute)
Arsenal honours League Championship 2003/2004
Arsenal record League: 3 (15) games, 1 goal; FA Cup: 1 (2) games, 0 goals;
League Cup: 3 (2) games, 4 goals; Europe: 0 (1) game, 0 goals; Community
Shield: 0 (1) game, 0 goals; Total: 7 (21) games, 5 goals

Manuel Almunia

Position goalkeeper **Squad number** 24
Born Pamplona, Spain, 19 May 1977
Other clubs Osasuna B, Cartagonova, Sabadell, Celta Vigo, Eibar on loan,
Recreativo Huelva on loan, Albacete on loan
Joined Arsenal from Celta Vigo in July 2004
Senior Arsenal debut 27 October 2004 v Manchester City at City of
Manchester Stadium (League Cup)
Arsenal record League: 10 games, 0 goals; FA Cup: 2 games, 0 goals; League
Cup: 3 games, 0 goals; Europe: 1 game, 0 goals; Total: 16 games, 0 goals

David Bentley

Position forward **Squad number** none
Born Peterborough, 27 August 1984
Other clubs Norwich City on loan
Joined Arsenal as scholar in summer 2000, professional in December 2001
Senior Arsenal debut 4 January 2003 v Oxford United at Highbury (FA Cup,
as substitute)
Arsenal record League: 1 game, 0 goals; FA Cup: 0 (2) games, 1 goal; League
Cup: 4 games, 0 goals; Europe: 0 (1) game, 0 goals; Total: 5 (4) games, 1 goal

Dennis Bergkamp

Position forward **Squad number** 10
Born Amsterdam, Holland, 10 May 1969
Other clubs Ajax, Internazionale
Joined Arsenal from Internazionale in July 1995
Senior Arsenal debut 20 August 1995 v Middlesbrough at Highbury (League)
Arsenal honours League Championship 1997/1998, 2001/2002, 2003/2004; FA Cup 2001/2002, 2002/2003, 2004/2005
Arsenal record League: 245 (46) games, 85 goals; FA Cup: 33 (5) games, 14 goals; League Cup: 15 games, 8 goals; Europe: 36 (8) games, 10 goals; Charity/Community Shield: 4 games, 0 goals; Total: 333 (59) games, 117 goals
Holland caps 79

Sol Campbell

Position defender **Squad number** 23
Born Newham, London, 18 September 1974
Other club Tottenham Hotspur
Joined Arsenal from Tottenham Hotspur in July 2001
Senior Arsenal debut 18 August 2001 v Middlesbrough at the Riverside (League)
Arsenal honours League Championship 2001/2002, 2003/2004; FA Cup 2001/2002
Arsenal record League: 113 (2) games, 6 goals; FA Cup: 18 games, 2 goals; Europe: 33 games, 0 goals; Community Shield: 2 games, 0 goals; Total: 166 (2) games, 8 goals
England caps 57

Gael Clichy

Position defender **Squad number** 22
Born Paris, France, 26 July 1985
Other club Cannes
Joined Arsenal from Cannes in August 2003
Senior Arsenal debut 28 October 2003 v Rotherham United at Highbury (League Cup)
Arsenal honours League Championship 2003/2004
Arsenal record League: 14 (13) games, 0 goals; FA Cup: 6 (3) games, 0 goals; League Cup: 6 games, 0 goals; Europe: 2 (1) games, 0 goals; Community Shield: 0 (1) game, 0 goals; Total: 28 (18) games, 0 goals

FIRST TEAM PLAYER PROFILES

Ashley Cole

Position defender **Squad number** 3
Born Stepney, London, 20 December 1980
Other club Crystal Palace on loan
Joined Arsenal as trainee in summer 1997, professional in November 1998
Senior Arsenal debut 30 November 1999 v Middlesbrough at the Riverside (League Cup, as substitute)
Arsenal honours League Championship 2001/2002, 2003/2004; FA Cup 2001/2002, 2002/2003, 2004/2005
Arsenal record League: 142 (3) games, 8 goals; FA Cup: 19 (1) games, 0 goals; League Cup: 2 (1) games, 0 goals; Europe: 39 (3) games, 1 goal; Community Shield: 3 games, 0 goals; Total: 205 (8) games, 9 goals
England caps 26

Patrick Cregg

Position midfielder **Squad number** 34
Born Dublin, Republic of Ireland, 21 February 1986
Joined Arsenal as scholar in summer 2002, professional in July 2003
Senior Arsenal debut 9 November 2004 v Everton at Highbury (League Cup, as substitute)
Arsenal record League Cup: 0 (2) games, 0 goals; Total: 0 (2) games, 0 goals

Pascal Cygan

Position central defender **Squad number** 18
Born Lens, France, 29 April 1974
Other clubs Valenciennes, ES Wasquehal, Lille
Joined Arsenal from Lille in July 2002
Senior Arsenal debut 1 September 2002 v Chelsea at Stamford Bridge (League, as substitute)
Arsenal honours League Championship 2003/2004
Arsenal record League: 41 (10) games, 1 goal; FA Cup: 4 (1) games, 0 goals; League Cup: 4 games, 0 goals; Europe: 14 (3) games, 0 goals; Community Shield: 1 game, 0 goals; Total: 64 (14) games, 1 goal

Johan Djourou

Position defender/midfielder **Squad number** 35
Born Ivory Coast, 18 January 1987
Other club Etoile
Joined Arsenal as scholar in summer 2003
Senior Arsenal debut 27 October 2004 v Manchester City at City of
Manchester Stadium (League Cup, as substitute)
Arsenal record League Cup: 2 (1) games, 0 goals; Total: 2 (1) games, 0 goals

Emmanuel Eboue

Position defender **Squad number** 27
Born Abidjan, Ivory Coast, 4 June 1983
Other clubs Abidjan, Beveren
Joined Arsenal from Beveren in January 2005
Senior Arsenal debut 9 January 2005 v Stoke City at Highbury (FA Cup)
Arsenal record League: 0 (1) game, 0 goals; FA Cup: 3 games, 0 goals;
Total: 3 (1) games, 0 goals

Edu

Position midfielder **Squad number** 17
Born São Paulo, Brazil, 16 May 1978
Other clubs São Paulo, Corinthians
Joined Arsenal from Corinthians in January 2001
Senior Arsenal debut 20 January 2001 v Leicester City at Filbert Street
(League, as substitute)
Arsenal honours League Championship 2001/2002, 2003/2004; FA Cup
2001/2002, 2004/2005
Arsenal record League: 41 (38) games, 7 goals; FA Cup: 13 (4) games, 3 goals;
League Cup: 8 games, 2 goals; Europe: 13 (8) games, 3 goals; Community
Shield: 1 (1) games, 0 goals; Total: 76 (51) games, 15 goals
Brazil caps 15

Francesc Fabregas

Position midfielder **Squad number** 15
Born Vilessoc de Mar, Spain, 4 May 1987
Other club Barcelona
Joined Arsenal from Barcelona in September 2003
Senior Arsenal debut 28 October 2003 v Rotherham United at Highbury (League Cup)
Arsenal honours FA Cup 2004/2005
Arsenal record League: 24 (9) games, 2 goals; FA Cup: 4 (2) games, 0 goals; League Cup: 3 (1) games, 1 goal; Europe: 4 (1) games, 1 goal; Community Shield: 1 game, 0 goals; Total: 36 (13) games, 4 goals

Mathieu Flamini

Position midfielder **Squad number** 16
Born Marseille, France, 7 March 1984
Joined Arsenal from Olympique Marseille in July 2004
Senior Arsenal debut 15 August 2004 v Everton at Goodison Park (League, as substitute)
Arsenal record League: 9 (12) games, 1 goal; FA Cup: 4 games, 0 goals; League Cup: 3 games, 0 goals; Europe: 2 (2) games, 0 goals; Total: 18 (14) games, 1 goal

Ryan Garry

Position defender **Squad number** none
Born Hornchurch, 29 September 1983
Joined Arsenal as scholar in summer 2000, professional in summer 2001
Senior Arsenal debut 6 November 2002 v Sunderland at Highbury (League Cup, as substitute)
Arsenal record League: 1 game, 0 goals; League Cup: 0 (1) game, 0 goals; Total: 1 (1) games, 0 goals

Gilberto

Position midfielder **Squad number** 19
Born Lagoa da Prata, Brazil, 7 October 1976
Other clubs America MG, Atletico Mineiro
Joined Arsenal from Atletico Mineiro in July 2002
Senior Arsenal debut 11 August 2002 v Liverpool at Millennium Stadium
(Community Shield, as substitute)
Arsenal honours League Championship 2003/2004; FA Cup 2002/2003,
2004/2005
Arsenal record League: 74 (6) games, 4 goals; FA Cup: 6 (2) games, 0 goals;
League Cup: 1 game, 0 goals; Europe: 17 (4) games, 2 goals; Community
Shield: 2 (1) games, 2 goals; Total: 100 (13) games, 8 goals
Brazil caps 30

Thierry Henry

Position forward **Squad number** 14
Born Paris, France, 17 August 1977
Other clubs AS Monaco, Juventus
Joined Arsenal from Juventus in August 1999
Senior Arsenal debut 7 August 1999 v Leicester City at Highbury (League,
as substitute)
Arsenal honours League Championship 2001/2002, 2003/2004; FA Cup
2001/2002, 2002/2003
Arsenal record League: 189 (16) games, 137 goals; FA Cup: 15 (6) games,
6 goals; League Cup: 2 games, 1 goal; Europe: 62 (5) games, 36 goals;
Community Shield: 3 games, 1 goal; Total: 271 (27) games, 181 goals
France caps 70

Justin Hoyte

Position defender **Squad number** 31
Born Waltham Forest, 20 November 1984
Joined Arsenal as scholar in summer 2001, professional in July 2002
Senior Arsenal debut 7 May 2003 v Southampton at Highbury (League,
as substitute)
Arsenal record League: 4 (3) games, 0 goals; FA Cup: 0 (1) games, 0 goals;
League Cup: 5 games, 0 goals; Europe: 1 (1) games, 0 goals; Community
Shield: 0 (1) game, 0 goals; Total: 10 (6) games, 0 goals

FIRST TEAM PLAYER PROFILES

Daniel Karbassiyoon
Position defender/midfielder/striker **Squad number** 46
Born Virginia, USA, 10 August 1984
Other clubs Roanoke Star, Ipswich Town on loan
Joined Arsenal from Roanoke Star in August 2003
Senior Arsenal debut 27 October 2004 v Manchester City at City of
Manchester Stadium (League Cup, as substitute)
Arsenal record League Cup: 1 (2) games, 1 goal; Total 1 (2) games, 1 goal

Sebastian Larsson
Position midfielder **Squad number** 39
Born Eskiltuna, Sweden, 6 June 1985
Joined Arsenal as scholar in summer 2001, professional in July 2002
Senior Arsenal debut 27 October 2004 v Manchester City at City of
Manchester Stadium (League Cup)
Arsenal record League Cup: 2 (1) games, 0 goals; Total: 2 (1) games, 0 goals

Lauren
Position defender or midfielder **Squad number** 12
Born Londi Kribi, Cameroon, 19 January 1977
Other clubs Utrera, Seville, Levante, Real Mallorca
Joined Arsenal from Real Mallorca in May 2000
Senior Arsenal debut 19 August 2000 v Sunderland at the Stadium of Light
(League, as substitute)
Arsenal honours League Championship 2001/2002, 2003/2004; FA Cup
2001/2002, 2002/2003, 2004/2005
Arsenal record League: 130 (7) games, 6 goals; FA Cup: 22 games, 2 goals;
League Cup: 1 game, 0 goals; Europe: 41 (6) games, 1 goal; Community
Shield: 3 games, 0 goals; Total: 197 (13) games, 9 goals
Cameroon caps 22

Jens Lehmann

Position goalkeeper **Squad number** 1
Born Essen, Germany, 10 November 1969
Other clubs DJK Heisingen, Schwarz-Weiss Essen, FC Schalke, AC Milan,
Borussia Dortmund
Joined Arsenal from Borussia Dortmund in July 2003
Senior Arsenal debut 10 August 2003 v Manchester United at the Millennium
Stadium (Community Shield)
Arsenal honours League Championship 2003/2004; FA Cup 2004/2005
Arsenal record League: 66 games, 0 goals; FA Cup: 10 games, 0 goals;
Europe: 17 games, 0 goals; Community Shield: 2 games, 0 goals; Total: 95
games, 0 goals
Germany caps 22

Fredrik Ljungberg

Position midfielder **Squad number** 8
Born Halmstads, Sweden, 16 April 1977
Other club Halmstads
Joined Arsenal from Halmstads in September 1998
Senior Arsenal debut 20 September 1998 v Manchester United at Highbury
(League, as substitute)
Arsenal honours League Championship 2001/2002, 2003/2004; FA Cup
2001/2002, 2002/2003, 2004/2005
Arsenal record League: 151 (22) games, 45 goals; FA Cup: 25 (4) games,
10 goals; League Cup: 2 games, 0 goals; Europe: 50 (9) games, 13 goals;
Charity/Community Shield: 2 games, 0 goals; Total: 230 (35) games, 68 goals
Sweden caps 51

Arturo Lupoli

Position forward **Squad number** 40
Born Brescia, Italy, 26 June 1987
Other club Parma
Joined Arsenal as scholar in summer 2004
Senior Arsenal debut 27 October 2004 v Manchester City at City of
Manchester Stadium (League Cup)
Arsenal record FA Cup: 1 game, 0 goals; League Cup: 3 games, 2 goals;
Total: 4 games, 2 goals

FIRST TEAM PLAYER PROFILES

Quincy Owusu-Abeyie
Position forward **Squad number** 42
Born Amsterdam, Holland, 15 April 1986
Joined Arsenal as scholar in September 2002
Senior Arsenal debut 28 October 2003 v Rotherham United at Highbury
(League Cup, as substitute)
Arsenal record League: 1 game, 0 goals, FA Cup: 0 (2) games, 0 goals;
League Cup: 2 (4) games, 1 goal; Europe: 0 (1) game, 0 goals; Total: 3 (7)
games, 1 goal

Jermaine Pennant
Position midfielder **Squad number** 21
Born Nottingham, 15 January 1983
Other clubs Notts County, Watford on loan, Leeds United on loan,
Birmingham City on loan
Joined Arsenal from Notts County as trainee in January 1999
Senior Arsenal debut 30 November 1999 v Middlesbrough at the Riverside
(League Cup, as substitute)
Arsenal record League: 2 (10) games, 3 goals; FA Cup: 1 game, 0 goals;
League Cup: 8 (1) games, 0 goals; Europe: 0 (3) games, 0 goals; Community
Shield: 1 game, 0 goals; Total: 12 (14) games, 3 goals

Robert Pires
Position midfielder **Squad number** 7
Born Reims, France, 29 January 1973
Other clubs Stade de Reims, FC Metz, Olympique Marseille
Joined Arsenal from Olympique Marseille in July 2000
Senior Arsenal debut 19 August 2000 v Sunderland at the Stadium of Light
(League, as substitute)
Arsenal honours League Championship 2001/2002, 2003/2004; FA Cup
2002/2003, 2004/2005
Arsenal record League: 136 (20) games, 55 goals; FA Cup: 21 (6) games,
8 goals; League Cup: 1 game, 1 goal; Europe: 48 (3) games, 9 goals;
Community Shield: 0 (1) game, 0 goals; Total: 206 (30) games, 73 goals
France caps 79

José Antonio Reyes

Position forward **Squad number** 9
Born Utrera, Spain, 1 September 1983
Other club Sevilla
Joined Arsenal from Sevilla in January 2004
Senior Arsenal debut 1 February 2004 v Manchester City at Highbury
(League, as substitute)
Arsenal honours League Championship 2003/2004; FA Cup 2004/2005
Arsenal record League: 32 (11) games, 11 goals; FA Cup: 8 (1) games, 3 goals;
League Cup: 1 game, 0 goals; Europe: 9 (3) games, 2 goals; Total: 51 (15)
games, 17 goals
Spain caps 12

Philippe Senderos

Position defender **Squad number** 20
Born Switzerland, 14 February 1985
Other club Servette
Joined Arsenal from Servette in June 2003
Senior Arsenal debut 27 October 2004 v Manchester City at City of
Manchester Stadium (League Cup)
Arsenal honours FA Cup 2004/2005
Arsenal record League: 12 (1) games, 0 goals; FA Cup: 6 games, 0 goals,
League Cup: 3 games, 0 goals; Europe: 1 game, 0 goals; Total: 22 (1) games,
0 goals
Switzerland caps 2

Frankie Simek

Position defender **Squad number** none
Born Missouri, United States, 13 October 1984
Joined Arsenal as scholar in August 2001, professional in summer 2002
Senior Arsenal debut 2 December 2003 v Wolverhampton Wanderers at
Highbury (League Cup)
Arsenal record League Cup: 1 game, 0 goals; Total: 1 game, 0 goals

FIRST TEAM PLAYER PROFILES

Ryan Smith
Position midfielder **Squad number** 47
Born Islington, London, 10 November 1986
Joined Arsenal as scholar in summer 2003, professional in November 2004
Senior Arsenal debut 28 October 2003 v Rotherham United at Highbury
(League Cup, as substitute)
Arsenal record League Cup: 2 (4) games, 0 goals; Total: 2 (4) games, 0 goals

Sebastian Svard
Position midfielder **Squad number** 32
Born Hvidovre, Denmark, 15 January 1983
Other clubs FC Copenhagen, FC Copenhagen on loan, Stoke City on loan,
Brondby on loan
Joined Arsenal from FC Copenhagen in November 2000
Senior Arsenal debut 27 November 2001 v Grimsby Town at Highbury
(League Cup, as substitute)
Arsenal record FA Cup: 1 game, 0 goals; League Cup: 1 (1) game, 0 goals;
Community Shield 0 (1) games, 0 goals; Total: 2 (2) games, 0 goals

Stuart Taylor
Position goalkeeper **Squad number** 13
Born Romford, 28 November 1980
Other clubs Bristol Rovers on loan, Crystal Palace on loan, Peterborough
United on loan, Leicester City on loan
Joined Arsenal as trainee in summer 1997
Senior Arsenal debut 1 November 2000 v Ipswich Town at Highbury (League
Cup)
Arsenal honours League Championship 2001/2002
Arsenal record League: 16 (2) games, 0 goals; FA Cup: 3 games, 0 goals;
League Cup: 4 games, 0 goals; Europe: 3 (2) games, 0 goals; Total: 26 (4)
games, 0 goals

Kolo Toure

Position defender **Squad number** 28
Born Ivory Coast, 19 March 1981
Other club ASEC Mimosas
Joined Arsenal from ASEC Mimosas in February 2002
Senior Arsenal debut 11 August 2002 v Liverpool at Millennium Stadium
(Community Shield, as substitute)
Arsenal honours League Championship 2003/2004, FA Cup 2004/2005
Arsenal record League: 80 (18) games, 3 goals; FA Cup: 12 (4) games, 2 goals;
League Cup: 3 games, 0 goals; Europe: 21 (4) games, 1 goal; Community
Shield: 2 (1) games, 0 goals; Total: 118 (27) games, 6 goals
Ivory Coast caps 33

Robin van Persie

Position forward **Squad number** 11
Born Rotterdam, Holland, 6 August 1983
Other club Feyenoord
Joined Arsenal from Feyenoord in May 2004
Senior Arsenal debut 8 August 2004 v Manchester United at Millennium
Stadium (Community Shield, as substitute)
Arsenal honours FA Cup 2004/2005
Arsenal record League: 12 (14) games, 5 goals; FA Cup: 3 (2) games, 3 goals;
League Cup: 3 games, 1 goal; Europe: 0 (6) games, 1 goal; Community Shield:
0 (1) game, 0 goals; Total: 18 (23) games, 10 goals

Patrick Vieira (Captain)

Position midfielder **Squad number** 4
Born Dakar, Senegal, 23 June 1976
Other clubs Cannes, AC Milan
Joined Arsenal from AC Milan in August 1996
Senior Arsenal debut 16 September 1996 v Sheffield Wednesday at Highbury
(League, as substitute)
Arsenal honours League Championship 1997/1998, 2001/2002, 2003/2004;
FA Cup 1997/1998, 2001/2002, 2004/2005
Arsenal record League: 272 (7) games, 28 goals; FA Cup: 46 (2) games,
3 goals; League Cup: 7 games, 0 goals; Europe: 67 (1) games, 2 goals;
Charity/Community Shield: 4 games, 0 goals; Total: 396 (10) games, 33 goals
France caps 79

Arsène Wenger (Manager)

Born Strasbourg, France, 22 October 1949

Clubs as player Mutzig, Mulhouse, Strasbourg

Clubs as manager/coach Strasbourg (youth section), Cannes (assistant), Nancy, AS Monaco, Grampus Eight Nagoya

Honours as manager/coach with AS Monaco: French League Championship 1987/1988, French Cup 1990/1991, France Manager of the Year 1987/1988; with Grampus Eight Nagoya: Emperor's Cup 1996, Japan Super Cup 1996, Japan Manager of the Year 1995; with Arsenal: League Championship 1997/1998, 2001/2002, 2003/2004; FA Cup 1997/1998, 2001/2002, 2002/2003, 2004/2005. Manager of the Year 1997/1998, 2001/2002, 2003/2004

Joined Arsenal 1996

PAT RICE (Assistant Manager)
Born Belfast, Northern Ireland, 17 March 1949
Clubs as player Arsenal, Watford
Honours as player with Arsenal: League Championship 1970/1971; FA Cup 1970/1971, 1978/1979. Won 49 caps for Northern Ireland
Joined Arsenal as coach 1984
Honours as Arsenal coach FA Youth Cup 1987/1988, 1993/1994 League Championship 1997/1998, 2001/2002, 2003/2004; FA Cup 1997/1998, 2001/2002, 2002/2003, 2004/2005

BORO PRIMORAC (First Team Coach)
Born Mostar, Yugoslavia (now Bosnia), 5 December 1954
Clubs as player Hajduk Split, Cannes, Lille. Captained Yugoslavia, winning 18 caps
Clubs as coach Cannes, Valenciennes, Grampus Eight Nagoya
Joined Arsenal 1997
Honours as Arsenal coach League Championship 1997/1998, 2001/2002, 2003/2004; FA Cup 1997/1998, 2001/2002, 2002/2003, 2004/2005

NEIL BANFIELD (Reserve Team Coach)
Born Poplar, 20 January 1962
Clubs as player Crystal Palace, Adelaide City, Leyton Orient
Clubs as coach Charlton Athletic
Joined Arsenal 1997

GERRY PEYTON (Goalkeeping Coach)
Born Birmingham, 20 May 1956
Clubs as player Fulham, Southend United (loan), Bournemouth, Everton, Bolton Wanderers (loan), Brentford, Chelsea (loan), West Ham United
Honours as player Won 33 caps for Republic of Ireland
Clubs as coach Vissel Kobe, AIK Solna, Fulham
Joined Arsenal 2003

GARY LEWIN (Physiotherapist)
Born East Ham, London, 16 May 1964
Clubs as player Arsenal (youth), Barnet
Joined Arsenal as physio 1983
England physio since 1996

COLIN LEWIN (Assistant Physiotherapist)
Born Plaistow, London, 15 September 1973
Joined Arsenal 1995

TONY COLBERT (Fitness Coach)
Born Paddington, London, 29 May 1963
Joined Arsenal 1998

CRAIG GANT (Assistant Fitness Coach/Masseur)
Born London, 27 February 1970
Joined Arsenal part-time 2000, full-time 2001

JOEL HARRIS (Sports Therapist)
Born Wimbledon, London, 28 August 1961
Joined Arsenal part-time 1994, full-time 1998

JOHN KELLY (Masseur)
Born Barking, 18 March 1957
Joined Arsenal 2002

STEVE ROWLEY (Chief Scout)
Born Romford, 2 December 1958
Joined Arsenal 1980

VIC AKERS (Kit Manager)
Born Islington, London, 24 August 1946
Clubs as player Slough Town, Cambridge United, Watford
Joined Arsenal as reserve team physio and kit manager 1986
General Manager of Arsenal Ladies

PAUL AKERS (Assistant Kit Manager)
Born Bromley, 3 February 1976
Joined Arsenal 2001

PAUL JOHNSON (Equipment Manager)
Born Hackney, London, 14 March 1961
Joined Arsenal 1981

RESERVES AND YOUTHS

ISSA ABDULKADIR
Position defender

NICKLAS BENDTNER
Position forward

ADAM BIRCHALL
Position forward

SEAN CLOHESSY
Position defender

MATTHEW CONNOLLY
Position defender

JORDAN FOWLER
Position midfielder

KERREA GILBERT
Position defender

BEN GILL
Position defender/midfielder

MATTHEW HISLOP
Position defender

MARK HOWARD
Position goalkeeper

MICHAEL JORDAN
Position goalkeeper

SEAN KELLY
Position midfielder

FABRICE MUAMBA
Position midfielder

MITCHELL MURPHY
Position midfielder

STEPHEN O'DONNELL
Position midfielder

AARON SAMUEL
Position forward

DOMINIC SHIMMIN
Position defender

DANIEL SPAUL
Position midfielder

ANTHONY STOKES
Position forward

LUKE WEBB
Position midfielder

CHRIS WRIGHT
Position goalkeeper

This list includes Reserve and Youth players with no senior appearances to date. These players were on Arsenal's books at the start of 2004/2005. Some may have since left the Club.

YOUTH DEVELOPMENT STAFF 2004/2005

LIAM BRADY (Head of Youth Development and Academy Manager)
Born Dublin, 13 February 1956
Clubs as player Arsenal, Juventus, Sampdoria, Internazionale, Ascoli, West Ham United
Honours as player with Arsenal: FA Cup 1978/1979; with Juventus Italian Championship 1981/1982. Won 72 caps for Republic of Ireland
Clubs as coach/manager Celtic, Brighton & Hove Albion
Joined Arsenal coaching staff 1996

DAVID COURT (Assistant Head of Youth Development and Assistant Academy Manager)
Born Mitcham, 1 March 1944
Clubs as player Arsenal, Luton Town
Joined Arsenal coaching staff 1996

STEVE BOULD (Under-18s Coach)
Born Stoke, 16 November 1962
Clubs as player Stoke City, Torquay United (loan), Arsenal, Sunderland
Honours as player with Arsenal: European Cup-Winners' Cup 1993/1994; League title 1988/1989, 1990/1991, 1997/1998. Won 2 caps for England
Joined Arsenal coaching staff 2001

DAVID WALES (Youth Team Physiotherapist)
Born Gateshead, 24 August 1972
Joined Arsenal 2001

JON COOKE (Youth Team Physiotherapist)
Born Colchester, 24 September 1976
Joined Arsenal full-time 2002

RESERVES

FA BARCLAYCARD PREMIERSHIP RESERVE LEAGUE (SOUTH)

Date	Opponents (Venue)	Score
Wed 8 Sept	West Ham United (A)	5–0
Mon 13 Sept	Derby County (H)	3–0
Mon 20 Sept	Coventry City (H)	4–0
Thu 30 Sept	Ipswich Town (H)	2–1
Tue 5 Oct	Portsmouth (A)	0–0
Mon 11 Oct	Fulham (H)	1–0
Tue 19 Oct	Southampton (A)	2–2
Mon 1 Nov	Watford (H)	3–2
Mon 8 Nov	Chelsea (A)	2–0
Mon 15 Nov	Leicester City (H)	1–1
Mon 22 Nov	Norwich City (A)	1–2
Mon 29 Nov	Charlton Athletic (A)	1–3
Mon 6 Dec	Tottenham Hotspur (H)	2–1
Mon 13 Dec	Crystal Palace (A)	1–1
Tue 21 Dec	Charlton Athletic (H)	2–2
Mon 10 Jan	West Ham United (H)	4–2
Wed 2 Feb	Crystal Palace (H)	2–0
Mon 7 Feb	Ipswich Town (A)	2–1
Wed 23 Feb	Fulham (A)	1–5
Tue 8 Mar	Coventry City (A)	2–3
Mon 14 Mar	Chelsea (H)	3–2
Sat 19 Mar	Portsmouth (H)	4–1
Mon 21 Mar	Southampton (H)	1–2
Mon 4 Apr	Norwich City (H)	4–0
Tues 12 Apr	Watford (A)	3–1
Mon 18 Apr	Tottenham Hotspur (A)	3–4
Tue 26 Apr	Leicester City (A)	4–2
Mon 2 May	Derby County (A)	2–0

APPEARANCES (SUBS IN BRACKETS) AND GOALS

Player	Apps	Gls	Player	Apps	Gls
ISSA ABDULKADIR	0 (2)	0	SEBASTIAN LARSSON	17	4
JEREMIE ALIADIERE	5	8	ARTURO LUPOLI	20 (2)	19
MANUEL ALMUNIA	3	0	FABRICE MUAMBA	7 (6)	0
NICKLAS BENDTNER	4 (10)	4	MITCHELL MURPHY	4 (2)	0
ADAM BIRCHALL	6 (5)	0	STEPHEN O'DONNELL	19 (3)	3
SOL CAMPBELL	3	0	QUINCY OWUSU-ABEYIE	17 (1)	4
GAEL CLICHY	2	0	JERMAINE PENNANT	4	1
SEAN CLOHESSY	4 (4)	0	AARON SAMUEL	1 (2)	0
MATTHEW CONNOLLY	9 (2)	0	PHILIPPE SENDEROS	4	0
PATRICK CREGG	14 (1)	1	DOMINIC SHIMMIN	5 (2)	0
PASCAL CYGAN	4	0	GILBERTO	3	0
JOHAN DJOUROU	12	0	FRANKIE SIMEK	11 (1)	1
EMMANUEL EBOUE	5	0	OLAFUR-INGI SKULASON	10	0
MATTHIEU FLAMINI	7	1	RYAN SMITH	12	1
JORDAN FOWLER	8 (1)	0	DANIEL SPAUL	0 (1)	0
KERREA GILBERT	17 (3)	1	JOHN SPICER	1	1
BEN GILL	1 (2)	1	ANTHONY STOKES	14 (6)	8
MATTHEW HISLOP	2 (3)	0	STUART TAYLOR	14	0
MARK HOWARD	5	0	ROBIN VAN PERSIE	3	4
JUSTIN HOYTE	9	0	LUKE WEBB	2 (4)	0
MICHAEL JORDAN	3	0	CHRIS WRIGHT	3	0
DANIEL KARBASSIYOON	14 (1)	2			
SEAN KELLY	2 (6)	0			

FA BARCLAYCARD PREMIER RESERVE LEAGUE SOUTH
FINAL TABLE

	P	W	D	L	F	A	Pts
Charlton Athletic	28	18	7	3	46	21	61
Southampton	28	18	4	6	68	29	58
ARSENAL	**28**	**17**	**5**	**6**	**65**	**38**	**56**
Crystal Palace	28	16	5	7	47	22	53
Tottenham Hotspur	28	13	8	7	47	35	47
Chelsea	28	10	8	10	28	28	38
Watford	28	9	9	10	32	33	36
Norwich City	28	10	4	14	24	40	34
Fulham	28	8	9	11	29	35	33
Derby County	28	9	6	13	29	48	33
West Ham United	28	7	9	12	33	51	30
Coventry City	28	7	8	13	29	50	29
Ipswich Town	28	6	6	16	24	35	24
Leicester City	28	5	9	14	36	49	24
Portsmouth	28	5	7	16	28	51	22

YOUTH TEAMS

FA ACADEMY LEAGUE UNDER-18

Date	Opponents (Venue)	Score
Sat 21 Aug	Bolton Wanderers (A)	1–4
Fri 27 Aug	Sheffield Wednesday (H)	3–1
Sat 4 Sept	Aston Villa (A)	3–2
Sat 11 Sept	Birmingham City (H)	1–4
Sat 18 Sept	Bristol City (A)	2–0
Sat 25 Sept	Cardiff City (H)	0–2
Sat 2 Oct	Norwich City (H)	2–1
Sat 9 Oct	Ipswich Town (H)	0–1
Sat 16 Oct	Crystal Palace (A)	2–1
Sat 23 Oct	Charlton Athletic (H)	1–2
Sat 30 Oct	Southampton (A)	1–2
Sat 6 Nov	Fulham (H)	0–0
Sat 13 Nov	Millwall (A)	1–0
Sat 20 Nov	West Ham United (A)	0–2
Sat 4 Dec	Chelsea (H)	1–0
Sat 11 Dec	Charlton Athletic (A)	2–0
Sat 8 Jan	Southampton (H)	2–1
Sat 15 Jan	Fulham (A)	2–1
Sat 22 Jan	Millwall (H)	6–1
Sat 5 Feb	West Ham United (H)	2–3
Sat 12 Feb	Chelsea (A)	0–1
Sat 19 Feb	Norwich City (H)	1–1
Sat 12 Mar	Crystal Palace (H)	1–1
Sat 2 Apr	Coventry City (A)	2–0
Sat 9 Apr	Leicester City (H)	4–1
Sat 16 Apr	Reading (A)	0–3
Sat 23 Apr	Tottenham Hotspur (H)	7–1
Sat 30 Apr	Ipswich Town (A)	0–1

FA YOUTH CUP

Date	Opponents (Venue)	Score
Thu 16 Dec	Crystal Palace (H) Rd 3	3–0
Mon 17 Jan	Preston North End (H) Rd 4	2–1
Tue 15 Feb	Southampton (A) Rd 5	0–1

LEAGUE APPEARANCES (SUBS IN BRACKETS) AND GOALS

Player	Apps	Gls	Player	Apps	Gls
ISSA ABDULKADIR	11 (3)	0	SEAN KELLY	24 (4)	2
MOSES BARNETT	3 (2)	0	PEGGY LOKANDO	0 (1)	0
NICKLAS BENDTNER	19	12	ARTURO LUPOLI	7	7
SEAN CLOHESSY	13 (3)	0	FABRICE MUAMBA	21	0
MATTHEW CONNOLLY	12 (2)	0	STEPHEN O'DONNELL	3	0
BILLY COYNE	0 (3)	0	MARK RANDALL	10 (5)	1
PATRICK CREGG	2	1	PAUL RODGERS	0 (2)	0
JOHAN DJOUROU	8	0	AARON SAMUEL	16 (6)	2
GIORGOS EFREM	2 (2)	0	DOMINIC SHIMMIN	11	0
MARC ELSTON	1 (1)	0	JAY SIMPSON	11 (6)	6
CEDRIC EVINA	1 (1)	1	RYAN SMITH	10	2
KERREA GILBERT	14	0	DANIEL SPAUL	9 (8)	0
BEN GILL	14 (6)	3	RENE STEER	1 (1)	0
MATTHEW HISLOP	12	0	ANTHONY STOKES	14 (1)	5
MARK HOWARD	17	0	LESLIE THOMPSON	3 (5)	0
JEFFREY IMUDIA	0 (1)	0	LUKE WEBB	15 (5)	2
MICHAEL JORDAN	5	0	CHRIS WRIGHT	6	0

FA YOUTH CUP APPEARANCES (SUBS IN BRACKETS) AND GOALS

Player	Apps	Gls	Player	Apps	Gls
NICKLAS BENDTNER	3	2	MITCHELL MURPHY	3	0
SEAN CLOHESSY	2 (1)	0	MARK RANDALL	0 (1)	0
MATTHEW CONNOLLY	3	1	DOMINIC SHIMMIN	1	0
KERREA GILBERT	3	0	JAY SIMPSON	0 (2)	0
BEN GILL	3	0	RYAN SMITH	3	1
MARK HOWARD	2	0	DANIEL SPAUL	0 (1)	0
SEAN KELLY	0 (1)	0	ANTHONY STOKES	3	0
ARTURO LUPOLI	2	1	LUKE WEBB	1	0
FABRICE MUAMBA	3	0	CHRIS WRIGHT	1	0

FA ACADEMY LEAGUE UNDER-18 GROUP A FINAL TABLE

	P	W	D	L	F	A	Pts
Southampton	28	23	2	3	62	25	71
Charlton Athletic	28	14	6	8	35	28	48
ARSENAL	28	13	3	12	45	39	42
Ipswich Town	28	11	6	11	39	39	39
West Ham United	28	11	4	13	37	53	37
Millwall	28	11	2	15	34	44	35
Chelsea	28	8	5	15	24	33	29
Crystal Palace	27*	7	7	13	35	51	28
Norwich City	28	6	7	15	26	38	25
Fulham	27*	4	5	18	23	54	17

* Crystal Palace v Fulham game not played

ARSENAL LADIES

Anything you can do... the Arsenal Ladies squad completed an unbeaten league season to equal the achievement of their male counterparts the previous year.

THE NEW 'INVINCIBLES'

Now the Gunners have another team of 'Invincibles'. In the season after their male counterparts defied the odds by going through a League campaign without losing a match, Arsenal Ladies equalled that sensational achievement.

After lifting their seventh Championship with a victory in their penultimate game against their closest rivals, Charlton Athletic, Vic Akers' imperious side finished in the best possible manner, crushing Fulham 6–2.

Having also won the League Cup in 2004/2005, and with six previous FA Cup triumphs to his credit, Vic is used to collecting silverware and passing milestones, but his appetite for success appears undiminished by the passing of the years.

As he said after watching Kelly Smith rise from the bench for her comeback following a long-term injury, then clinch Arsenal's fourth Premiership crown in five seasons with a truly majestic strike: 'I'm absolutely delighted. To win such an important game with a wonderful goal like that is fantastic. It's just an amazing feat. It's not about management. It's about who you put out on the field of play, and I'm fortunate to

have such great players, such a marvellous group of girls.'

Charlton Athletic, who mounted spirited season-long resistance to the Gunners' supremacy, provided the opposition in the League Cup Final, which Arsenal won by a comfortable 3–0 margin.

Free-scoring Scottish international striker Julie Fleeting – who was named as National Players' Player of the Year by her peers after hitting the target 23 times in all senior club competitions in 2004/2005 – supplied the first goal against the Addicks, then skipper Faye White added the other two, climaxing with a 30-yard screamer into the top corner.

At one point of their memorable campaign, Arsenal Ladies nursed genuine prospects of an unprecedented quadruple, but they fell to Everton in the FA Cup semi-finals, then went out of the UEFA Cup at the last-four stage, going down to Djurgården of Sweden after a tense semi-final.

The European reverse, by a 2–1 aggregate, was particularly disappointing after Arsenal had excelled in securing a 1–1 draw in Stockholm, but Vic was magnanimous at the end of the tie! 'I think

Vice-captain Jayne Ludlow's performances in central midfield played a major part in Arsenal Ladies' Championship-winning season.

After a frustrating season on the bench, Kelly Smith scored a cracking 30-yarder against Charlton to secure the league title for the Club.

Djurgården deserved it over 180 minutes. We played out of our skins over there, but at home we never threatened their goal enough. We had 1,800 or so people come to watch us in the home leg and their support was fantastic. We're really grateful to them for coming out and they did make a difference.'

For Vic, though, there was another personal triumph to record, as he lifted the Nationwide Manager of the Year award.

The affable north Londoner, a former full-back who made more than 150 appearances for Cambridge United and Watford during the 1970s, remains one of the busiest men at the Club as he balances his twin duties as kit manager for Arsène Wenger's team and his inspired stewardship of Arsenal Ladies.

He is a passionate advocate of the women's game, the standard of which has risen markedly in recent seasons, and hopes it continues to go from strength to strength.

Arsenal Ladies celebrate with the league trophy after beating Fulham 6–2 on the last day of the season.

FIRST-TEAM FIXTURES

(FA Women's National Premier League, except where indicated)

Date	Opponents (Venue)	Score
Sun 22 Aug	Charlton Athletic (H)	2-2
Sun 29 Aug	Fulham (A)	0-0
Sun 5 Sep	Liverpool (A)	4-0
Tue 14 Sept	Athletic Club de Bilbao (*) UEFA Cup	2-2
Thu 16 Sept	AE Aegina (*) UEFA Cup	7-1
Sat 18 Sept	Djurgården/Älvsjö (*) UEFA Cup	1-0
Sun 3 Oct	Liverpool (H)	4-1
Sun 10 Oct	Bristol City (H) League Cup Rd 2	4-1
Wed 13 Oct	Birmingham City (A)	5-2
Sun 17 Oct	Leeds United (H)	2-0
Sat 23 Oct	Torres Terra Sarda (A) UEFA Cup QF	0-2
Sun 31 Oct	Torres Terra Sarda (H) UEFA Cup QF	4-1
Sun 7 Nov	Fulham (H) League Cup Rd 3	3-0
Sun 14 Nov	Everton (H)	2-0
Sun 21 Nov	Bristol City (A)	3-2
Sun 28 Nov	Bristol Rovers (H)	2-0
Sun 5 Dec	Doncaster Belles (H)	3-0
Sun 12 Dec	Birmingham City (A) League Cup SF	3-1
Sun 9 Jan	Wimbledon (H) FA Cup Rd 4	2-0
Sun 23 Jan	Bristol City (H)	7-0
Sun 30 Jan	Leeds United (A) FA Cup Rd 5	3-1
Sun 6 Feb	Everton (A)	1-1
Sun 20 Feb	Birmingham City (A) FA Cup QF	3-0
Sun 27 Feb	Doncaster Belles (A)	1-0
Sun 6 Mar	Charlton Athletic (League Cup Final)†	3-0
Sun 20 Mar	Everton (A) FA Cup SF	0-3
Wed 23 Mar	Birmingham City (H)	8-1
Sun 27 Mar	Leeds United (A)	2-1
Sun 3 Apr	Bristol Rovers (A)	5-1
Thu 7 Apr	Djurgården/Älvsjö (A) UEFA Cup SF, FL	1-1
Fri 15 Apr	Djurgården/Älvsjö (H)UEFA Cup SF, SL	0-1
Sun 24 Apr	Charlton Athletic (A)	1-0
Sat 7 May	Fulham (H)	6-2

* played in Stockholm

† played at Griffin Park, Brentford

ARSENAL LADIES OFFICIALS

VIC AKERS General Manager

CLARE WHEATLEY Development Manager

CIARA GRANT Assistant Development Manager

FAYE WHITE Assistant Development Manager

JAYNE LUDLOW Medical Officer

FRED DONNELLY Academy Director

*With **23 goals in 27 appearances** National Players' Player of the Season star striker Julie Fleeting has many reasons to celebrate with the league trophy.*

APPEARANCES (SUBS IN BRACKETS) AND GOALS

Player	League Apps	Gls	League Cup Apps	Gls	FA Cup Apps	Gls	London County Cup Apps	Gls	Totals Apps	Gls
ANITA ASANTE	14	1	2(1)	0	1(2)	0	7	0	24(3)	1
ANGELA BANKS	14(2)	13	4	0	4	0	6(1)	3	28(3)	16
LISA BURROWS	0(1)	0	0	0	0	0	0	0	0(1)	0
EMMA BYRNE	18	0	4	0	4	0	7	0	33	0
LEANNE CHAMP	14(2)	0	2(2)	0	4	0	4(1)	0	24(5)	0
CORI DANIELS	0	0	0	0	0	0	1	0	1	0
GEMMA DAVISON	0(2)	0	0	0	0	0	0(1)	0	0(3)	0
JULIE FLEETING	14	12	4	5	3	3	6(1)	3	27(1)	23
CIARA GRANT	16(2)	5	4	2	4	0	7	2	31(2)	9
AMBER HEARN	1(6)	0	0(1)	0	0(1)	0	0(4)	0	1(12)	0
HAYLEY KEMP	2(2)	0	1	0	0	0	2(1)	1	5(3)	1
KELLY LAWRENCE	0	0	0(1)	0	0	0	0	0	0(1)	0
JUSTINE LORTON	5(6)	4	0(1)	0	1	0	1(2)	0	7(9)	4
JAYNE LUDLOW	15(3)	5	4	1	4	2	7	2	30(3)	10
KIRSTY McBRIDE	3(5)	0	0(3)	0	1	0	0	0	4(8)	0
ELAINE O'CONNOR	1(4)	0	0	0	0	0	0	0	1(4)	0
KIRSTY PEALLING	17	1	4	0	3(1)	0	7	0	31(1)	1
MARY PHILLIP	17	0	4	0	3(1)	0	7	0	31(1)	0
LIANNE SANDERSON	18	9	4	3	4	1	4(3)	0	30(3)	13
KELLY SMITH	2(1)	2	0	0	0(1)	0	0	0	2(2)	2
DUNIA SUSI	0	0	0	0	0(1)	0	0(1)	0	0(2)	0
YUKI TOZAKI	0	0	0	0	0	0	0(1)	0	0(1)	0
YVONNE TRACY	3(3)	0	0(2)	0	1	0	0(1)	0	4(6)	0
CLARE WHEATLEY	16(2)	0	4	0	3	0	7	1	30(2)	1
FAYE WHITE	8(1)	3	3	2	4	1	5(1)	2	20(2)	8

FA WOMEN'S NATIONAL PREMIER LEAGUE FINAL TABLE

	P	W	D	L	F	A	Pts
ARSENAL	18	15	3	0	57	13	48
Charlton Athletic	18	13	2	3	43	17	41
Everton	18	11	4	3	45	24	37
Birmingham City	18	9	3	6	37	28	30
Bristol Rovers	18	9	1	8	35	28	28
Leeds United	18	8	2	8	31	34	26
Fulham	18	3	5	10	18	39	14
Doncaster Belles	18	3	3	12	10	38	12
Liverpool	18	3	2	13	21	49	11
Bristol City	18	2	3	13	12	39	9

TRAVELLING WITH ARSENAL

ASTON VILLA

Villa Park, Trinity Road,
Birmingham B6 6HE
Tel: 0121 327 2299
Tickets: 0121 327 5353
Website: www.avfc.co.uk

TRAVEL INFO
By Car
Take the M1 to junction 19, then the M6. Leave the M6 at junction 6 for the A38 (M) Aston Expressway. Take the first exit at the roundabout onto Victoria Road, then at the next roundabout take the right exit into Witton Road.
Car parking Please where possible try to use the official car parks, most of which are within five minutes walk from the ground.

By Train
Villa Park is a two-minute walk from Witton station. Aston station is a ten-minute walk. Connecting trains run from Birmingham New Street.

League position 2004/2005 10th

BIRMINGHAM CITY

St Andrews, Birmingham B9 4NH
General Equiries
and Tickets: 0871 226 1875
Website: www.bcfc.com

TRAVEL INFO
By Car
From the North and North-East Exit M6 at junction 6 and take the A38(M) Aston Expressway. Take the second exit. At the roundabout along Dartmouth Middleway, take the first exit. After about a mile, turn left into St Andrews Street.
From the South-West Exit M5 at junction 3A and follow signs for the north on to the M42 northbound. Exit M42 at junction 4 and turn left at the roundabout on to the A34. Continue over four roundabouts, through suburb of Sparkbrook to Camphill Circus roundabout. Take third exit on to A4540. At roundabout go straight on to ground.
From the South-East Exit M40 at junction 3A on to the M42 northbound. Exit M42 at junction 4 and turn left at the roundabout onto the A34. Continue over four roundabouts, through suburb of Sparkbrook to Camphill Circus roundabout. Take third exit on to A4540. At roundabout go straight on to ground.

By Train
The nearest stations are Birmingham New Street or Birmingham Moor Street, a 20-minute walk from the ground.

By Bus
Numbers 15, 15A and 17 run from Birmingham New Street station along Coventry Road. Numbers 96 and 97 run from Carrs Lane (behind High Street) to Garrison Lane.

League position 2004/2005 12th

BLACKBURN ROVERS

Ewood Park, Nuttall Street,
Blackburn BB2 4JF
General Enquiries
and Tickets: 08701 123 456
Website: www.rovers.co.uk

TRAVEL INFO
By Car
Exit the M6 at junction 31, or take the A59/A677, following signs for Blackburn, then the A666. After 1¹/₂ miles turn left into Kidder Street. From the east, use the A679 or A667 and follow the signs for Bolton Road (then follow directions as above). There are extensive secure private parking facilities immediately adjacent to the stadium, allowing for up to 800 vehicles.

Ewood Park is signposted from junction 4 off the M65 (which leaves the M6 at junction 29).

By Train
The nearest stations are Blackburn (1¹/₂ miles from the ground) and Mill Hill (1 mile from the ground).

By Bus
Use any bus from Blackburn town centre heading for Darwen and it will drop you off two minutes from the ground.

League position 2004/2005 15th

BOLTON WANDERERS

Reebok Stadium, Burnden Way,
Lostock, Bolton BL6 6JW
Tel: 01204 673673
Tickets: 0871 871 2932
Website: www.bwfc.co.uk

TRAVEL INFO
By Car
From the North Follow signs for the M61 towards Manchester/Bolton and leave at junction 6. Take the first exit off the sliproad roundabout onto the A6027 Mansell Way.

From the South Follow signs for the M61 towards Preston. (Do NOT take the A666 towards Bolton). Turn off the M61 at junction 6 and take the third right exit from the sliproad roundabout onto the A6027 Mansell Way.

By Train
Horwich Parkway railway station serves the stadium, with regular trains from Bolton's main station. Horwich Parkway is only a few minutes walk from the ground.

By Bus
Bus station at Trinity Street. Football specials run from Bolton city centre to the stadium, otherwise catch the number 11 from outside the court house in Black Horse Street.

League position 2004/2005 6th

CHARLTON ATHLETIC

The Valley, Floyd Road, Charlton,
London SE7 8BL
Tel: 020 8333 4000
Tickets: 020 8333 4010
Website: www.cafc.co.uk

TRAVEL INFO

By Car

From the M25 The easiest way to get to the Valley is to use the A2, accessed from junction 2 of the M25. Heading into London, the dual carriageway becomes the A102M – the approach road to the Blackwall Tunnel. Leave at the junction after the A2 exit and take the right-hand exit at the roundabout – the A206 Woolwich Road. After the major set of traffic lights at Anchor and Hope Lane and Charlton Church Lane, travel around second roundabout and take the last exit to drive back on yourself. Then take the first left into Charlton Lane. Cross the railway line and continue up the road, then right into Harvey Gardens. The stadium is on the left. Access to Floyd Road and Harvey Gardens is restricted on matchdays.

Via the South Circular Follow the A205 South Circular Road to Woolwich and turn left into the Woolwich Road at the roundabout for the free ferry. You should then turn left into Charlton Lane and proceed as described above.

From Central London From north of the Thames, take the A102 through the Blackwall Tunnel. Come off at the second junction and take the first exit at the round-about. Go along the A206 Woolwich Road as above.

Car parking You can park in many roads around the ground but some restrictions are in force on match-days. Yellow lines apply at weekends, as well as weekdays, though most parking bays are free – except around the railway station. The use of some of the bays, however, is suspended on matchdays. Restrictions are vigorously enforced, and local retail car parks operate a clamping policy. The club recommends using public transport whenever practical.

By Train and Tube

Connex runs train services to the railway station at Charlton, from Central London in the west and north Kent to the east. The station is a short walk from the ground. Frequent services depart from Charing Cross, Waterloo East and London Bridge, with limited departures from Victoria and Cannon Street. Some services come through Dartford and continue to Charlton, while connections for others can be made at Blackheath, Lewisham and London Bridge. The Docklands Light Railway from east London connects with rail services from Greenwich and Lewisham to Charlton, while the Jubilee Line underground station at North Greenwich is a short bus ride from the Valley.

By Bus

Numerous bus routes serve the ground. They include the 53 (Plumstead, Woolwich, Blackheath, New Cross, central London), the 54 (Lewisham, Catford, Beckenham, Elmers End) and the 161 (Chislehurst, Mottingham, Eltham, Woolwich, North Greenwich). Others are the 177 (Thamesmead, Plumstead, Woolwich, Greenwich, New Cross, Peckham), the 180 (Thamesmead, Plumstead, Woolwich, Greenwich, Lewisham), the 422 (Bexleyheath, Welling, Plumstead, Blackheath, North Greenwich), the 472 (Thamesmead, Plumstead, Woolwich, North Greenwich), and the 486 (Bexleyheath, Welling, Shooters Hill and North Greenwich). These services discharge passengers on the A206 Woolwich Road, or in Charlton Village, both a five-minute walk from the ground.

League position 2004/2005 11th

CHELSEA

Stamford Bridge, Fulham Road,
London SW6 1HS
Tel: 0870 300 1212
Tickets: 0870 300 2322
Website: www.chelseafc.co.uk

TRAVEL INFO
By Car
From the North, East or West Use the M25 to take you round to junction 15 and turn off onto the M4 towards London, follow the M4 which becomes the A4 up to Hammersmith. Stay on it over the Hammersmith fly-over and for a further 1^1/$_2$ miles before turning off for Earl's Court. Go past Earl's Court station and down the one way system until you hit Fulham Road, turn right at the traffic lights. Go straight on for 600 yards and the ground is on your right.

From the South Head for Wandsworth Bridge to cross the river and head straight up Wandsworth Bridge Road. At the junction with New King's Road turn right and then immediately left. This will take you up to Fulham Broadway, turn right onto Fulham Road and the ground is 400 yards on your left.

Car parking Parking is difficult close to the ground so you may want to look a bit further away.

By Tube
The nearest tube station is Fulham Broadway on the District Line. Take a train to Earl's Court and change for Wimbledon bound trains. West Brompton station is also a ten-minute walk from the ground.

By Bus
There are plenty of buses to the ground from Central London.

League position 2004/2005 1st

EVERTON

Goodison Park, Goodison Road,
Liverpool L4 4EL
Tel: 0151 330 2200
Tickets: 0870 422 1878
Website: www.evertonfc.com

TRAVEL INFO
By Car
From the North Approaching on the M6, exit at junction 26 onto the M58 and continue until the end. At junction 7 turn left onto the A59 Ormskirk Road. Continue on this road until it becomes Rice Lane and cross over the roundabout into County Road. After ^{1}/$_4$-mile turn left into Everton Valley and then Walton Lane. Goodison Road and the ground are on the left.

From the South Approaching from the M6, exit at junction 21a onto the M62. Exit the M62 at junction 4 and get onto the A5080. At the junction with A5058 turn right and continue along this road as it becomes Queen's Drive. Continue to the junction with Walton Road and turn left onto the A580 Walton Lane. Goodison and the ground are on the right.

From the East Approaching from the M62, exit at junction 4 and get onto the A5058 and then follow the route above.

By Train
Liverpool Lime Street Station is about 2 miles from Goodison Park. Kirkdale Station is a 10-minute walk from the ground.

By Bus
Numbers 17 or 217 from stand L outside Lime Street station.

League position 2004/2005 4th

FULHAM

Craven Cottage, Stevenage Road,
Fulham, London SW6 6HH
Tel: 0870 422 1222
Tickets: 0870 442 1234
Website: www.fulhamfc.com

TRAVEL INFO
By Car
From the North Take the A1/M1 to the North Circular A406 follow signs for Harlesdon A404, then take the A219 to Hammersmith. When on Broadway follow signs for Fulham, turn right after 1 mile into Harboard Street then left at the end for the ground.
From the South/East Take the South Circular A205, follow signs for Putney Bridge A219, cross the bridge and follow signs for Hammersmith for $\frac{1}{2}$ mile, take a left into Bishop's Park Road, then right at the end.
From the East Take the M4 to the A4, after 2 miles branch left into Hammersmith Broadway, then follow signs for Fulham, turn right after 1 mile into Harboard Street then left at the end for the ground.

Please note that Fulham Football Club advises all fans to use public transport where possible.

By Tube
Putney Bridge, on the District Line, is approximately 10 minutes walk from the ground. Hammersmith, on the Hammersmith & City, Piccadilly and District Lines, is approximately 20 minutes walk away.

By Bus
From Kingston-upon-Thames bus station take either the number 85 or C4 bus to Putney Bridge. The ground is approximately 10 minutes walk from there. From Hammersmith catch either of the following numbers which run down Fulham Palace Road: 190, 211, 295, 220. From Putney catch either the 74 or the 220 to Fulham Palace Road.

League position 2004/2005 13th

LIVERPOOL

Anfield Road, Liverpool L4 0TH
Tel: 0151 263 2361
Tickets: 0870 220 2345
Website: www.liverpoolfc.tv

TRAVEL INFO
By Car
From the North Take the M6 until junction 28 then follow signs for Liverpool on A58. Continue straight on into Walton Hall Avenue past Stanley Park and turn left into Anfield Road.
From the South Take the M6 then M62 until the end of the motorway. Then turn right at signs for the A5058 into Queen's Drive. After 3 miles, turn left into Utting Avenue. Then turn right into Anfield Road.
From the West Take the Mersey Tunnel into Liverpool city centre, then follow signs for Preston A580 into Walton Hall Avenue. This will turn into Walton Lane. Take a right into Anfield Road.
From the East Take the M6 until junction 28 then follow signs for Liverpool on A58. Continue straight on into Walton Hall Avenue past Stanley Park and turn left into Anfield Road.

By Train
Liverpool Lime Street is about 2 miles away from the ground. A taxi is about £3.50. Sandhills is just over a mile from the ground. To walk it, turn right out of the station. At the lights go up the hill with the park on the right. Turn right before the Lambeth pub. After 100 yards swing a left into Whittle Street. At Kirkdale Road turn left, then go right and up the hill. Go straight over the lights then turn right into Walton Breck Road when you see a signpost to the ground.

By Bus
Numbers 17,17c, 17d, or 217 run from Queen's Square by Lime Street station. Numbers 26 and 27 run from Paradise Street.

League position 2004/2005 5th

MANCHESTER CITY

City of Manchester Stadium,
SportCity, Rowsley Street,
Eastlands, Manchester M11 3FF
General Enquiries and
Tickets: 0870 062 1894
Website: www.mcfc.co.uk

TRAVEL INFO
By Car
From the South Leave M6 at junction 19, follow A556 towards Stockport. Join M56 towards Stockport and then take M60 heading towards Ashton Under Lyne. Or leave M60 at junction 23 and take A635 towards Manchester, then branch off onto A662 towards Droyslden. After about 3 miles you will see the stadium on your right.
From the M62 Leave the M62 at junction 18 and then join the M60 towards Ashton Under Lyne. Then follow directions as above.

By Train
The nearest station is Manchester Piccadilly which is a 20 minute walk away from the ground. To walk from there, leave the station by the exit for Fairfield Street and then bear right towards London Road. With the station now to your right, take another right down Store Street which will take you through a tunnel under the station. From here simply follow the blue CityLink signposts that lead to the stadium.

By Bus
Numbers 53, 54, 185, 186, 216, 217, 230, 231, 232, 233, 234, 235, 236, 237,X36 and X37 all go close to the stadium.

League position 2004/2005 8th

MANCHESTER UNITED

Old Trafford, Sir Matt Busby Way,
Old Trafford, Manchester M16 0RA
Tel: 0870 442 1994 868 8000
Tickets: 0870 757 1968
Website: www.manutd.com

TRAVEL INFO
By Car
From the North Exit the M60 at junction 12 for M602. At the end of the M602 follow signs for Salford Quays and Trafford Park. At roundabout turn right into Trafford Road (A5063). At the bridge over Manchester Ship canal turn right. At Trafford Wharf Road turn left onto Watersreach. Continue through traffic lights onto Sir Matt Busby Way.
From the South Exit the M6 at junction 19, and take the A56 in the direction of Manchester Airport. Follow the M56 to Manchester, past the airport and follow signs to M60 Leeds and Liverpool. Exit M60 at junction 7 (A56 Chester Road) following signs for Manchester United Football Club. Turn left into Sir Matt Busby Way.
From the West Take the M62 then M63 until junction 4. Leave motorway and follow signs for Manchester A5081. After 1^1/$_2$ miles turn right into Sir Matt Busby Way and ground is on the left.
From the East Exit M62 at junction 17, then take the A56 into Manchester. Follow signs south, then for Chester into Chester Road. In 2 miles turn right into Sir Matt Busby Way and ground is on the left.

By Train
Trains from Piccadilly and Manchester Oxford Road stop at the ground. The Old Trafford Metrolink station is ^{1}/$_2$ mile away from the ground.

By Bus
Bus numbers 252, 253, 254, 525, 256, 257, 17, 114 and 236 run from Manchester Piccadilly to Old Trafford.

League position 2004/2005 3rd

MIDDLESBROUGH

Riverside Stadium, Middlesbrough,
Cleveland TS3 6RS
General Enquiries and
Tickets: 0870 421 1986
Website: www.mfc.co.uk

TRAVEL INFO
By Car
From the North Take the A19 and turn left onto the Northern Route (A66) eastbound. Exit the A66 when you see the sign for St Hilda's and take the first left exit off the roundabout. Follow through to traffic lights into Dockside Road. The stadium is on the right hand side.
From the South Take the A19 all the way to Middlesbrough, until the junction with the A66, south of the River Tees. Turn right onto the Northern Route and follow for 2 miles. Exit the A66 when you see the sign for St Hilda's and take the first left exit off the roundabout. Follow through to traffic lights into Dockside Road. The stadium is on the right hand side.
From the West Take the A66, crossing the river on the Tees Bridge, and follow round to the Northern Route, eastbound. Exit the A66 when you see the sign for St Hilda's and take the first left exit off the roundabout. Follow through to traffic lights into Dockside Road. The stadium is on the right hand side.

By Train
Middlesbrough station is under a mile from the ground. To walk it, come down the steps and turn left, avoiding the ticket office. Turn right, and go straight at the crossroads towards the Bridge pub in Bridge Street East. Turn right into Windward Way and you will see the ground.

By Bus
Numbers 36, 37 and 38 run from the bus station to North Ormesby. Take the underpass from here to the ground.

League position 2004/2005 7th

NEWCASTLE UNITED

St James' Park,
Newcastle-upon-Tyne NE1 4ST
Tel: 0191 201 8400
Tickets: 0191 261 1571
Website: www.nufc.co.uk

TRAVEL INFO
By Car
From the South Follow the A1, A68 then A6127 to cross the Tyne. At the next roundabout, take the first exit into Moseley Street. Turn left into Neville Street, then right at the end for Clayton Street and then Newgate Street. Then turn left for Leazes Park Road.
From the West Take the A69 towards the City Centre. Turn left into Clayton Street for Newgate Street, then left again for Leazes Park Road.
From the North Take the A1, then follow signs for Hexham until you get to Percy Street then turn right into Leazes Park Road.

By Train
Newcastle Central is half a mile from the ground. A taxi will cost about £3.00. To walk it, cross the road towards the Bakers Oven and turn right down Central Street. Turn left into Grainger Street and left again into Westgate Road. Turn right into Bath Lane and the ground is on your right.

The Metro station is right next to the stadium, though if you are taking the Metro it may be quicker to walk from Monument station instead.

By Bus
There are many buses which head in the direction of the ground. Get off at Gallowgate.

League position 2004/2005 14th

PORTSMOUTH

Fratton Park, Frogmore Road,
Portsmouth PO4 8RA
Tel: 023 9273 1204
Tickets: 0871 230 1898
Website: www.pompeyfc.co.uk

TRAVEL INFO
By Car
From the North and West Take the M27 and M275 to the end then take the second exit at the roundabout and after ¼ mile turn right at the T-junction into London Road (A2047). After 1¼ miles cross the railway bridge and turn left into Goldsmith Avenue. After ½ mile turn left into Frogmore Road.
From the East Take the A27 following Southsea signs (A2030). Turn left at the roundabout (3 miles) onto A288, then right into Priory Crescent and next right into Carisbrooke Road.

By Train
The Portsmouth mainline train station is at least 30-minutes walk from Fratton Park. However, most trains to Portsmouth also stop at Fratton station, which is only a ten-minute walk to the ground. When you arrive walk over the bridge and turn left into Goldsmith Avenue. Carry on till you reach Apsley Road and the visiting supporters' turnstiles are directly ahead.

By Bus
Number 13 stops at Commercial Road South, Fratton Bridge, Goldsmith Avenue, White House and Furze Lane. Numbers 17 and 18 stop at the Hard Interchange, Commercial Road, Victoria Road North/Elm Grove, Highland Road Post Office, White House, Goldsmith Avenue, Fratton Bridge and Commercial Road. Other services which stop close to the ground: 3, 13, 16, 16A, 24, 27 (all Fratton Bridge), 4, 4A, 6 (all Milton Road).

League position 2004/2005 16th

SUNDERLAND

The Stadium of Light,
Sunderland SR5 1SU
Tel: 0191 551 5000
Tickets: 0191 551 5151
Website: www.safc.com

TRAVEL INFO
By Car
Leave the A1 at the Durham/Sunderland exit and take the A690 towards Sunderland. After about 8 miles, turn left onto the A19, signposted for the Tyne Tunnel. Stay in the left-hand lane and take the slip road over the River Wear. Turn right onto the A1231 following the signs for Sunderland. Go straight over four roundabouts into the city. Then go through two sets of traffic lights and you will see the stadium car park on your right, about a mile after the traffic lights.
Car parking There is only limited parking at the ground, but you can park in the city centre and walk (about 10-15 minutes). There is also a free park-and-ride scheme in operation on matchdays. This is situated at Sunderland Enterprise Park just off the A1231. Buses run every five minutes for 90 minutes before kick-off and after the game.

By Train
Sunderland station is about 15 minutes walk from the stadium. From the station, exit between W.H.Smith and the bakery. Turn left and walk down High Street West, then turn left again up Fawcett Street to the Wear Bridge from where you can see the ground.

Two new Metro stations, Stadium of Light and St Peters, also go to the ground and both are only a few minutes walk, although away supporters should alight at St Peters as that is closer to their entrance. Please note that after the game the Stadium of Light Metro station only operates northbound (towards Newcastle) and St Peters Metro station only operates southbound (towards Sunderland centre).

League position 2004/2005 1st in Championship

TOTTENHAM HOTSPUR

White Hart Lane, Bill Nicholson Way,
748 High Road, Tottenham,
London N17 0AP
General Enquiries and
Tickets: 0870 420 5000
Website: www.spurs.co.uk

TRAVEL INFO

By Car
From the East or West Take A406 North Circular Road to Edmonton and at Fore Street traffic lights follow signs for Tottenham (A1010, High Road) and for White Hart Lane Stadium. From Waltham Cross or Tottenham Hale use North-South route Meridian Way (A1055) to Tottenham (Northumberland Park area).

By Train
White Hart Lane Station is about 5 minutes' walk from the ground. Services from Liverpool Street to Enfield Town and Cheshunt/Hertford East run every 15 minutes. Northumberland Park station is about 10 minutes walk from the ground.

Main Line services from Liverpool Street to Cheshunt/Broxbourne/Cambridge/Bishops Stortford/Stansted Airport and Hertford East (peak times only).

By Tube
Seven Sisters Station (Victoria Line), is within 20 minutes walking distance or change onto main line to White Hart Lane station. Alternatively change on to bus routes 149, 259 or 279, that operate directly to the stadium every 12 minutes (Mon-Sat day-times).Tottenham Hale Station (Victoria Line), is 20 minutes' walking distance, or take a taxi from the rank.

By Bus
The following bus services frequently pass the ground: 149, 259, 279.

League position 2004/2005 9th

WEST BROMWICH ALBION

The Hawthorns, Halfords Lane,
West Bromwich,
West Midlands B71 4LF
Tel: 0870 066 8888
Tickets: 0870 066 2800
Website: www.wba.co.uk

TRAVEL INFO

By Car
From the M5 Exit the M5 at junction 1. Take the A41, signposted Birmingham. The stadium is visible from here, and stands about 600 metres to the Birmingham side of junction 1. Turn right into Halfords Lane for stadium.

By Train
The Hawthorns railway station is situated on Halfords Lane, 250 metres south of the stadium itself. There is also a Metro tram link which services the main route from Birmingham to Wolverhampton. Otherwise, from New Street, head for Smethwick Rolfe Street (10 minutes walk).

By Bus
Numbers 74, 77-79 and 450 all pass by the ground.

League position 2004/2005 17th

WEST HAM UNITED

Boleyn Ground, Green Street,
Upton Park, London E13 9AZ
Tel: 020 8548 2748
Tickets: 0870 112 2700
Website: www.whufc.com

TRAVEL INFO
By Car
Go to M25 junction 27, then join the M11 southbound.
Follow that until it divides to join the A406 (North
Circular Road). Take the left fork signposted A406
South. Do not follow the signs for the City. The end of
the motorway joins the A406 from the left, creating a
four-lane road for a short distance. You need to be in
one of the outside two lanes. Proceed south passing
the junctions for Redbridge and Ilford. Leave the
A406 at the Barking junction. At the roundabout at
the bottom of the slip road, turn right, taking the third
exit towards East Ham (Barking Road). Proceed west
along Barking Road through several sets of traffic
lights until you have passed the lights at East Ham
Town Hall (big red Victorian building on the left just
before the lights). Three-quarters of a mile further
on, you pass the ground on your right (behind a
parade of shops, including the Hammers Shop). At
the next lights (Boleyn Arms Pub on right-hand
corner), turn right into Green Street. The main
entrance to the ground is 200 yards on your right.

Car parking On Saturday matchdays, parking is very
restricted with little or no off-road space. The best
areas to look are on roads left of Barking Road, once
you are past the lights at East Ham Town Hall.

By Tube
The nearest Tube station is Upton Park which is on the
District and Hammersmith & City lines. The station is
a short walk from the ground. Please note that West
Ham Tube station is nowhere near the ground.

League position 2004/2005 6th in Championship.
Promoted via the play-offs.

WIGAN ATHLETIC

The JJB Stadium, Robin Park Complex,
Newtown, Wigan WN5 0UZ
Tel: 01942 774000
Tickets: 0870 112 2552
Website: www.wiganlatics.co.uk

TRAVEL INFO
By Car
From the South Leave the M6 at junction 25, then
take the A49 to Wigan. After around 2 miles you
should pass an Aldi store on your left, before
reaching a large roundabout that is traffic light
controlled. Turn left at this roundabout into Robin
Park Road and continue into Scot Lane. The ground
is down Scot Lane on your right.

From the North Leave the M6 at junction 26 and
follow the signs for Wigan town centre (this road
meets the A49) then turn left into Robin Park and
continue into Scot Lane. The ground is down Scot
Lane on your right.

Car parking There is a large free car park at the
stadium, behind the away end.

By Train
Wigan's central railway stations (Wigan North
Western and Wallgate) are a good 20-minute walk
from the ground. On exiting from either station head
under the railway bridge and keep to the right. Follow
the road (A49), making sure you stick to the right for
around 10 minutes. You should pass the Seven Stars
Hotel and then pass under a second railway bridge.
The Robin Park complex and the JJB Stadium
should then be visible. Turn down Robin Park Road
and you are there.

League position 2004/2005 2nd in Championship

EMIRATES STADIUM

On their feet: *60,000 Gunners fans will undoubtedly give the thumbs up to the magnificent Emirates Stadium when it hosts its first match in 2006.*

QUANTUM LEAP

When Arsenal's fabulous, state-of-the-art new home opens for business at the start of the 2006/2007 campaign, it will be packed with 60,000 fans, a quantum leap from the 38,000-plus capacity of dear old Highbury.

But while the scale of the £357 million Emirates Stadium will be truly colossal, traditionalists need not despair. One of the key points in the Club's intricately detailed brief to the design team for the Gunners' 21st-century headquarters was to create the environment for an exhilarating, uplifting atmosphere.

Crucially, too, it was specified that the new pitch must be the equal of Highbury's famously impeccable, multiple-award-winning surface, so that it will be perfectly suited to the team's thrilling, free-flowing style of football.

Here are a few more facts and figures about the Emirates Stadium:

- 1,800 new jobs will be created in the Borough of Islington as a result of the project.

- More than 2,000 new homes will be built in Islington as part of the development.

- More than 2,500 legal documents were signed to give the project full clearance.

- At the peak of activity, approximately 1,000 construction workers will be engaged on the sumptuous new venue.

- The site of the new stadium is 17 acres.

- The height of the stadium will be 41.9 metres from pitch level to the top of the roof.

- An anticipated 1,140,000 supporters will attend Premiership matches at the new stadium in one season, compared with the Highbury average of 722,795.

- There will be 150 executive boxes at Arsenal's new home, compared to 48 boxes at Highbury.

- The executive boxes will have the capacity to serve up to 2,000 meals on a matchday.

- There will be approximately 250 catering serving points.

- There will be more than 900 WCs, together with 370 metres of urinals and 113 toilets for the disabled.

- There will be 41 TV camera positions throughout the stadium, as well as 215 seats for the media.

- Fans will be able to shop at a new 1,000-square-metre merchandising megastore.

- It was January 2002 when Arsenal appointed Sir Robert McAlpine Ltd to carry out the construction work.

- Previous projects which Sir Robert McAlpine have been responsible for are the new Hampden Park Stadium in Glasgow, the Centenary Stand at West Ham United, the Millennium Dome and the Bullring at Birmingham.

A glimpse of the future: the sight that will greet the eyes of the first Arsenal fans to walk into Emirates Stadium when it opens next season.

- The new stadium is designed by HOK Sport, the architects of Stadium Australia in Sydney, the English National Stadium at Wembley, Royal Ascot racecourse and Wimbledon Centre Court.

- More than 25,000 cubic metres of contamination has been removed from the sites, to make way for the project.

- There will be capacity for up to 250 wheelchair-users. The positions will be provided at all public and corporate levels throughout the building.

- Size of the grass area will be 113 metres by 76 metres, compared to 105 metres by 70 metres at Highbury.

Building for the future: *construction work continues on the Emirates Stadium, Arsenal Football Club's new citadel.*

- More than 60,000 cubic metres of concrete will be used in the structure. That's sufficient to fill the team bath at Highbury more than 7,500 times, or to fill the area of the pitch three stories high.

- Some 10,000 tons of steel reinforcement will be used, the equivalent of the weight of more than 300 team coaches.

- There will be 3,000 tons of tubular steel in the main roof, as against 100 tons in Highbury's North Bank.

- There will be 33,000 metres of concrete terracing.

- The new stadium will house 15,000 square metres of glass, the equivalent area of two football pitches.

- Metal hand railings will stretch for 4,500 metres.

- The complex will contain 2,000 doors.

- There will be 100 flights of stairs, which is enough to go to the top of Canary Wharf twice. Also there will be 13 elevators and five escalators.

- The four tiers of seating will all be covered by a roof of approximately 30,000 square metres. To place this in context, a football pitch covers approximately 8,600 square metres.

- To improve the potential quality of the pitch at the new stadium, extensive computer modelling is being carried out to study the sunlight and ventilation at pitch level.

Statistics courtesy of arsenal.com

THE FUTURE OF HIGHBURY

Future perfect: *an artist's impression of the future of the Highbury Stadium site, where the pitch will be converted into a garden square.*

What will happen to Highbury when Arsenal vacate the famous ground which has been their home since 1913? That's a burning question for countless Gunners fans who, while looking forward keenly to the brave new world of the Emirates Stadium, retain a deathless attachment to the scene of so many former glories.

A comprehensive answer has been provided by Martin Letts, director of Vision Four Developments – the company handling the ambitious Highbury regeneration project – in an interview in the Club's matchday programme.

Most fascinating of all, what will become of the hallowed turf, bestrode so majestically down the decades by all-time great footballers such as Alex James, Joe Mercer, Tony Adams and Thierry Henry? Mr Letts revealed: 'The pitch is being retained and converted into a formal garden square, which will include a variety of spaces created by glass, water and light walls, formal hedging and tree planting.'

Regarding the stadium as a whole, he recapped that Arsenal received planning permission in May 2002 to provide a mix of uses at Highbury, including residential apartments, a community health centre, a gym and a nursery. Since then there have been refinements to the design and alterations were being considered by the London Borough of Islington at the time of writing.

However, most of the details have been finalised, including the retention of the East and West Stand facades, together with the legendary Marble Halls, which will be included in the new development. Mr Letts continued: 'The North and South Stands will be replaced, but items such as the clock will either be retained or incorporated into the Emirates Stadium. New apartment buildings will replace both stands. These have

The hallowed turf: the Highbury pitch will be converted into a garden square. The public will be able to walk where Arsenal heroes once played.

been designed to reflect the scale of the former stands, maintaining the stadium atmosphere and framing the new garden square.'

At present it is intended to create 711 flats at Highbury and, although prices had not been finalised when this yearbook went to press, they were expected to start at around £240,000 rising to above £500,000 for a penthouse. The blocks will consist of seven storeys each, and the development will be known as 'The Stadium, Highbury Square.'

A new footpath will be created to link Avenell Road with Highbury Hill and will be open to the public. Mr Letts added that the former pitch

would be open to local people by arrangement with the management company. A memorial garden will be part of the project and the Marble Halls will be retained as the main gateway to the scheme.

Supporters who want to buy old Highbury fittings which are not being transferred to the new headquarters may get their chance at an auction, though no firm plans have been finalised.

The redevelopment will commence in the summer of 2006, directly following Arsenal's move to the Emirates, and it is hoped that the work wll be completed in 2007.

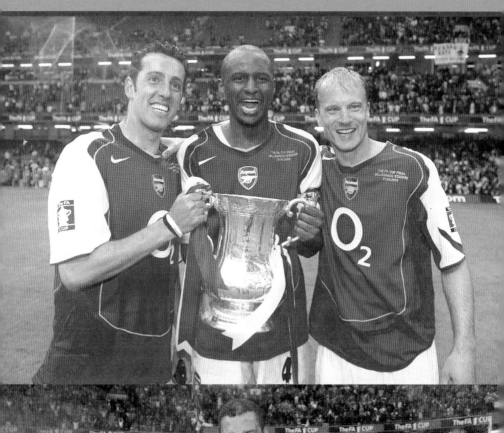